HELICOPTERS

THE BRITISH COLUMBIA STORY

Peter Corley-Smith and David N. Parker

VICTORIA • BRITISH COLUMBIA • CANADA

Sono Nis Press

Copyright © 1998 Royal British Columbia Museum

ALL RIGHTS RESERVED

Canadian Cataloguing in Publication Data

Corley-Smith, Peter, 1923-
   Helicopters

   Includes bibliographical references and index.
   ISBN 1-55039-094-5

   1. Helicopter transportation–British Columbia–History. 2.
Helicopters–British Columbia–History. I. Parker, David N. II.
Title.
HE9793.C22B7 1998   387.7'3352'09711   C98-910883-X

We acknowledge the support of the Canada Council for the
Arts publishing program.
We acknowledge the assistance of the Province of British
Columbia through the British Columbia Arts Council.

FRONT COVER: Vancouver Island Helicopters pilots Bob Reimer
and Ken Norie hone their waterbombing skills in a Bell 204;
Durrance Lake, August 1984.

Cover design by Jim Brennan
Interior design by Jim Bennett

Published by
SONO NIS PRESS
P.O. Box 5550, Stn. B
Victoria, British Columbia V8R 6S4

http://www.islandnet.com/sononis/
sono.nis@islandnet.com

Printed and bound in Canada by Friesen's

*To Carl Agar and Alf Stringer,
two people who,
with courage, resourcefulness
and intelligence,
pioneered a whole new industry.
They deserve to be remembered
for a long time.*

CONTENTS

PREFACE

In the first edition of this book we began by emphasizing that it did not presume to be a definitive history of the helicopter in British Columbia because we had neither the time nor the resources to embark on such an ambitious venture. Instead we brought together the story of helicopter flying as recalled by some of the participants–people who were clearly pioneers in a new technology.

While this remains true, we have, through additional research, been able to clarify some descriptions of events that were either ambiguous or erroneous. As well, we have updated our history, mainly in the chapters dealing with public sector helicopter operations: such areas as provincial ambulance services and search and rescue operations; in the private sector, a scheduled city-to-city service, and advances in helicopter logging. Once again, though, this does not represent a comprehensive history of helicopter flying in B.C.

In fact the history of helicopter operations in British Columbia is comparatively brief, a mere 50 years, or about half that of fixed-wing aircraft. Perhaps for this reason, published sources are still few in number, though this has begun to change over the past decade–no doubt because people are becoming more aware of the important part helicopters have played in the overall development of this province. Initially, and because of this, we placed much reliance on the recollections of those actually involved in the events described; and these were corroborated, and in some instances expanded upon, when personal records such as logbooks or similar primary sources were consulted as part of the review process.

Other sources we have investigated include company annual reports, reports of government agencies, trade-journals and newspaper articles. These have often been useful in establishing or confirming a chronology of events and technological developments and their significance. They also provided clues to further contacts or information. Additionally, we have been given access to a considerable body of primary source material.

Interviews were conducted to elicit certain information and then transcribed. Excerpts chosen for inclusion were carefully edited. This involved removal of interviewers' questions, normal repetitiveness in conversation, and speech habits that made translation from transcripts to prose difficult. Each person interviewed read, and approved, the appropriate excerpts.

Personal experience has inevitably provided the basis for the "Life in the Bush" chapters; to write from secondary sources would have reduced this central aspect of the story, to rather uninteresting expository prose that sacrificed the desired intimacy.

In preparing this book, the authors needed much assistance. Fortunately, it was always available.

Our most valuable help in the area of commercial flying came from A. H "Barney" Bent, one of the original partners in Okanagan Air Services and, until the summer of 1982, a member of the board of directors of Okanagan Helicopters Limited. Barney had prepared a manuscript on the history of the company; generously, he allowed us full access to it and the company files.

We also thank Cherry Graf of Okanagan Helicopters, who could always find exactly the document or photograph we needed. Both she and Barney spent considerable time reviewing the material for us, as did Walter Pulubiski, the late Don MacKenzie and Ken Blackwood. Ken was our liaison through much of this project.

Alf Stringer (sadly now the late Alf Stringer) of Vancouver Island Helicopters, contributed much time helping us assemble information on the early days of both the Okanagan and Vancouver Island companies, as did his wife, Lynn. Alf and Eric Cowden preserved us, we hope to a large extent, from technical errors, particularly in the evolution of the Bell 47 series of helicopters.

Lieutenant-Colonel Gordon Diamond, former Commanding Officer of 442 Squadron, Canadian Armed Forces, outlined the operation of the Search and Rescue facilities on the West Coast and reviewed the SAR chapter for accuracy. Ensign Jeff Vail, Lieutenant-Commander Dennis Maclean and Commander Paul Milligan of the United States Coast Guard offered their records and reviewed our material, while Lieutenant Richard Wall, United States Navy, provided material about the Perfect Pass crash.

Bob Jones and Ian Duncan of the Canadian Coast Guard were very helpful in providing photographic material of Coast Guard operations, and helped with suggestions for additions to the manuscript.

Harvey H. Lippincott and Bob Carrol of United Technologies supplied information and photographs relating to the development of Sikorsky helicopters and their operation by Okanagan Helicopters in British Columbia.

Members of various British Columbia Ministries provided considerable assistance. Helmut Braditsch, Jack McClelland and Hugh Lyons in Forestry provided the bulk of material on inventory/evaluation techniques and read the manuscript for accuracy. Peter Robbin at the Forestry photo lab spent time with us to ferret out suitable photographic material; Don Pearson of Environment provided photographic material and assisted in verifying British Columbia place names.

In our own institution, the Royal British Columbia Museum, we had the support of Director R. Yorke Edwards, and of his successor, Bill Barkley. Our friend and colleague, curator Bob Turner, read the manuscript and insisted on the same high standards he maintains with his own writing. Curator of Modern History, Dan Gallacher, read the manuscript and offered advice. Terry Hanna (now Eade) spent many hours typing the original manuscript (in pre-computer days). Museum Publications Editor Harold Hosford provided his customary helpful editing, and administrator Doug Lockhart arranged for transcripts of all the interviews. For this edition, we have also had the help of Tina Strange's computer expertise, and help from Jim Wardrop, Bob Griffin, Robin Patterson, and Phil Nott; and finally, thanks to Chief of Publications, Gerry Truscott, for making the publication of this new edition possible.

Dr. Paul Spitzer, Corporate Historian for the Boeing company in Seattle, also contributed many helpful suggestions.

Inevitably, we had to borrow material from other sources, and the support of the following publishers is sincerely appreciated: *Scientific American*, New York; William Heinmann Ltd., London, Paris; Dodd, Mead and Company, New York; MacDonald's, London; *Approach*, Norfolk, Va.; J. B. Lippincott Ltd., New York; Max Parrish, London.

Other institutions allowed us to use photographic material: the Victoria *Times-Colonist*; Provincial Archives of British Columbia; National Archives of Canada; United States Coast Guard; United States Navy; Canadian Armed Forces; Vancouver *Province*; Vancouver Public Library; and Victoria City Archives.

More recently, Henry Stevenson has contributed information about the invention of the monsoon bucket for forest-fire fighting, and both Bob Petite and George Williamson enlightened us with new information about very early helicopter operations.

Finally, we are sincerely grateful to Diane Morriss of Sono Nis Press for making this new edition possible, and to Jim Bennett and Jim Brennan for their very talented designs.

Peter Corley-Smith
Dave Parker
Victoria, B.C., August 25, 1998

INTRODUCTION

Helicopters were the answer to the problems of flying in British Columbia's mountains. Few people realized it to begin with, not even the first crew working in the Okanagan Valley in 1947; but the great mountain barriers of the province, which for so long had been cruel obstacles to travel, construction and exploration, were where the unique potential of helicopters would be realized.

Mere months after the first commercial certification had been granted to a helicopter manufacturer in North America, a small company began agricultural spraying with a helicopter in B.C. As it turned out, the spraying operation was not a success, but another spraying operation the following year, this time on forests rather than orchards, quickly convinced the company that the opportunity for commercial success lay in flying the mountains; in providing quick access to the vast interior of B.C., dominated as it was by range after range of rugged mountains that, before this, were virtually inaccessible.

The opportunities and the needs were certainly there – access for mapping, mineral exploration, forestry, search and rescue and construction – but a whole range of new flying techniques had to be developed and perfected. It was a dangerous, nerve-testing period for the early pilots, but it was also a great adventure. By 1947, the Royal Canadian Air Force, using Sikorsky H-5s, began operating in a search and rescue capacity and commercial operations were becoming established. By the late 1950s helicopters had proved their worth beyond question and were in use throughout the province. By the early 1960s, the Canadian Coast Guard had been equipped with them not, as many people assumed, to undertake search and rescue operations – that was the responsibility of the RCAF – but to supply and service lighthouses and other marine navigational aids, and to serve as pathfinders for the icebreakers in the Arctic during the summer months. In 1973, the Royal Canadian Mounted Police added helicopters to their air service division. A decade later, the Helijet company was providing scheduled intercity service between Victoria and Vancouver and the provincial government had established a comprehensive air ambulance service.

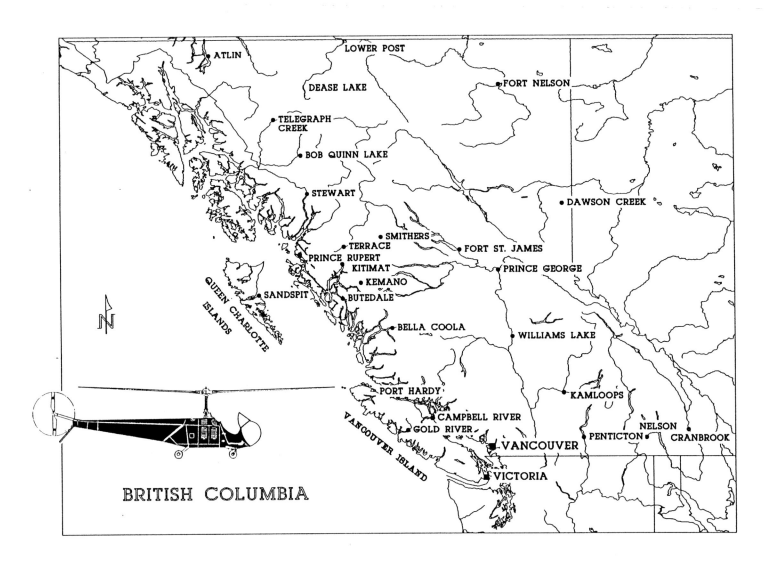

ATLIN

LOWER POST

DEASE LAKE

FORT NELSON

TELEGRAPH CREEK

BOB QUINN LAKE

STEWART

DAWSON CREEK

SMITHERS

TERRACE

FORT ST. JAMES

PRINCE RUPERT

KITIMAT

PRINCE GEORGE

KEMANO

QUEEN CHARLOTTE ISLANDS

SANDSPIT

BUTEDALE

BELLA COOLA

WILLIAMS LAKE

PORT HARDY

KAMLOOPS

CAMPBELL RIVER

GOLD RIVER

NELSON

PENTICTON

CRANBROOK

VANCOUVER ISLAND

VANCOUVER

VICTORIA

N

BRITISH COLUMBIA

But it was the commercial crews who led the way and, because of this, while attempting to do justice to all the organizations who flew helicopters in the early days of the new technology, it was inevitable that this book became in large part the story of one company: Okanagan Helicopters Limited. It was the Okanagan crews who first tackled and finally solved the problems of mountain flying. It was to them that the military and other government departments turned when they wanted to learn this new art. In short, Okanagan's crews established a second era of bush flying.

Bush flying in Canada got its start in the 1920s and 1930s, when legendary pilots like Punch Dickens, Doc Oakes, Fred Stevenson, Wop May, Herbert Hollick-Kenyon, Tommy Thompson, and Walter Gilbert were opening up northern Canada to more than the missionaries and the Hudson's Bay traders. Accompanied by their engineers, people like Pete Darbyshire, Bill Nadin, Alex Milne, Stan Knight, Al Cheesman, Don Goodwin and Emil Kading, their sleeping bags and some emergency rations in the back, they set off, often with no maps, to explore the country in machines which were still balky and temperamental. They had to feel their way as they went; and in order to learn, of course, they had to make mistakes. They had to find out by experience what a reasonable ice or snow surface for a landing looked like from the air. They had to discover the hard way what happened when they tried to land on glassy water without instruments. They had to learn to read the wind and the waves on the lakes, the furrows on the snow, the dull, opaque appearance of soft ice; and with a bit of luck and enough skill and resourcefulness, they would survive to profit from their mistakes and pass on their new knowledge to their successors.

Much the same thing happened when helicopters made their appearance in the Canadian bush. Those involved in this second wave of bush flying were, like their predecessors, people of strong character. In British Columbia for the first ten years, nearly all of them worked for the same two companies: Okanagan Air Services (which became Okanagan Helicopters in 1952) and Vancouver Island Helicopters. The very first crew was Carl Agar as pilot and Alf Stringer as engineer. They were soon training others: pilots Bill McLeod, Deke Orr, Fred Snell, Peter Cornwall, Ted Henson and Bob Taylor; engineers Jock Graham, Sig Hubenig, Bill Smith, Gordy Askin, Eric Cowden and Art Johnson.

These people, too, were self-reliant, resourceful and courageous. They had to be, for now they too were doing something no one else had ever done. They had to learn to estimate the wind and turbulence on high mountain ridges, or judge from the air the firmness of a swamp in a forest clearing. They had to try out new techniques, hoping their experiments would not prove fatal. They, too, were working in remote areas,

They had to learn to estimate the wind and turbulence on high mountain ridges, or judge from the air the firmness of a swamp in a forest clearing. They had to try out new techniques, hoping their experiments would not prove fatal.

affected by the tensions that small groups of people living in the closest proximity are bound to experience. In short, it was a hard life and, in the early days particularly, the financial rewards were negligible.

Fortunately, there were some compensations. Time and familiarity have made us indifferent now; but in the late 1940s and early 1950s there was still a touch of magic about the helicopter–the frontiers of flight have always captured the imagination.

And because of this, when a helicopter landed anywhere at that time, and there were people about, they would come running to look at it; to take photographs of the people in it and tap the plastic bubble and marvel at its flimsiness. It was heady stuff. Helicopter crews had become people of some distinction, successful and with a sort of pleasant self-confidence which had nothing to do with arrogance.

In our research for this book, we interviewed not only helicopter crews, but some of the people who first employed them in what sometimes seemed like the combat zone of bush and mountain flying. All of these employers spoke with respect of the intelligence and all-round competence of the crews they worked with. To give just one example, Ernie McMinn, of the Provincial Topographic Surveys: "This was one of the great things about Okanagan; the kind of guys they had were just top rate; they were interested in the job; they got to know the requirements of the job within a very short time, and they could just about do the job themselves."

The early fixed-wing bush pilots of the 1920s and 1930s had a somewhat similar rapport with their customers; but in helicopters this closeness was emphasized because, whereas the fixed-wing pilots were usually engaged in a supply and transport role, the helicopter pilots became an integral part of the job. They took surveyors out on the line and sometimes worked with them as rod-men or helped cut line for theodolite sightings. In geology, they spent so much time with the geologists that they became knowledge-able–though not very often, as far as we know, when it came to stock exchange transactions. They learned a great deal about oil exploration techniques and came to know much about our forests and how they were being managed.

It was this personal involvement, so different from the concept of an airborne taxi driver, that made helicopter crews an interesting and vital part of British Columbia's history. While the pilot was out devising new techniques to accelerate the progress of the job, the engineer would very often be working to improve living conditions in camp–constructing a shower with a ten-gallon (45 *l*) drum propped in the trees and a perforated plastic bottle for a shower head; or repairing a balky electric generator; or working on the camp's two-way radio, which broke down more often than a teenager's jalopy.

[Helicopter pilots] took surveyors out on the line and sometimes worked with them as rod-men or helped cut line for theodolite sightings. In geology, they spent so much time with the geologists that they became knowledgeable–though not very often, as far as we know, when it came to stock exchange transactions. They learned a great deal about oil exploration techniques and came to know much about our forests and how they were being managed.

However, to convey the impression that that life in a bush camp was an image of harmony would be misleading. Just as the helicopter crews were strongly individualistic, so also were the surveyors, geologists and foresters. And in the confinement and isolation of a bush camp, personality clashes were the rule rather than the exception.

For the pilot, there was an obvious danger: the very qualities of a helicopter gave him a sense of power. He could quite literally vault over a two-storey building – or a mountain for that matter. He was, in many ways, the centre of the operation. Without him virtually nothing could be accomplished, and it required a strong character, indeed, to withstand the temptation to try to usurp the party chief's authority.

With the engineer, on the other hand, an entirely different problem emerged. For the engineer had to do his work in the evening, very often when the mosquitoes and black-flies were at their worst. While the rest of the camp were relaxing, talking about what they had done and seen during the day – in short, enjoying what small social life there is in a bush camp – the engineer was out on his lonely job, greasing, cleaning, fixing the small mechanical snags the pilot had reported – or perhaps even a more serious one.

During the day, he would be left in camp with the cook. At first, those ingenious and productive things he did to improve living conditions were very much appreciated; but as time wore on, they began to be taken for granted. Worse yet, he began to be looked upon as a sort of camp handy man. He would be expected to gather wood for the stoves, to carry water for the cook – there were any number of things that might be expected of him, sitting all day in camp with very little to do. Some handled this sort of thing tactfully; others with growing resentment. In either case, it was all part of the dynamics of life in a helicopter operation bush camp.

Meanwhile, there was the question of progress. The advantages of improved technology are not always immediately apparent, and this was particularly evident in the development of helicopters. The first Bell machines – the 47-B3, 47-D and 47-G – were equipped with wooden blades; blades which were inclined to soak up moisture, thus altering their delicate balance and causing vibrations. As well, they were fragile, tending to split if they struck a willow no thicker than one's little finger, or break off altogether if they struck anything more substantial.

Then came the metal blades that could chop off the tops of small trees without damage to the blades. But this led to a new problem. If the tree tops were thick enough, or the object happened to be a rock instead of a tree, the blade didn't break; instead the whole helicopter would be hurled in the opposite direction to the path of the blade – usually to the detriment of both the helicopter and the pilot.

Then came the metal blades that could chop off the tops of small trees without damage to the blades. But this led to a new problem. If the tree tops were thick enough, or the object happened to be a rock instead of a tree, the blade didn't break; instead the whole helicopter would be hurled in the opposite direction to the path of the blade–usually to the detriment of both the helicopter and the pilot.

Similarly, the first Bell offered marginal performance in the mountains. Pilots yearned for more engine power, for the superchargers with which so many fixed-wing aircraft engines were equipped. The advent of the helicopter turbocharger in the late 1950s, which maintained sea-level power up to 10,000 feet (3 050 m), took much of the terror out of mountain flying. As always, though, there was a penalty. If one did have an accident, fuel nearly always spilled onto the red-hot turbo-charger and the machine would catch fire.

The next development, eagerly awaited by many, was the turbine engine. This, it was claimed, would bring significant advantages: the power to weight ratio was a big improvement over the conventional piston engine; maintenance would be minimal; performance and reliability remarkable.

The first claim was incontestable; the second and third something of a joke to begin with. One unfortunate pilot set off across Canada on a demonstration flight with a light turbine helicopter. He experienced four engine failures. The last one, which occurred while he was flying through Rogers Pass, in British Columbia, earned him some grey hairs. He had lined up for a forced landing on a pull-off viewpoint beside the highway. Just as he settled into his final approach, a camper drove slowly into the middle of the parking area and stopped while its occupants admired the view. The pilot managed to slip over the edge of the viewpoint and go on down for a landing on the rocky bank of the Illecillewaet River. He was a professional. He managed to put down with very little damage to the helicopter.

The results of this disparity between the promise and the reality were interesting. When the first light turbine machines – the Bell 206, the Hiller 1100 and, a little later, the Hughes 500 – began to appear in commercial flying, they were all flown by senior pilots. A year and many flame-outs and forced landings later, the senior pilots were all back in piston-engined machines; the turbines were being flown by the "young turks." Some time passed before the grizzled veterans would climb back into the turbine machines. They were wise, because it turned out that the unreliability lasted for some time and, in the case of one of the new models, there was a fundamental defect which resulted in its disappearance from the British Columbia scene for some years.

Since both the Canadian Coast Guard and the RCMP first operated helicopters somewhat beyond our definition of the early days, we have devoted only one chapter to them. This does not imply a hierarchy of importance: both these organizations have and still do provide a very valuable service to the province; but they were not among the pioneers of helicopter flying in B.C.

There is one factor, however, that should be mentioned: a misunderstanding. The name Coast Guard suggests rather clearly to the general public a search and rescue role, and they are frequently criticized in the media for failing to fulfil this function. The simple truth is that the federal government long ago made a political decision that the armed forces would deal with rescue and the Coast Guard with supply and maintenance of marine navigational aids. It would cost vast sums of money now to reorganize and re-equip the Coast Guard for SAR duties; and in any case, they would merely be duplicating the remarkably efficient service provided by the armed forces. We sympathize with the Coast Guard people for having to bear criticism for something over which they have absolutely no control.

As for the Search and Rescue services provided by the RCAF and, more recently, the integrated armed forces, and the ambulance services provided by the provincial government, theirs is a story that deserves a book of its own. Within the limits of our resources, we can only hope that we have done these government services at least a measure of justice.

Central Airways Bell 47-B at Yakima, Washington State, 1947. Carl Brady is demonstrating the helicopter's versatility by picking up a message from a person on the ground without having to land.

CARL BRADY

CHAPTER ONE

A Trip to Yakima

*And that's how it started:
through Carl and Barney Bent and
some of the others sitting in a
coffee shop in Penticton and reading
this magazine.*

ALF STRINGER

The history of the helicopter goes back a long way; all the way to such distinguished minds as Archimedes and Leonardo da Vinci. Da Vinci, using principles proposed by Archimedes some 700 years earlier, produced a design for a "helix" which appeared in a 1505 manuscript. But this was a theoretical design, and as it turned out, the aerodynamics and the engineering involved in the actual production of a helicopter were so complex that another 400 years of experimentation–of trial and error, often comic, sometimes tragic–were to pass before the first practical examples of the concept took to the air more or less simultaneously in Europe and the United States, in the late 1930s.

In British Columbia, the first commercial helicopter flight took place only a decade later, in August, 1947, over the fruit orchards of Penticton and Summerland in the Okanagan Valley. Although it aroused some interest, and possibly excitement, amongst the local population, few people at the time seem to have realized what an impact this new machine was going to have on the future of the province.

The principals in this pioneering venture, Carl Agar, Alf Stringer and Barney Bent, were all ex-RCAF people, and all at the time were struggling to stay in the flying business after the Second World War. Carl and Barney were both pilots; they had served together as flying instructors at Abbotsford, in the Fraser Valley. Alf Stringer had served with them as a maintenance engineer.

All three were discharged from the RCAF as soon as the war ended. As with most people in their situation, Agar and Bent, together with another ex-RCAF pilot, Andy Duncan, began their civilian careers in aviation with an attempt to run a flying club–in this case at Penticton. One of the first things they had to do was to find a competent maintenance engineer to look after their machines, and Agar travelled to Vancouver to persuade Alf Stringer, who was then working as a garage mechanic in the lower mainland, to join them. Alf didn't really regard it as a golden opportunity.

Carl Agar came down to Vancouver; he spent some time talking to me and decided, I guess when he went back to the people who were going to form this club, that I'd be a likely subject to tighten the nuts and bolts for them, and so they decided to hire me and I headed up to the Okanagan Valley. In fact this deal in Penticton didn't sound too awe-inspiring but there wasn't much going on in aviation at that time anyway, so I thought I'd give it a whirl.

And business was slow. Few people at the time could afford to fly for pleasure and there was a surplus of ex-service pilots ready to fill any commercial jobs which did become available. So the new partners soon decided to branch out into the charter business. They set themselves up as Okanagan Air Services Limited, and began to investigate what seemed then the most likely road to success: the potential for aerial spraying. The Okanagan Valley is the prime fruit growing area in the province, producing apples, pears, peaches, apricots, cherries, plums and grapes, all of which were sprayed to protect them from insects in the short summer season.

Yet if aerial spraying seemed the most obvious commercial possibility at hand, some familiarity with American spray operators over the border in the Wenatchee district of Washington State tended to be discouraging. "We were shocked at the mortality rate of their pilots and aircraft," Barney Bent recalls. "We looked around at one another; there was Carl Agar and myself as pilots and Alf Stringer as the engineer. I think it was Alf who summed it up. 'Well,' he said, 'we could last at least six months with you two.'"

Alf Stringer describes the next move:

In 1946, Carl and a couple of the people who were involved with the flying club were sitting in the coffee shop in Penticton. I guess Carl had picked up the mail and read in one of the aviation magazines that a company called Central Aircraft, who operated out of Yakima in Washington, and who had been in the aerial spray business for years, were going to go into helicopters because they looked like the answer for spraying [The principal advantages were slow speed and remarkable manoeuverability, as well as the fact that the downwash from the rotor blades tended to drive the insecticide down into the foliage of the plants below].

We were thinking of equipping one of our Tiger Moths to do spraying. So we thought . . . well, since we didn't know anything about spraying, we might as well start out with two unknowns. If we could get some people interested in helicopters–we knew the fruit growers were interested in spraying because their livelihoods depended on it–and get some money collected together, we'd get into the helicopter business. And that's how it started: through Carl and Barney Bent and some of the others sitting in a coffee shop in Penticton and reading this magazine.

Unlike Agar and Stringer, Barney Bent had other resources besides flying. His family was involved in the metal fabrication business–one of the offshoots of which was to manufacture ground spray equipment for the fruit growers in the Okanagan Valley. As a consequence, he was perhaps naturally interested in the potential advantages of using helicopters for this purpose, and he readily agreed to a preliminary visit to evaluate the experimental helicopter operation in Yakima. He, Agar and Stringer went down

Alf Stringer and Carl Agar. Carl was presumably just back from the bush before his wife made him shave off the beard.

OKANAGAN COLLECTION

together, experienced their first demonstration helicopter rides in an open-cockpit Bell 47-B3 and returned to Penticton with a firm conviction that helicopters would provide all the answers to the problems of spraying fruit orchards. As it turned out, they were wrong about the spraying, but fortunately for them the helicopter had other potentials.

To continue with Alf's description:

So we went down to Yakima, where the Bell Company had a helicopter [The Bell Company's main plant was in Buffalo, New York]. They were actually testing–they weren't even at FAA [Federal Aviation Administration] certification yet–but they took us up for demonstration rides in this thing. Then we got back and tried to work up some enthusiasm among the fruit growers, then formed this public company and got the helicopter business started. In the spring of 1947 I went down to Yakima and started on a maintenance engineer's course. After a while Carl came along and started on the pilot's course and we went from there.

But while the three principals of Okanagan Air Services Limited may have been confident that helicopters were the answer, persuading businessmen to invest in their convictions was another matter–until, as is probably the case with most successful business ventures in their early stages–luck intervened. A group of businessmen in Penticton had decided to form a new airline to service the interior of the province. Led by Douglas Dewar, a distinguished New York chartered accountant who had retired in Penticton; Ernie Buckerfield, owner of a large feed supply company; O. St. P. Aitkens; Gordon Butler and James B. Kidston, they had applied to the Air Transport Board for a licence to operate. Their application was turned down; Canadian Pacific Airlines got the licence instead.

Okanagan Air Services were quick to spot the potential. As Barney put it:

So we said to ourselves, well, here's a fine opportunity; here are two or three people of substance who have obviously had their financing put together for this other airline–let's see if we can interest them. Which we did. They weren't exactly overjoyed to get into the helicopter business because they'd had their hearts set on the fixed-wing deal. But Mr. Dewar did agree to head up the company–Okanagan Air Services Limited. Even so, we had all sorts of problems raising $50,000 to buy the first copter. A helicopter at that time cost $35,000, plus a few spares and plus some training for Alf Stringer as an engineer and Carl as a pilot.

The machine they were considering was the Bell 47-B3, powered by a 178-horsepower Franklin aircraft engine. Instead of sitting horizontally as it did in fixed-wing aircraft, the engine was mounted vertically, with fuel tanks beneath it and the transmission and rotor mast above. The early models required a great deal of maintenance. Grease nipples and grease boots were still in the future, so the helicopter had to be virtually taken apart every 25 hours of flying time to be greased. The transmission, too; it had to be taken

Barney Bent served, with Carl Agar, as a flying instructor in the RCAF.

Flight-Lieutenant Carl Agar was a flight instructor in the RCAF during the Second World War.

DOROTHY AGAR

apart and have bearings replaced every 25 hours. The maintenance man had his hands full.

Fortunately for Alf, he was trained by an expert. Joe Beebe, of Central Aircraft in Yakima, had originally worked with the Bell company right from the early design stages during the Second World War; thus he knew as much about that particular type of machine as any engineer alive. For Carl, however, things were different. He was trained, coincidentally, by another Carl, Carl Brady, who had only 25 hours of helicopter flying time. So the two Carls were very much learning together; and Brady, like Carl Agar, went on to a distinguished career in helicopters. He began operating his own helicopter in Alaska in 1948. In 1957, he was co-founder of Economy Rotor Aids, and he is still active in the parent company, Rowan of Houston, who operate 110 helicopters.

When they actually started operating in British Columbia, everything looked promising. Dr. James Marshall, an entomologist at the Dominion Experimental Station in Summerland, gave them considerable support because he was aware that the fruit growers in the Okanagan were in danger of unintentionally sterilizing their land with too much insecticide. In their attempts to wipe out the pest insects, they had been using as much as 1,000 gallons (4 545 *l*) of dilute sprays to the acre (.40 ha). From the air, they could achieve the same effect with perhaps 5 or 6 gallons (23-27 *l*) to the acre. But there were to be some setbacks before they discovered this. The first operational flight took place, with insecticidal dust, over a test plot laid out on the Wally Mutch orchard, just outside Penticton. The downwash from the rotor blades bounced off the ground, forcing the dust up into the air again and the helicopter promptly disappeared from sight before it started to move into forward flight. They changed to liquid spray equipment for the next test.

Now they discovered that their troubles were connected with the functioning of the spray equipment and the logistics involved. Alf found himself spending far more time working on clearing plugged-up spray nozzles than on maintaining the helicopter; and when he did manage to keep the spray equipment operating for any length of time, they made a second disconcerting discovery: they found that they could spray at the rate of an acre a minute.

This would have been enormously encouraging if they had been dealing with large acreages. But the orchards in the Okanagan were small and diverse, and each one required a different kind of spray mixture. Thus, had they fully succeeded in solving the spray equipment problem, they would have needed a dozen helicopters all working at once to meet the demand during the relatively short season. Ironically, their very success made the operation unmanageable. For they would also have needed a large staff, equipped with a fleet of fuel and chemical tankers and other vehicles to support the fleet of helicopters. In addition, of course, there was the problem of what to do with all this staff and equipment when the short spraying season was over.

Then, just as they were facing these problems, disaster struck. Carl flew into some power lines and seriously damaged the helicopter–though fortunately not himself. It was a discouraging moment for the fledgling company, but their backers apparently never wavered. As Barney recalls: "We had a quick meeting right after it happened and Mr. Dewar and Mr. Buckerfield put it to the three of us: 'Do you want to carry on or don't you?' As far as I was concerned, it was up to Carl–he was flying the thing–and there was no question in his mind: 'Get the thing fixed; let's get back at it,' he replied, and that's just what we did."

They had started work at the beginning of August with their first machine, registered CF-FZX; now, less than a month later, it was grounded–damaged beyond immediate repair. But there were still two or three weeks of contract spraying to be done and they managed to lease another Bell 47-B3 helicopter, CF-FZN, from a Winnipeg company called Skyways Services Limited, that had decided to open a base in Vancouver but couldn't find any work for its machine. Having completed their first contract with the leased machine, Alf put FZX on a truck and drove it down to Yakima in the fall to take advantage of the facilities of the Bell company. He spent most of the winter rebuilding it from scratch–the first of many helicopters he was to rebuild in the years to come.

Now, in the spring of 1948, Okanagan learned another fact about helicopters that, in retrospect, seems very obvious. While a sizeable majority of the population might suffer from natural disasters, helicopter operators almost invariably benefit from them. When floods, landslides, avalanches or forest fires occur, the helicopter's versatility makes it invaluable; and the spring of 1948 brought one of the biggest floods in the history of the lower Fraser Valley. Among the many consequences of this flooding was a plague of mosquitoes severe enough to endanger people's health. Okanagan Air Services was awarded a contract by the government to spray portions of the valley. This turned out to be a much more practical proposition than orchard spraying in the Okanagan. Carl was faced with wide open fields and sloughs, and the spray consisted of a mixture of 99 per cent fuel oil laced with DDT–a mixture which did not clog the jets of their equipment. It was a very successful operation.

Meanwhile, however, Okanagan had doubled its fleet of helicopters. The machine they had leased from the Skyways company the previous summer, FZN, had been returned to the company in Winnipeg at the end of the season and it, too, was wrecked

Carl Agar in CF-FZX spraying to control a Hemlock Looper infestation near Windermere, July 1948.

BC MINISTRY OF FORESTS

Carl Brady, later president and chairman of the board of Economy Rotor Aids (ERA) Helicopters, a large Alaska-based company with over 100 helicopters and 15 fixed-wing aircraft. ERA was established by Brady in Yakima in 1948 as Economy Pest Control-Economy Helicopters, the year after he trained Carl Agar.

CARL BRADY

in an accident. Skyways ran into financial problems; they were unable to rebuild the machine and went out of business. After some skirmishing with the insurance company involved, Okanagan took over the remains for, in Barney's words: "a dollar down and dollar when they caught us sort of thing. The insurance company was happy to make almost any kind of a deal to get it off their hands."

The spraying job in the Fraser Valley had attracted a good deal of attention and publicity, and this led directly to another worthwhile operation–a contract with the provincial forest service to spray the Windermere Valley in the East Kootenays, where the forests were suffering from a heavy infestation of the "False Hemlock Looper" (*Nepytia canosaria*). This operation lasted from July 1 to July 24, and again it was very easy spraying; the only potential problem was that they would be working at altitudes between 2,500 feet and 4,500 feet (760-1 070 m)–altitudes that even the maker of the helicopter considered to be marginal for operations because, as you go higher, the air becomes less dense, the rotors provide less lift and the power of the engine diminishes.

But Carl Agar was more than equal to the challenge, and he began to develop the mountain flying techniques for which he became celebrated. He found that flying over mountains, and landing in small clearings or on sandbars in the creeks and rivers were not only feasible but thoroughly exhilarating; and what was perhaps more important, the forest service people were delighted with the results. Now, for the first time, everyone involved began to realize the huge potential of the helicopter for other tasks beside spraying. People could be lifted over mountains and dropped in small clearings– perhaps even dropped on top of mountains. The future looked very promising if they could make their machine do what Carl Agar felt it could do.

Before he accomplished that, though, Carl had much to overcome. For example, when learning to drive a car, the driver has to rehearse certain movements. He or she has to think consciously about how to change gear–right foot off the accelerator, left foot down on the clutch, move the gear shift, left foot up, right foot down—and so on. In time, of course, this becomes a reflex, requiring no thought. The difficulty faced by early helicopter pilots was that they had to unlearn the reflexes they had developed in flying fixed-wing aircraft and learn an entirely new set of reflexes. The first, most important reflex was this: in a fixed-wing aircraft, you must maintain forward speed because it is the relative airflow, acting on the wing, that provides lift. If you let the speed drop below a certain limit, you will stall and drop out of the sky. In a helicopter, because the wing is rotating at a more or less constant speed, you do not have to worry about forward speed as a means of staying in the air–unless you are high in the mountains,

During the Windermere operation in July 1948, Alf Stringer followed Carl and the B3 in a pickup truck stocked with fuel and spare parts. The spray bars seem to be receiving attention in this photo.

This closed-cockpit Bell 47-B was in use in Yakima when Carl Brady trained Carl Agar in 1947, and may have been the one Brady landed on the Tiedemann Glacier in B.C. the following year.

Carl Agar and Alf Stringer with their new Bell 47-B3 after its arrival in British Columbia early in August 1947. The castoring forward wheels allowed manoeuvring on the ground. This was a throwback to fixed-wing taxiing and not really needed on a helicopter, which can move slowly in any direction a foot or two above the ground. The hoppers and discharge tubes for insecticide are behind the cockpit. Agricultural models of the 47-B had open cockpits.

STOCKS FAMILY COLLECTION / INTERIOR PHOTO BANK

Power lines are virtually invisible to low-flying helicopters and an encounter with them will often have drastic results. Carl Agar had just such an accident in 1947 and Alf Stringer spent the following winter rebuilding the machine. (*Top*) Alf Stringer is removing the rotor blades. A truck-mounted A-frame was used while dismantling the helicopter.

ANDY DUNCAN PHOTO / OKANAGAN COLLECTION

Towers such as this one were used in triangulation. It was important to establish these benchmarks as high as possible. Helicopters on occasion replaced them by simply hovering at the required height over the spot.   BC MINISTRY OF ENVIRONMENT

Before turbocharging, helicopters like this 47-B3 would be pushed to performance limits when operating in the mountains, particularly in hot weather. In late fall or winter, as in this photo, colder air provided greater lift. From a landing pad right on the side of a hill, the pilot could literally drop the helicopter over the side and dive to gain air speed and lift.

BILL MCLEOD

where the air is thin.

In practice, though, forward speed does provide more lift to a helicopter, and this was the problem Carl Agar had to solve. He had discovered the difficulties of getting into the air on hot days even at relatively low altitude. The trick was to lift off and then move rapidly into what is called translational lift: the extra airflow, and thus lift, generated by forward speed. In short, you had far more lift once you had achieved 30 to 40 mph (50-60 km/h), than you had when hovering. It wasn't an easy problem to solve because in physics there are no miracles, and the helicopter pilot has another anxiety. He has to maintain rotor speed–a speed that decays quickly if too much load is put on rotary wings.

On the early Bell helicopters, the engines had to operate at between 2,900 and 3,100 revolutions per minute, the rotor at about one tenth of this speed–from 290 to 310 revs. The "collective" lever that controlled this aspect of helicopter flying lay to the left of the pilot's seat. Moving it up and down altered the pitch on the main rotors, giving more or less lift, and the twist-grip throttle on the end of the collective fed in more or less power to maintain the desired revs.

Another difference between the aeroplane and the helicopter is that the wing on an aeroplane is relatively rigid and supports the weight of the aircraft by its structural strength, whereas the helicopter's blades, which are wings, are much more flexible, relying on the centrifugal force imparted by rotation to support the weight of the aircraft. Consequently, if the revs drop too low, the rotor blades will simply fold up like the spokes of an umbrella in a gale, and the helicopter will fall out of the sky. At the other end of the scale, if the revs are allowed to climb too high, the blades are likely to break loose from too much centrifugal force, with a similarly undesirable consequence.

Another thing Carl learned was that, if the helicopter was lifted off the ground with some vigour, even on hot days the momentum in the rotor system would keep the revs up for some seconds before they began to decay. After thinking about this and the problem of high-altitude landings and take-offs, Carl came to a conclusion: he knew that if he came into a high landing with some airspeed, killing forward motion just as he reached the landing spot, he could land–at least as high as 5,000 feet (1 525 m). When it came to the take-off, momentum alone wouldn't be enough to keep in the air long enough to attain translational lift. The answer was to land at the edge of a cliff, or very steep drop off. Then, when it came to the take-off, jump the machine over the edge and push the "cyclic" stick* forward to pick up speed in a dive and fly to the next landing.

All this, like most other good ideas in retrospect, seems obvious but it required a good

* Movement on the horizontal plane–forwards, backwards and sideways–was controlled by the conventional control column between the pilot's knees. Called the "cyclic," it provided differential pitch to the blades through a mechanism known as the swash plate. If the pitch of the blade sweeping in front of the bubble was decreased (less lift), and the converse occurred on the blade sweeping past the tail (more lift), the machine would tilt forward and begin to move forward, as it would in any direction if this differential was applied. This same differential pitch mechanism also solved the most enduring problem faced by early helicopter designers. If the blades maintained equal pitch when the machine was in forward flight, the one moving forward into the airflow would provide far more lift than the one retreating into the airflow and the helicopter would roll over. The swash plate, once again, maintained differential pitch to overcome this problem.

Carl Agar dropping off the edge. Note that originally the 47-B3 was flown from the right seat. This soon changed because all the early pilots had converted from fixed-wing, and they felt more comfortable on the conventional left seat for fixed-wing flying.

deal of intelligence to work out, and must have taken a great deal of courage to put into practice for the first time. Fortunately, Carl possessed both attributes and, by the time Okanagan Air Services had been approached by the provincial government – the Surveys Branch of the Land Department – to experiment with the helicopter in the mountains, Carl was ready to demonstrate what could be done, even though he still had much to learn.

The genesis of this venture is intriguing because the suggestion actually came from a university student on a temporary summer job. The late Ernie R. McMinn, who would in time become Director of Surveys and Mapping in the provincial government, recalled the exact beginnings: "In 1947, on my first survey job up in Terrace, we had a university student on the crew, and we'd gone out to do a little practice mountain climbing to see how the crew could handle it. We got up on top of this hill at Terrace and I said, 'My God, it's taken us five hours to get here, and look at it – you could land a bomber up here. This kid looked around. He said, 'Well, why don't you use one of these new-fangled things, a helicopter?' We all laughed about that; but when we got back to camp, we mentioned it to the party chief, Gerry Emerson. He was a really bright and resourceful person, and instead of laughing he took to the idea, and followed it up."

The Topographic Survey crews were engaged in triangulation. Using theodolites to measure angles and distances, they were laying out a survey grid from which the cartographers could make their maps. In triangulation, the longer the base lines the more accurate the grid and the less work has to be done to complete it. Obviously, therefore, the higher they could place their instruments, the longer the base lines. But getting high with all the equipment they required was backbreaking work on foot; so they were naturally interested in any machine that might relieve them of this burden.

Gerry Emerson, with the support of the Surveyor-General, Norman Stewart, contacted Okanagan Air Services and arranged a contract for 25 hours of flying time during the late summer of 1948. They were to work on a map sheet in the Chilliwack area – in the Wahleach Mountain Range that runs southeast towards Chilliwack Lake. The cost was to be $85 an hour for the helicopter. It is interesting to note that Carl Agar was earning only $350 a month for this very dangerous experimental flying, and Alf Stringer only $300 for maintaining a very complex machine. Carl Agar and Alf Stringer arrived with their helicopter at Chilliwack airport, Ernie McMinn recalls, "and we went down and looked at it. Gerry showed Carl on the map where he wanted to go. He wanted to land on a mountain called Cheam Peak. Carl went off by himself and had a look.

The late Gerry Emerson, shown here refuelling the B3, was party chief on the first Topographic Survey conducted and supported solely by air. He was quick to realize the remarkable advantages of helicopters for survey work, but also appreciated their limitations. His enthusiasm and leadership did much to advance helicopter use and technology in the very early days.

New instruments and techniques were introduced as helicopter use increased in topographic surveys. In the left foreground is a tellurometer, which transmits a signal to a dish mounted at the foresight and the backsight. By measuring the time the signal takes to bounce back, distance can be determined. On the right is a theodolite to measure the angle. Both could be readily moved by helicopter, which in this case, is a Hiller 12E.

The late Ernie McMinn, shown here on the side rack of a 47-D1, was involved with helicopters almost from the beginning of their operations for the Topographic Surveys Branch.

BC MINISTRY OF ENVIRONMENT PHOTOS

When he got back, he said, 'Fine, I found a spot back there and landed on it. Had to chase a black bear off it first—but it's no problem.'"

In fact, Carl had spent some time working out the best procedure for a landing and take-off from a small, frozen lake in a cirque at the 5,300-foot (1 615-m) level. First he approached it at 40 miles an hour (64 km/h), peeling off while he still had room to drop off the edge of the cirque and pick up speed again if he needed to. Then he tried it at 30 miles an hour (48 km/h). Finally, he decided to commit himself, gradually dropping his speed as he let down until he arrived at the ice surface just as he reached zero forward speed. He was anxious about the strength of the ice at that time of the year, but on wheels, it provided a temptingly flat landing surface. As it turned out, the lake was sheltered from the sun most of the time and it bore his weight. The take-off was a little more difficult, but by over-revving the engine slightly he got away all right.

Norman Stewart, the Surveyor-General, was his first passenger. They landed on the ice again but decided it was not reliable for repeated landings; so they climbed up onto the ridge in front of the lake, found a flat spot and cleared away the rocks until they had a satisfactory landing site. Carl left Stewart there and went back for Gerry Emerson and then Ernie McMinn. As Ernie described it:

We got on this ridge and found we had to climb about half a mile to get to the mountain top. In fact, as we realized later, the ridge Carl had chosen was far from ideal for a helicopter landing. It was at the foot of a glacial cirque—a ridge of gravel in front of a little lake with a wall of ice behind it; and of course the cold air was coming down off this ice like a waterfall. Not a good place for any kind of flying machine. Anyway, we climbed the mountain and on the way up we walked into the remains of a [Lockheed] Lodestar. It had piled into the mountain in '42, I think. It was an Air Force machine and the engines were burned right into the rock. Just a pile of aluminum down at the bottom of a cliff. We got back to the landing and Carl picked us up just as the fog was rolling in. The weather really socked in. I think we were grounded in the pouring rain for the next five days.

Thus began the first of many, many helicopter survey operations in which Ernie McMinn was involved. He remembers being excited rather than nervous on those first experimental flights:

We thought it was a great thrill—sailing over this ground at 60 miles an hour [96 km/h]. We could see how long it would take to walk through it; if you could walk a mile an hour [1.6 km] you were doing pretty well. And Carl didn't like heights. The only place he felt safe was sitting in this flaming helicopter. Getting out on the ridge of a mountain, he'd walk over to the edge and suck his breath in. This became a familiar affectation: a mountain pilot claiming fear of heights invariably raised a chuckle. But, we had a lot to learn.

The biggest problem to begin with was the wheels. the helicopter had four little wheels, and they were a menace. It was awfully hard to find somewhere really flat to land—and if you landed on a slope, the

"We thought it was a great thrill—sailing over this ground at 60 miles an hour [96 km/h]. We could see how long it would take to walk through it; if you could walk a mile an hour [1.6 km] you were doing pretty well. And Carl didn't like heights. The only place he felt safe was sitting in this flaming helicopter. Getting out on the ridge of a mountain, he'd walk over to the edge and suck his breath in."

ERNIE MCMINN

machine would start to roll. There were no brakes. I remember once they tried to take off from the top of a snow slide and couldn't quite make it, so they had to land again on the slope and rolled all the way down the snowbank–about three or four hundred yards [274-366 m]. Eventually, they reached a flat space and stopped. After a good deal of soul searching, they took off again.

But still, apart from the wheels, the biggest problem was getting off with a load when you were high–up about five or six thousand feet [1 500 or 1 800 m]. You had to carry a theodolite and tripod, which weighed about 35 pounds [16 kg], and a camera, which in those days weighed about 30 pounds [15 kg]. So Carl soon came up with the idea of landing on the edge of a drop off. He'd take some extra revs. I can remember some of those take-offs: the rpm's were dropping back from 3,600 to about 2,800, and the thing was falling, but it was falling clear, and gradually we'd pick up the revs again. [Clearly, Carl Agar did not pay much attention to the maker's red line on the tachometer: 3,200 was supposed to be the maximum.]

Alf Stringer responded to the problem of the wheels by improvising his own braking system. He cut some strips from an old car tire and wedged them between the axle and the tire. This worked after a fashion, but they had advised the Bell helicopter people of this problem, and Bell responded by putting hydraulic brakes on the wheels. Stringer advised them at the same time that the real answer was to come up with some sort of fixed undercarriage; the helicopter didn't really need wheels, except when it was being moved in and out of a hangar, and then a simple dolly could be used. The first skid gear appeared in 1949, and after that only the very large helicopters had a wheeled undercarriage.

The other advantage of the skid gear, when it appeared, was that it lent itself to the fixture of loading racks on either side of the helicopter. Trying to carry tripods, instruments and back-packs in the small cockpit was obviously unsatisfactory. But these improvements were to come later; in the meantime, the first experimental operation with the Topographic Survey was a qualified success. The weather was bad much of the time and they did not accomplish as much as they had hoped. Nevertheless, they managed to occupy eight or ten survey stations and needed no more persuading that the potential was there.

From Chilliwack, Carl and Alf went straight to another job at Knight Inlet. It was a short job, only 12 hours of flying, but it broke new ground again. They were engaged in a timber cruising survey from the air, and the customer was delighted with the results: the ease with which they could pick out routes for the cruisers to travel on the ground and the simplicity of deciding where potential logging roads should be constructed.

That was the end of the second season. In most ways it had been a very successful one. They had made large strides from simple agricultural spraying to a much more versatile role for the helicopter; and this in turn meant that some firm decisions had to be made during the coming winter.

CHAPTER TWO

Okanagan Air Services: From Orchards to Mountains

No one knew at the time what the Kitimat project was about—we had no idea; it was a hush-hush deal.

BARNEY BENT

Alf Stringer was boarding with Carl Agar and his wife Anne in Penticton during the winter of 1948, and they spent endless hours discussing what the future should be. They had already concluded that aerial spraying was out. Now they decided that the future lay in competing with the horse–the packhorse trains which had always been used in the summer to take people and supplies into remote areas for surveying, mining exploration or timber cruising. By now, too, they also realized the problems of their isolation in the Okanagan Valley. To win the sort of contracts they were beginning to contemplate, they needed to be closer to the seats of industry and government: Vancouver for the one; Victoria for the other. They settled for the former, renting hangar space at Vancouver airport in the spring of 1949. The company was still in the red; they had yet to earn a profit.

The year began with two jobs: one, a spell of mining exploration at Herbert Arm, operating out of Tofino on the west coast of Vancouver Island; the other, the building of the Palisade Lake dam in the mountains north of Vancouver, which was to augment the city's water supply. The latter was particularly valuable because it was such a visible operation. Practically everyone in greater Vancouver could see the helicopter at work; at least some of them must have begun to realize its potential in their own fields.

For this job Okanagan Air Services had hired the pilot of the defunct Skyways company, Paul Ostrander, to fly the second helicopter, while Carl flew FZN on the mining job. Between them they flew long hours, moved many people and a great deal of equipment, and did much to bring the helicopter out of the category of a curiosity into the realm of genuine utility. But the fundamental economic problem still faced them: they were only working in the summer, perhaps from June until early September. How to survive the seven months of winter with $100,000 worth of helicopters sitting idle in the hangar?

Nevertheless, things were beginning to look up, and in a letter to David Forman, Manager of the Bell Company's Helicopter Division, dated July 7, 1949, President

Douglas Dewar was able to say: "You will be interested in knowing that we have just concluded a contract on a twelve-month basis with the B.C. Electric Company and the Greater Vancouver Water District; for the former we will make a monthly patrol of their power lines, and for the latter we expect to move 500,000 pounds [226 800 kg] of construction materials to their new dam site at the head of Capilano.

"We are also concluding a contract with the Provincial Government Mapping Division for a topographical survey in difficult country in Northern B.C., following a similar successful operation last year."

They were busy and enjoying the satisfactions of accomplishment if not yet much in the way of financial reward. When Carl finished his job out of Tofino, he went at once to another spell of timber cruising with the company he had worked for the previous fall–this time round Elaho Lake, north of Squamish. From there he went to Lytton to fly two geologists, McKenzie and Warren, to a landing close to the 8,000-foot (2 400-m) level of Mount Gott, where he left them, with their camping and prospecting gear, to walk down when they had finished. While he was in Lytton, he received a message to return to Vancouver and meet what turned out to be one of the most important customers he was ever to meet–Wilfred Heslop, a professor of Civil Engineering at the University of British Columbia, who was acting as a consultant to B.C. International Engineers. Carl took him for demonstrations of the helicopter's capabilities in and around the mountains on the north shore. Heslop did not have much to say at the time, but he asked Carl to meet him in Terrace on August 31, for two or three weeks of flying.

Meanwhile, Paul Ostrander was more than pulling his weight on the Palisade dam job, flying as many as 30 round trips a day, carrying everything from lumber and nails to concrete, together with a concrete-mixer. The mixer barrel weighed 400 pounds (180 kg) and became the first sling-load to be carried beneath a helicopter. A landing platform was constructed with a hole large enough to allow the barrel to be lowered into it. The helicopter landed above it. Four wires were slung from each of the undercarriage legs and hooked onto the bowl, which was then eased out of its hole in the platform and flown up to the dam site.

While this was going on, Carl left for Hazelton to begin the operation with the Topographic Survey people mentioned in Dewar's letter to the Bell company. Although he did not know it at the time, this was the first phase of the Survey's plans for a three-year project, under the direction of Gerry Emerson, to cover the area from Hazelton up to Atlin. Seven weeks later, with one Topo job finished, he received a request to go to the Indian village of Kitimat to assist Ernie McMinn, in charge of the government

A typical Surveyors' alpine fly camp.

mapping project for the valley. After three months of difficulties with bad weather, rain-forest jungles and river crossings, the project was completed in eleven hours flying time. Then Carl flew to Terrace for his pre-arranged meeting with Heslop. With him, he returned to the Indian village of Kitimat, where a stock of fuel and oil for the helicopter had been landed by boat during the summer. They stayed and worked out of there for the next two weeks.

This was the beginning of the Aluminum Company of Canada's Kitimat-Kemano project which, if not actually the largest, was certainly one of the largest industrial development projects ever undertaken in British Columbia. It was also the turning point for both Okanagan and the entire helicopter industry; and luck was with them right from the start. Barney Bent remembers it with a gleam of satisfaction in his eye:

No one knew at the time what the Kitimat project was about—we had no idea; it was a hush-hush deal. However, Carl met Professor Heslop at Terrace on the appointed day, and they were extremely fortunate with the weather; they had about two weeks of absolutely clear CAVU [ceiling and visibility unlimited] weather—which is certainly not a common occurrence in that area. As it turned out, the engineer was looking for a route for the power line. They had pretty well established from aerial photographs where they were going to locate the dams and the hydro generating station, but the big question mark was the routing of the power line from Kemano to Kitimat. Carl flew them over some thirteen potential routes in the two weeks they were together.

They flew every day for long hours and they not only covered the power line routes, but also the lake areas where they were planning to reverse the existing flow of the drainage with their dams. They did so much work that everybody concerned was completely satisfied with the operation of the helicopter. They estimated they had saved one year, and possibly a good two years of engineering in that two weeks of clear flying. As a consequence, they assured us that if this project did go ahead, we were right in there, solid—and from day one. And the Kitimat project was the big break for Okanagan because it got us over the problem of seasonal flying. From now on we could plan, hire our crews, train them and know we were going to get a steady income. It made all the difference.

While this was going on, an interesting development had taken place in Vancouver. Okanagan Air Services had been approached by a well-known mining entrepreneur who had asked for comprehensive details about helicopter operations. Confident that another job was in the offing, they gave him all the information he wanted. A week or two later, management discovered that this individual was setting up a rival helicopter company. The new company never materialized but the incident created some excitement. Almost simultaneously, Ostrander left to return to Ontario, and now it became necessary for Carl to train a replacement to fly their second machine. Bill McLeod, the man he chose, was a seasoned fixed-wing bush pilot whose background, since it was so typical of a post-war bush pilot, is worth recording in some detail.

This was the beginning of the Aluminum Company of Canada's Kitimat-Kemano project which, if not actually the largest, was certainly one of the largest industrial development projects ever undertaken in British Columbia. It was also the turning point for both Okanagan and the entire helicopter industry; and luck was with them right from the start.

McLeod was born in Nanoose, north of Nanaimo on Vancouver Island, but his parents moved to Ladysmith shortly afterwards and he received his education there. The year after he graduated from high school, he took a course in aircraft engineering with a small company called the Brisbane Aviation School in Vancouver. It was a correspondence course, lasting for nine months, after which he completed three months of practical training and promptly went to work for a flying school called Foggin Flying Services. While working as an engineer (mechanic) for the flying school in 1939, Bill learned to fly on a Fleet 2 biplane.

By now, the war had started, and Bill volunteered for the RCAF. He could not get in as aircrew because at that time the RCAF required at least two years of university education for potential pilots. So he joined as an aero-engine mechanic, went to work in an Elementary Flying Training School, and promptly applied to remuster to pilot.

After completing his aero engine mechanic's training at St. Thomas, Ontario, he was posted to Ucluelet on the west coast of Vancouver Island. Here he worked on Stranraer flying boats until his reclassification came through and he was posted to an Initial Training School in Edmonton, an Elementary Flying Training school in High River, and a Service Flying Training School in Calgary. From there he went on to learn how to instruct in Arnprior, Ontario, before finally ending up as an elementary flying instructor in Fort William.

His next move was to be a significant one as far as Bill McLeod's future was concerned. He was sent to Abbotsford, in the Fraser Valley, and here, for the first time, he met Carl Agar, Commanding Officer of the flight he was posted to. Teaching students in de Havilland Tiger Moths, and talking endlessly as pilots do about flying, they got to know each other rather well. Then the war ended, and each went his own way – Carl to found the Penticton Flying Club, and Bill to run a small flying club for B.C. Airlines in Vancouver.

Bill's next move was to Queen Charlotte Airlines, this time as a pilot on Stranraers. Later he flew Norseman floatplanes (the predecessor of the de Havilland Beaver) and Waco's. Then, in 1948, he moved up to Prince Rupert to open up and manage a base there. There followed a period of coastal flying which broadened his experience tremendously: six days a week into the Queen Charlotte Islands; one day a week into Alice Arm and Stewart, interspersed with unscheduled charter work which might take him almost anywhere in the province. Flying the west coast in an aircraft with only basic flight instruments was at once the purest and perhaps the most difficult flying in the world. For much of the year, if you didn't fly in the rain, you didn't fly at all. The coast

The configuration of the Okanagan 47-B3s changed considerably during their operational lives. The first stage was to add a full bubble and remove the engine panels, as in this photograph. Next, the wheels were replaced by skids and the covering removed from the tail boom. Finally, the tail skid was replaced by a harp and the fuel tanks were moved up behind the mast to provide gravity feed to the carburetor. At this stage, the model designation changed to 47-D1.

A worker unloading supplies from the racks of CF-FZN at the Palisade Lake Dam site north of Vancouver in 1949.

A substantial helicopter pad in the mountains; many were far smaller.

ALF STRINGER

Ada Carlson joined Okanagan when things were starting to look up.

ADA CARLSON

is a baffling maze of inlets, sounds, bays, arms, islands and canals; and if the pilot could see more than half a mile ahead, he felt as a motorist does after emerging from the rush hour traffic of a city onto a quiet country lane.

But clearly there were compensating factors, and when Bill left QCA it was because of personal problems and not because he disliked the job or the company. He had, he said,

left QCA and come down to Vancouver with nothing in my mind, really – I didn't know what I was going to do. In the first three days I was offered five different jobs. The aviation community was still relatively small and you got to be pretty well known. One of the people to offer me a job was Carl Agar – so this was where the helicopter thing started.

We met in the coffee shop [where so much of the business of flying seems to have been transacted], and Carl said to me, "How would you like to fly a helicopter?" I looked at him to make sure he was serious. He was. "I've never even seen one," I replied. And I hadn't – I had never even seen a helicopter at that stage of my career. And he said, "Well, you come over with me and have a look. I've got a little job to do. You can come along on this job and that'll give you an idea of what you can do with a helicopter."

The job turned out to be a remarkably effective demonstration of the versatility of a helicopter:

There was this big smoke stack at one of the mills, over on the Fraser, and they had to hang a rope on it – a hook attached to an endless rope which would drop down and allow the steeplejacks to climb the stack and pull up the equipment they needed to work on it. So I climbed into this stupid machine – at that time I figured it was a stupid machine – it was the open-cockpit Bell 47-B3 with the four wheels. They had had a hook manufactured – a home-made thing with a sort of a loop on the bottom and a long arm welded to it so I could reach out and clip it over the edge of the steel chimney. The rope went through the loop, and I had the rest of it, a big coil of heavy rope, in my lap.

So we took off and chugged off along the Fraser. There was a nice brisk wind blowing from the west, about 25 miles an hour [40 km/h], which gave us a bit of added lift. Carl steamed up alongside this smokestack and I found I couldn't handle the pole sitting down. I had to put the rope on the floor, undo my seat belt, climb half out of the machine and put one foot on the wheel leg to hold the pole properly. Anyway, I got the hook on, picked up the rope and threw it down and got back into my seat. Then I realized that the long handle of the hook was against my stomach and if Carl started to move forward I was going to end up with a bad stomach-ache. So I got back out again, held on to the door frame, put my foot against the smokestack and gave a good shove. The machine moved away and the handle dropped out. I sat down again and gave Carl the thumbs up and away we went. By the time we got back to the airport, I was thinking: "anything you can do that with, I've got to learn to fly."

Bill McLeod was trained by Carl Agar in the winter of 1949-50. When he left to work on his first operation he had some 60 hours of helicopter time. But his mountain flying experience consisted of four demonstrated landings and perhaps 20 landings and take-offs on his own, all on three locations.

The coast is a baffling maze of inlets, sounds, bays, arms, islands and canals; and if the pilot could see more than half a mile ahead, he felt as a motorist does after emerging from the rush hour traffic of a city onto a quiet country lane.

The job he started on was the Topographic Survey operation, beginning where the previous year's crew had left off. They started north of Kispiox, up the Nass River, at Brown Bear Lake, and worked north up the valley of the Nass to the Bell-Irving River. This was the first time the Topographic Survey had worked entirely with air support. Fixed-wing aircraft took in the equipment and supplies; helicopters moved the surveyors from one occupied survey station to the next. They had finally abandoned the pack horse.

Bill recalls the encouragement he received at the start of this, his first helicopter operation:

When the machine was loaded up and I was ready to leave for Kispiox, Carl came out and shook hands with me and he said: "Well, Bill, remember one thing – if you get through this season without breaking a helicopter, you'll be the first man who's ever managed to do so." With those happy words ringing in my ears, I climbed into the machine and took off. As it turned out, I did manage to get through that first season without breaking a helicopter, but I sure scared the hell out of myself a few times.

You see, the truth was, you had to learn a whole new ball game. Remember that in an airplane you're trained right from day one to approach a landing, and to take off, into wind. If you persist in this in a helicopter in mountain terrain, you're dead – you're going to kill yourself; it's just that simple. Because it means that if you're approaching a mountain and you're into wind, you're also in the down draft. If you do that, pretty soon you'll find yourself looking up at the place you were going to land, instead of down at it. So you get a few more grey hairs and you scare yourself a couple of times and you say, there's got to be a better way, and you develop these ways. You approach downwind and turn into wind at the last minute – something like that.

An awful lot of what I learned that first season wound up in the mountain training manual Okanagan produced, because I wrote a lot of it; but only after I'd discussed my experiences with Carl Agar. That was Carl's great talent: he had a very special ability to talk to a pilot after the pilot had had some shaky experience and reduce it to its elements. He seemed to be able to see through what you were saying to the essence of what had happened. I guess this came from his long experience as an instructor. I think it was this ability to sort out the meat of an experience and then analyze it that made Okanagan Helicopters what it became.

You see, the learning experience had to depend on making mistakes – that was the only way you could learn. If you're going into the unknown and there's nobody to guide you, you're going to make mistakes and, if you survive, you hand your knowledge down to others so that they won't make the same mistakes. The trouble is you have to go through some awfully hairy experiences to start with.

I'll give you one example. I had landed on a ledge at about 6,500 feet [2 000 m], a ledge jutting out from the mountain. There was a short cliff on one side and a sheer drop on the other, and the ledge would be about, oh, perhaps 150 feet [46 m] wide. I landed about 60 feet [18 m] in from the edge on a nice flat spot. On this particular day, I landed facing the cliff. What I learned then was that you never land unless you have figured out how you are going to take off again. Remember, we were at 6,500 feet, and the only way you can get back into the air at that height is to over-rev the engine and jump

The job he [Bill McLeod] started on was the Topographic Survey operation, beginning where the previous year's crew had left off. They started north of Kispiox, up the Nass River, at Brown Bear Lake, and worked north up the valley of the Nass to the Bell-Irving River. This was the first time the Topographic Survey had worked entirely with air support. Fixed-wing aircraft took in the equipment and supplies; helicopters moved the surveyors from one occupied survey station to the next. They had finally abandoned the pack horse.

off over the edge. You'll lose your revs, but after picking up airspeed for a thousand feet or so [300 m], you'll pick up your revs again as well. But this time I did my jump take-off too far from the edge. The body of the machine was going to go over the edge all right, but I knew the tail wasn't. I was already losing revs by the time I realized this. I shoved hard forward on the stick and then kicked on full rudder. I cartwheeled over the edge – cart-wheeled so far that I was inverted at one stage and then I pulled out and got clean away with it. Right there, it was another few grey hairs. But after that I always landed very close to the edge of a drop off; and I always jumped sideways off a ledge.

When he had successfully completed the Topographic Survey contract for the season, McLeod's next job was to fly men and equipment into the Reco Copper Mine. Although this was a relatively small job, it was an important one because the take-off and landing site was at Laidlaw, about 15 miles (25 km) west of Hope, right alongside the Trans-Canada Highway. Like the Palisade dam job, it was very visible and attracted a lot of attention.

By this time, another new employee, Jock Graham, had joined the company. He was an ex-Royal Air Force aviation mechanic who had been working, like so many of the early staff, for Queen Charlotte Airlines on the curiously diverse fleet of aircraft they had assembled (insiders said that QCA stood for Queer Collection of Aircraft). Graham was based in Vancouver and so, by now, was Okanagan Air Services Limited. They had leased a corner of a hangar and applied for certification of it as a permanent base. Graham, who worked in the same hangar, became intrigued by the curious machines Alf Stringer and Carl Agar were working on. He was single, with nowhere in particular to go in the evenings and he took to visiting them when his own work was finished.

He remembers the first meeting because it seemed to exemplify their ability to handle problems without getting excited. Carl was running up a machine after a transmission overhaul. The engine had to be run for something like an hour, after which filters were pulled and checked to see if there was any metal in them – metal shavings which would indicate that something was amiss in the transmission. The covering over the tail boom had been removed during the overhaul, and a large and determined swarm of bees had settled on the boom. The bees weren't troubling Carl in the cockpit, so they finished the run up, shut down and went to find a bee-keeper to remove the swarm before attempting to check the filters.

Some months later, with the Kemano contract in their pockets, Alf Stringer and Carl Agar decided to offer Jock Graham a job. He accepted, and his apprenticeship was to rebuild the second helicopter, the wrecked FZN which had been bought from the insurance company the previous winter and shipped to the coast from Winnipeg in a boxcar. Apparently, they all spent a great deal of their time in and around the hangar, often sleeping on a couch in a sleeping bag. It was a time of considerable excitement and tension for them all. The future looked very inviting, but none of them had enough experience yet to be sure that the helicopter would do all the things they were planning. Now they were setting up a formal company structure, and they had to start looking for other help besides pilots and engineers. Ada Carlson recalls how she was hired:

> My husband was a vocational teacher in Vancouver and somebody from Okanagan phoned him to ask if he could find them a stenographer. He said he couldn't and mentioned it to me when he got home. I said, "Why didn't you suggest me?" He said, "Well, you're too old." Anyway, he phoned them back the next day and said I was a good steno and they told him to send me over. That's how I became their first secretary in Vancouver. It wasn't much of a job to begin with—just a corner of the old Queen Charlotte Airlines' hangar. They didn't even have a ladies' washroom; I had to go across to the airport terminal.

Carl's widow, Anne, remembers more clearly than anything else the difficulty her husband was encountering at the time in his attempts to raise working capital, particularly from the more affluent members of the community. Both she and Ada recall that Douglas Dewar, a millionaire who had recently retired as president of the Wall Street accounting firm of Peat Marwick Mitchell, was also very much a Scotsman. As Ada put it: "He did have some money in, but it was really a small amount. I was amazed when I got there to find out that one director had one share, and somebody else had a share and it was nothing, you know."

Ada Carlson stayed with the company as an executive secretary until her retirement in 1963. When Okanagan's prosperous years began, she remembers that Carl decided to have a large and very attractive house built on the corner of Angus Drive and 71st Avenue in Vancouver. Typically, Carl was determined that it should be well built, plumb and true, and he asked his engineers for an accurate carpenter's level so that he could check construction as it progressed. His staff provided one, but only after they had rigged the bubble to give a false reading. We have no record of Carl's relations with his builder after that.

Meanwhile, Jock Graham stayed in Vancouver, making forays to the Reco Copper operation near Hope to do maintenance, and attending to the other helicopter which was still working on the Palisade Lake job. Then came Kemano.

The Aluminum Company of Canada's Kitimat project was an imaginative one, but it was not greeted by everyone as enthusiastically as it was by the helicopter operators. Many people were seriously concerned about its effects on the environment and the salmon fishery. Dams were to be built on Whitesail Lake, Des Lake, the east end of Tahtsa Lake, and at the Canyon dam site on the Nechako River—thus reversing the flow of several very large lakes which normally drained into the Nechako River. This created a 335-square-mile (870-km^2) reservoir in Tweedsmuir Park, which was not to be cleared of trees before flooding. The water from this reservoir was to be released through a ten-mile (16-km) tunnel through the mountains from the west end of Tahtsa Lake, which in turn would drop it 2,600 feet (600 m) into the powerhouse turbine generators at Kemano. The powerhouse itself was constructed in a giant cave excavated out of the mountain. The power generated would then be transmitted to the aluminum smelter plant to be built at Kitimat.

For Okanagan Helicopters, though, it was a time of expansion and optimism. The initial crew, pilot Bill McLeod and engineer Jock Graham, arrived in February, 1951, before the first barge-load of supplies had been brought in up Gardner Canal. They began with a visit to a test tower which had been erected in Kildala Pass the previous summer by Carl Agar. This was the pass though which ALCAN were hoping to construct the transmission line. The tower was at 5,000 feet (1 525 m), and its purpose was to record the build-up of ice over the winter. Evidently the tests were successful because that was the pass chosen for the transmission line.

Things moved quickly after that. Bill McLeod recalls the first few weeks:

When we went in on the Kemano project, my first commitment was for eight weeks. Our reason for being there was to move the survey crews. The survey crews were going in only two weeks ahead of the road construction crews, who were going to build ten miles [16 km] of road from tidewater on Gardner Canal up to the actual powerhouse site on the Kemano River. The idea was that they could get the road surveyed up the valley and get far enough ahead of construction and maintain this lead so the construction crews coming on their heels would have a surveyed line and a surveyed road to work on; and of course, years later, the helicopters are still there.

I found that I was not only flying the surveyors, but I was flying all the construction people as well. At the end of eight weeks, you couldn't have got that thing out of there with a bull-dozer. They'd have killed you if you had tried to take the helicopter away from them.

Jock Graham remembers it as a time of adjustment. He had not previously worked out in the bush so he was not quite sure what to expect. Both he and many others on the project needed to come to terms with the area and its people. For example, on their way to Kemano, they landed on a large scow in Butedale. Bill McLeod had gone to visit someone, leaving Jock to look over the machine before they continued on the next leg of their flight. While he was doing so, an Indian strolled down to look at the helicopter. Jock addressed him in the Hollywood version of an Indian lingua franca. "How!" he said. "Heap big machine, eh?" The Indian studied the small Bell for a few seconds. "Mmm," he agreed gravely, "but not nearly as big as the Sikorsky S-51."

"I found that I was not only flying the surveyors, but I was flying all the construction people as well. At the end of eight weeks, you couldn't have got that thing out of there with a bull-dozer. They'd have killed you if you had tried to take the helicopter away from them."

BILL MCLEOD

Kemano, circa 1953. Two
Bell 47-D1s and ALCAN's first
Sikorsky S-55.

A United States Air Force B-36 bomber, en route from Alaska to Fort Worth in Texas, had encountered severe icing. After it had lost two of its engines, 12 of the crew had baled out, landing on Princess Royal Island. Five more stayed on board. As was learned much later, they had jettisoned an atomic bomb before attempting to continue the flight. The wreck of the bomber was found several years later near Prince George. The five remaining crew members were never found. The 12 on Princess Royal Island were rescued with the help of a Sikorsky S-51 helicopter. Presumably it landed at Butedale on its way to the search area.

The construction people experienced a similar culture shock. To begin with they worked off a scow tied up to the shore of Gardner Canal, living in a float camp rented from a lumber operator. Bill McLeod's first task was to put out the survey crews so that they could survey the initial line up to the Kemano site. George Smith, the surveyor in charge (who, in the course of time, became Jock Graham's father-in-law) went off to an Indian village to hire a crew to do the actual cutting. He sought out the Chief and, like Jock, spoke in a mythical argot. "You fit to cut trees for white man?" he inquired. "Yeah, okay," the Chief replied, "I presume you'll be paying union rates?"

While Bill was moving the line-cutting crews and the surveyors back and forth, Fred Snell came up with the other machine to join them. He went to work on the tunnel survey. As we have seen from McLeod's description, things went remarkably well from the very start. The performance of the helicopters lived up to their most optimistic expectations. In a matter of months, the pressure was on for more helicopters to meet the demands of the engineers as well as the surveyors.

Consequently, as the Kemano project swung into high gear, so did Okanagan Air Services Limited. During the first six months of 1951, they earned their first profits, $10,000. At the same time, their first two machines were converted by Alf Stringer to use skids instead of wheels, and he fitted the now familiar full plexiglass bubble instead of the original open cockpit with windshield. Now, too, they bought another helicopter from the Kenting company, CF-FJA, for $15,000 (this had been the first commercially licensed helicopter in Canada). Meanwhile, training of the crews proceeded apace. After D. K. "Deke" Orr, and Fred Snell, came Peter Cornwall, Leo Lannon and Don Poole as pilots; Sig Hubenig, Bill Smith and Gordon Askin joined Jock Graham as engineers. By the end of that year, they had three Bell helicopters, FZX, FZN and FJA, and ALCAN had bought two, GZX and GZJ, Okanagan having first offer if ALCAN decided to sell them.

By now the original concept of using the helicopter just to move the survey crews had long been forgotten. Innovations began to emerge. For example, a large boatload of material had to be moved from the east end of Tahtsa Lake to the west end, where the tunnel would begin. The lake was still frozen, so the old spraying equipment was installed on one of the helicopters. A mixture of soot and coal oil was sprayed in a 50-foot (15-m) swathe, stretching some 18 miles (29 km) along the ice. The black soot did not reflect the heat from the sun; consequently the swathe thawed much more rapidly than it would have unassisted, and the boat was able to move some two weeks sooner than it could have otherwise. Another innovation was the installation of landing pads as construction fanned out for the various phases of the development. They had to be built on the side-hills of the mountains so that engineers and drill crews could keep up with a project which was already well in advance of its original schedule.

Carl Agar and his wife, Anne, attended the investiture at Government House in Victoria in 1954 to receive the Air Force Cross awarded to him in 1945.

ANNE AGAR

Such obvious, in fact dramatic, progress brought about by the helicopter was bound to attract attention throughout industry and government, both in Canada and elsewhere. This resulted in some tension among the directors of Okanagan Air Services. Carl Agar, whose official position at this time was general manager, was eager to take advantage of the situation and wanted to expand. By now he was getting requests from Ottawa to train pilots to operate on icebreakers; the Army wanted mountain training for their pilots; geophysicists in the federal Department of Mines and Technical Surveys wanted a machine; the provincial Topographic Survey people wanted to expand their operations; and numerous mining companies were making inquiries. The demand for more helicopters was so insistent, Agar became convinced that if they, Okanagan, did not supply them, other companies would spring up to benefit from the pioneering that he and Alf Stringer had done. But Douglas Dewar, the president, tended to be more conservative. The capital costs required for expansion were formidable, and he wanted to proceed with more caution. There were some lively directors' meetings during this period. In the end, though, they reached a compromise. They did expand, but neither as fast as Carl would have liked, nor as slowly as Dewar would have preferred. History suggests that it was a successful compromise. They did not lose control through sudden over-expansion, and they did not lose business to any competitor. In fact, their first competitor in the west failed to appear until 1954.

In the meantime, much was happening to encourage everyone. Carl Agar was constantly in demand as a consultant and as a speaker; he was gaining almost month by month a sort of snowball of public recognition which, although it was gratifying, made it very difficult for him to keep pace with his workload. First, he was invited to attend an investiture in Victoria, where he was presented with the Air Force Cross—a decoration he had earned in 1945 but had not yet collected. Then in April, 1950, when he was at

Kemano, he learned that he had been awarded the McKee trophy, the most prestigious award in Canadian aviation. This in turn resulted in an invitation to speak at the International Air Transport Association's annual convention at Harrison Hotsprings.

Carl, in short, had become a celebrity. Soon after he returned from Harrison Hotsprings, he was invited to be the guest speaker at the annual convention of the Helicopter Association of America in Washington, D.C. Here he met for the first time Igor Sikorsky, the most veteran of helicopter designers. They took to each other from the first—in fact, Sikorsky had arranged to have Agar sit beside him at the head table—and this led to another significant development for Okanagan Air Services, the procurement of the first two large Sikorsky S-55 helicopters. But we are jumping ahead of our story.

Igor Sikorsky, Alf Stringer and Carl Agar discuss helicopters at a Vancouver hotel in 1954. Sikorsky and Agar were close friends by then.

CHAPTER THREE

Okanagan Helicopters: Kemano and New Horizons

When the noise finally died down,
I was still 30 feet [9 m] from the
ground in the trees, inverted,
swaying gently up and down and
listening to the pitter-patter
of the rain drops.

BILL MCLEOD

Except for some bulldozers parked in a clearing amongst the trees, the campsite at Kemano in the fall of 1951 looked very much like the construction camps in photographs taken at the turn of the century. The campsite was situated in the flats formed by the confluence of two streams with the Kemano River. The rows of wooden-walled tents squatted like tiny, angular mushrooms beneath the towering mountains; but the inhabitants of this small canvas city, erected the previous year by the Morrison-Knudsen and the Northern Construction companies, seldom felt the weight of those brooding mountains pressing down on them. The mountains were usually lost in the clouds which swirled in from the warm Pacific Ocean.

Normally the view was restricted to the muddy river and the dark, sombre trees, dripping with rain. All one could see of the mountains was an occasional sliver of snow in a deep gully, reaching up into the overcast. It was on just such a morning that Joan McLeod, wife of the Okanagan pilot, was tending the primus stove in her tent. She was baking an upside-down cake in the tin oven which surrounded the stove pipe. She remembers that oven with affection because in it she could cook large roasts of meat and serve everything from well done to extremely rare. This was important because, as the sole woman in the camp in the early days of the project, Joan had discovered that her tent was the only alternative to the company cook-tent. She found herself having to prepare a lot of meals. Apart from the fact that Joan was an excellent cook, there was another reason why her meals were so popular. The newly created society of Kemano was a very stratified society; supervisors could only associate with other supervisors; workmen only with each other. Yet in Joan's tent, because she was the wife of a helicopter pilot, the company could be mixed. It is an interesting fact, and one not easy to explain, but helicopter pilots and their families were nearly always acceptable in any gathering. For the moment, Joan found it very satisfying because, as she points out: "There were some fascinating people up there; people recently over from Europe. There was one chap who was literally digging ditches. He was an Austrian. He had been a Colonel—a very, very literate chap who got on awfully well with a lot of the others who were supervisors, and we could have him at the tent, and the supervisors as well and there was never any problem. Whereas he couldn't invite them to his tent, nor expect an invitation from them."

Joan was born in Toronto, spent some years in England, then returned to be educated in her home town. Armed with a degree in Modern Languages, she grew bored with Toronto and headed west, with no plans for a vocation. She worked for a while in an advertising agency, one of whose clients was the largest flying company in British Columbia at that time, Queen Charlotte Airlines. The advertising agency went bankrupt and she moved to QCA as traffic agent, radio operator and dispatcher in Prince Rupert. Here she met her husband, Bill, just before they both decided to leave QCA and Prince Rupert and head back to Vancouver.

The period before they were married, while Bill was taking his training as a helicopter pilot, was a lean one. Joan tried unsuccessfully to find a job, and they were forced to live on Bill's salary which, while he was training, was $200 a month.

But once Bill had made the transition from the Stranraers, Norsemen and de Havilland Rapides of QCA to helicopters, things began to improve. In Kemano in the fall of 1951 he had been working with the construction crew, putting in the road from tidewater to the new settlement. Now the project had expanded and he was flying construction crews into the newly-installed helicopter pads on the sidehills of the mountains. Work had begun on the tunnel from the west end of Tahtsa Lake, and on the main excavation for the power house. The two helicopters, one flown by Bill, the other by Fred Snell, were constantly in demand.

Joan McLeod made a good start on her upside-down cake that day, but it was never baked. Just as she was about to put it in the oven, she heard a commotion outside her tent. She stuck her head out of the fly to see what was going on and saw the engineering supervisor sprinting towards her along the lane between the row of tents.

"Where's Bill?" he demanded as he reached her. "Fred Snell's killed himself."

"Fred's not flying today–Bill is."

"Then where's Fred? Bill's killed himself."

Not surprisingly, Joan abandoned her cake and followed the supervisor in his search for Fred Snell. Failing to find him, they returned to the river, where the accident had occurred. Standing on the far shore, looking depressed but obviously not dead, was Joan's husband. After shaking his head, he turned and disappeared into the trees again.

Bill recalls that it had been raining so hard that day neither he nor Fred Snell had flown:

A sidehill pad
overlooking Kemano.

That was a bad year. We had one of those flash floods up at Kemano. Horetzki Creek, which flowed down into the Kemano River, was rising at a rate of about a foot an hour and a log jam had developed. They were afraid the camp would be flooded. A bulldozer went out to try to clear the jam and it dropped into a hole. There were three people on the "cat." One fell off and managed to swim ashore; the other two were up on the canopy, ankle-deep in the water. The water was still rising and two of the supervisors came to me and said, "those guys are going to drown; you'll have to get them off." So I said okay, but here's where I made my mistake: I didn't go over and tell those guys on the "cat" what to do myself—I told the others to tell them while I ran for the helicopter.

The instructions Bill wanted relayed to the men on the bulldozer canopy were to wait until Bill had put one skid on the canopy then, and only after Bill had given them the nod, they were to climb into the helicopter, one at a time. Bill had taken the doors off and when he got to within two or three feet of balancing one skid on the canopy, one of the catskinners made a wild leap and grabbed the front of the skid. The helicopter dropped violently and the nose of the skids actually went into the water. The only thing Bill could do now was to pull up hard on the collective (the control which makes a helicopter rise or drop vertically), and twist on as much throttle as he could. But the weight of the man on the front of the right skid pulled the helicopter down and to the right. There was, as Bill says, "nothing on the right but trees," and he went barrelling right into them.

"When the noise finally died down," Bill recalls, "I was still 30 feet [9 m] above the ground in the trees, inverted, swaying gently up and down and listening to the pitter-patter of the rain drops. The fellow who was riding the skid was still there; he was half in the machine and half out; he was sort of pinned. Of course the bubble was gone and I noticed the battery was smoking. You know those braided battery straps? Well, believe it or not, you can tear one of those apart with your hands if you're desperate enough."

The over-eager passenger was unconscious. Bill's first attempt to get him out of the machine failed. So he climbed down to the ground and found a branch to use as a pry. This time he was able to free the passenger and get him down to the ground. It was a ticklish business because Bill was afraid the whole helicopter might break lose and come crashing down. He managed to work the passenger free of the helicopter, ease him onto his shoulder and climb down to safety. The passenger recovered consciousness a few minutes later, but they were on the wrong side of the river and Bill emerged from the trees to see what was going on. What he saw made him shake his head in dismay after a minute or two and turn back into the trees.

There were some 400 people on the far bank and they were in the grip of a remarkable panic. One man was rushing into the water with a first-aid kit. He would rush in until the water reached his thighs, realize that he couldn't go any further, retreat to the shore, only to rush back into the water again, sobbing with frustration. A little further along, somebody had backed a bulldozer with a logging boom on it up to the water. A man was standing on the logging boom with a coil of rope, hurling it towards the far bank. It never reached more than half way across the river, but doggedly he retrieved it, coiled it and tried again. An hour later he was still doing exactly the same thing. "It was just unbelievable," Bill recalls. "All that crowd of people–it was mass hysteria."

Joan McLeod, surrounded by irrational panic, finally did the one thing that is effective for hysteria. She ran up to the engineering supervisor and booted him as hard as she could in the backside.

Shocked, he turned to look at her. "What did you do that for?" he demanded.

"To make you start thinking."

It worked. The engineer sent for a mobile crane. They strapped a large log to the boom, lowered it across the river and succeeded in rigging up a sort of bosun's chair that got Bill and his passenger back across the river safely, as well as the man still stranded on the bulldozer. Kemano at that time boasted a hospital of sorts and they were taken there to be treated. It turned out that Bill was more seriously damaged than his passenger. He had broken off the instrument pedestal in the helicopter with his shin, and he was in considerable pain and some shock.

Joan McLeod, by her own account, still had a rough night ahead of her:

The regular staff doctor was out on holiday and he had been replaced by a pathologist who had decided to take a busman's holiday in Kemano. He hadn't done any general practice work for some years. But he patched Bill up and gave him some pain killer which contained codeine. Later on we discovered that Bill was allergic to codeine. But at the time he seemed to settle down and we went back home to the tent. By now it was getting late, so I got Bill settled down in bed and then joined him and went to sleep.

Sometime in the small hours I woke up to find Bill standing with one foot on my face. He was talking very strangely, not very rationally, so realizing that something was obviously very wrong, I got up, wrestled him down onto the bed and got the dog to lie on top of him to keep him still while I went for help. I ran to the engineer's tent and woke him and he went for the doctor while I went back and lay on top of Bill with the dog to keep him still until the doctor arrived. This time the doctor gave him some morphine and Bill did finally settle down for the night.

Fortunately, Bill's injuries were not serious and he was very quickly back flying again. But there were two more accidents that summer. In the first, a construction worker walked into the tail rotor of GZJ, resulting in serious injuries. In the second, Fred Snell suffered an engine failure. He had to autorotate (the equivalent of a glide in a fixed-wing

Joan McLeod, surrounded by irrational panic, finally did the one thing that is effective for hysteria. She ran up to the engineering supervisor and booted him as hard as she could in the backside.

This 1949 photograph of a Topographic Surveys Branch crew was taken north of Hazelton in the Kispiox River Valley. Carl Agar is sitting on the rack directly below the rotor mast. To his left are the cook and Frank Speed. The rest are local men hired for the job.

BC MINISTRY OF ENVIRONMENT

As always very humble, Okanagan crews at Kemano felt obliged to record their achievements, including passengers scared, bulldozers lifted and lakes thawed. Here, clockwise from top left, are Bill Brookes, Deke Orr, Gordy Askin, Ivor Barnett, "Frenchie" (a Morrison-Knudsen employee) and John Porter.

GORDY ASKIN

In 1951 this helicopter, not yet fully converted from its original B3 configuration, was working on the Kitimat side of Kildala Pass and was required for a job back at Kemano. Bad weather in the Pass, and the urgency of the situation, meant that it had to be loaded on the stern of a vessel and shipped back.

GORDY ASKIN

ALCAN officials shortly before an inspection flight at Kitimat in May 1951: *(left to right)* A.W. Whitaker Jr., Vice President and General Manager; P. E. Radley, Manager; and J. S Kendrick, Assistant Manager, B.C. Project.

ALCAN

Okanagan's 47-D1, CF-GGC, on the Kemano project in 1953.

The Morrison-Knudsen construction camp at Kemano, circa 1950.

Joan McLeod, who initially had lived "downtown" in the middle of a row of tents, soon moved out to the suburbs of Kemano. Later, accommodation was in steel Quonset huts.

BILL MCLEOD

Bell 47-D1s, similar to those used on television's *MASH* series, were vital in the early days of the Kemano project.   ALCAN

Jock Graham was in charge of the engineering crew at Kemano.

JOCK GRAHAM

The ALCAN S-55s proved valuable at Kemano, their sling load being more than three times as great as that of the Bell 47-D1s. While owned by ALCAN, these machines were identified by a silver ingot on the nose. Okanagan soon purchased the ALCAN machines and subsequently operated more than 20 S-55s on the Mid-Canada Line.

ALCAN

Carl Agar stands beside ALCAN's
first S-55, CF-GHV; Bill McLeod
in cockpit.

According to Alf Stringer, the original tail boom on this S-55 was damaged and, because the aircraft was needed quickly, Pratt and Whitney (Sikorsky's representative in Canada) sent a replacement out that was originally intended for the RCAF. It was later repainted.

ERIC COWDEN

Carl Brady (centre) was elected president of the Helicopter Association of America, succeeding Carl Agar in 1957. The photo, taken at the Sheraton-McAlpine Hotel in New York, also includes Elynor Rudnick of Kern-Copters, Bakersfield, California, a former president of the Association.

CARL BRADY

aircraft) into some rocks and, though Fred was unharmed, the machine was badly damaged. These accidents appear to have been accepted as more or less inevitable in the circumstances; they did not cause too much anxiety, except, perhaps, to the pilots involved.

But less than a year later there was an accident that caused a great deal of concern for everyone. Bill was extraordinarily fortunate to survive it:

I was just heading back out of the pass [Kildala] when the machine started to develop a very heavy bounce; it was bouncing up and down about a foot, and it kept getting worse. I was about 1,500 feet [460 m] above the ground when it started and I let down as fast as I could. Then the bubble broke; finally, the engine quit and the tail rotor let go–it was bouncing so badly the tail rotor driveshaft tore right out of the transmission–and I had to dump collective. Even then, I was spinning. All the controls went; the whole bottom end of the engine fell out. I had cartons tied on the racks and they all flew off.

I was lucky, though, I hit on the only patch of snow in the whole area. It was about 80 feet [24 m] wide and a hundred [30 m] long, on a steep slope. I hit right in the middle of it. I slid down and hung up on boulders. Eighty feet [25 m] further on, there was a drop-off of some 500 feet [150 m] down onto a glacier. When stopped, I looked up and I could see the sun shining. I said, "Boy, that's a nice looking landing field!" Because I really didn't expect to come out of that one.

In fact, Bill came out of the wreck with a cracked vertebra; his passenger suffered cuts and bruises but no broken bones. The people on the spot were dismayed about this accident because, apart from an engine failure, there had been no mechanical failures worth mentioning. Jock Graham, who by this time was Okanagan's base engineer at Kemano, was determined to find the cause. If he did not, both pilots and their passengers would be nervous and edgy every time they took off. Jock describes how he went to work to do this:

It was a broken yoke [the hub on top of the rotor mast to which the main rotor blades are attached]. Bell had come out with aluminum yokes to save weight, and they sent out a directive that, if you ever had a blade strike, you had to throw away the aluminum yoke. We had bought the machine, JAA, from another company and I went back through the log book. Sure enough, I found an instance where they changed the blades. The obvious question was, "why had they changed them?" It took me some time, but I managed to get in touch with the engineer working on the machine when they had changed the blades, and he admitted they had done so because the tip had hit an oil drum. They were a small outfit. They didn't want to spend the money on a new yoke, so they didn't throw it away.

Quite apart from accidents, though, the helicopter crews began to become restive about their salaries. Their dissatisfaction was brought into focus by a recent immigrant who spoke very little English and whose job was to clean up around camp and to wield a shovel when called upon. The labourer had heard that the pilots were only earning $350 a month, while he was earning over $500. Every time he saw the helicopter crews he

"I was lucky, though, I hit on the only patch of snow in the whole area. It was about 80 feet [25 m] wide and a hundred [30 m] long, on a steep slope. I hit right in the middle of it. I slid down and hung up on boulders. Eighty feet [25 m] further on, there was a drop-off of some 500 feet [150 m] down onto a glacier. When stopped, I looked up and I could see the sun shining. I said, 'Boy, that's a nice looking landing field!' Because I really didn't expect to come out of that one."

BILL MCLEOD

would shake his head and begin to laugh. And now that some of the initial glamour was beginning to wear off and the danger becoming more apparent, the helicopter crews grew increasingly resentful. They had played a vital part in the accelerated progress of the whole project and, at the same time, were its lowest paid employees. This, too, led to some lively exchanges between Carl Agar and his fellow directors down in Vancouver–particularly since profits, which had stood at $10,000 in June, had risen to $58,000 by the end of August, 1951.

During this period, as well, Carl Agar's connection with Igor Sikorsky began to pay off. For some time ALCAN had been considering the possibility of getting larger helicopters to move the heavier construction equipment. Carl phoned Sikorsky and asked him if there was any hope of getting hold of two S-55s, capable of loads up to 1,500 pounds (680 kg), as compared to the 400-pound (180 kg) capacity of the Bells. There were two immediate problems: the Korean War was absorbing all the helicopters the Sikorsky plant could produce; and the S-55 had not yet been certified for commercial operations. However, Sikorsky was confident that certification would be granted and, towards the end of 1951, Jock Graham was sent down to the Sikorsky plant in Bridgeport, Connecticut, to take a course on the S-55. When his course was almost completed, Carl Agar joined him for his conversion training.

The first certified commercial machine off the line was going to Los Angeles Airways; the second would be theirs. The first was ferried down to Los Angeles in March 1952. The pilot gave a demonstration of its capabilities to the board of directors of the airline when he arrived. Unfortunately, he experienced a tail rotor failure during the demonstration. Several people were hurt; consequently all S-55s were grounded until the manufacturer had found a solution to the problem and incorporated a modification.

This delayed the Okanagan crew for three weeks, but finally, on April 10, they set off for Vancouver. Coincidentally, Bill McLeod had been visiting his wife's parents in Toronto, so he was picked up in Cleveland and, with instruction from Carl, he did his conversion training by flying the machine back to Vancouver.

Okanagan's first S-55, CF-GHV, was taken straight up to Kemano by Bill. With it he began to lift the materials for a camp of 60 men in Kildala pass; and then, once the camp was established, he began to fly in the machinery and aluminum tower structures to complete the power line between Kemano and Kitimat. Moving lumber for the camp required another innovation, Bill recalls:

We rigged a rather novel idea for packing the lumber. At first we were packing it in bundles and slinging it; but that didn't work very well; it was slow and tedious. So what we did was to rig a cable

During this period, as well, Carl Agar's connection with Igor Sikorsky began to pay off. For some time ALCAN had been considering the possibility of getting larger helicopters to move the heavier construction equipment. Carl phoned Sikorsky and asked him if there was any hope of getting hold of two S-55s, capable of loads up to 1,500 pounds (680 kg), as compared to the 400-pound (180 kg) capacity of the Bells.

between the front wheels. Then we put the choker on the bundle of lumber so that it was very tail heavy on the sling. This meant that the front end of the load would snug up against the wire between the wheels, and the rear end would hang down below the horizontal. Then we had the sling cable rigged with a pressure switch so that a light came on in the cockpit as soon as the load touched the ground and took some of the weight off it. We never had to stop. We kept moving at 5 to 10 miles an hour [8-16 km/h] and kicked off the load as soon as the light came on. That really speeded things up.

A few months later ALCAN bought a second S-55 for Okanagan crews to fly and Deke Orr became its pilot. As with the Bells, the Sikorskys proved reassuringly reliable. Jock recalls that they had one main transmission failure in the early days, but the failure did not cause an accident, and once the transmission had been replaced they had no more than routine maintenance to worry about.

By the end of 1952, the operation had settled down and become probably the biggest helicopter operation in North America. ALCAN had constructed a hangar for the fleet of helicopters, which now consisted of two S-55s and four 47-Ds, with a crew of six pilots and six engineers.

Meanwhile, for Joan McLeod, life had become a little more complicated; in January of 1952 the birth of her first child was imminent:

In January our first daughter became very due, so it was decided that we'd better get out; get up to the hospital in Prince Rupert. It was terribly rough; the ship could not come in and they couldn't get a tender out to her; instead, they brought the ship as close to the dock as they could and then swung out a net on a derrick and hoisted us aboard. It was even worse after Paddy was born and we came back. It wasn't quite so rough this time and they managed to get a tender out to us. We were taken down into the cargo hold, where they opened up the big cargo doors and laid a plank across to the tender. We had Paddy in a clothes basket and two men to push us off and two more waiting on the tender to grab us. Bill carried the clothes basket and made a mad dash and got across all right. I was still bent double at that stage of the game, but they threw me from one side and caught me on the other very handily. You travelled in style in those days.

On her return to Kemano, Joan moved out of the wooden-walled tent into a Quonset hut, which was far less comfortable because condensation inside the hut dripped steadily onto them in cold weather. When Paddy was nine months old, Bill was transferred to the Tahtsa Lake camp and Joan returned to Vancouver.

Bill joined her at the beginning of December for a Christmas break. Two weeks later Carl Agar phoned and apologetically suggested that it was desperately urgent for Bill to return immediately to the Tahtsa Lake camp. As an inducement, he was to take Joan and the baby with him. Joan describes their arrival:

We were in Tahtsa for Christmas, in a Quonset hut again. But it was colder at Tahtsa than Kemano, and foolishly they had bulldozed all the snow away from the walls so that we could walk around. This removed the insulation, and we were horribly cold inside. The baby was starting to crawl and stagger by that time. I used to take her out of bed in the morning and virtually sit her on the stove to dress her. I had cut down a pair of Bill's old grey socks and I'd pull those up to her hips; then the usual diapers and vest, followed by layers of sweaters, a snow suit, boots and mittens. Then I could put her down on the floor to crawl. But by this time the poor child was practically helpless–so many clothes she could hardly move.

The McLeod's second child, Jean, was also born in Prince Rupert, in October 1953. With two children to look after, Joan left the Kemano project for good and returned to Vancouver, probably with a sigh of relief. The helicopter crews were growing bored with the operation and they started to look around for new worlds to conquer. Jock Graham wanted to be trained as a pilot. He had a private pilot's licence and he had unofficially flown the 55s a good deal in Kemano–they were equipped with dual controls and the pilots helped him as much as they could–but he needed a formal training course. In spite of repeated requests, Carl always put him off with the suggestion that he was more valuable to the company as an engineer. In the end, because he felt that he was being held back and that he might be able to get the flying training he wanted else-where, Jock accepted a job as technical representative with Pratt and Whitney, the manufacturers of the S-55 engine.

By 1954, the work was beginning to wind down in Kemano. ALCAN cut their fleet of helicopters to one S-55 and two 47-Ds. The remaining machines, a 55 and two 47-Ds were bought by Okanagan under the option they had. Fortunately, Jock, in his new capacity, had contacts in Calgary by this time. He heard rumours that Shell Oil, who were carrying out exploration work up the Mackenzie, were looking for something bigger than a Bell. He contacted Peter Leigh-Jones, executive assistant to Shell's president. At a breakfast meeting with Leigh-Jones and John Stuart, Shell's chief pilot, Jock advised them to phone Glenn McPherson, Okanagan's new president. Terms were quickly agreed upon and Okanagan had a three-month contract for their S-55.

Bill McLeod flew on this operation and he describes it as the most enjoyable one of his career:

That was the first year that Shell had used a helicopter. They got a 55 and a Bell and I flew the 55. We did a preliminary geological survey of the Mackenzie mountains, starting at Fort Liard and working our way not quite to the Arctic coast. We were back in the Richardson range by the time we finished up.

They were surveying a swathe of country approximately 40 to 60 miles [65-100 km] west of the river, depending on where the pre-Cambrian rock occurred; in other words, it was soft rock geology. That was extremely interesting because we stayed only ten days to two weeks in any one location; then we moved on.

They had three geologists, three helpers, my engineer George Chamberlain, myself and a cook on our part of the operation. In the morning I would load all six of the geology crew and put two crews out to measure sections and take samples. Then I would travel with the third crew until it was time to pick up the others in the evening. Dr. Matthews from UBC was the geologist and I became a one-man classroom for him for the season. By the end of it, he would pick up a fossil, hand it to me and say, "Well, what is it, Bill?" and I'd reply, "Oh, that's Middle Devonian; it's a Brachiopod." I could reel it all off and it made the job much more interesting.

But that was one of those good years. Even the cook was good, and we were on the move all the time. We got to the point where the engineer and I, we slept in the helicopter. We didn't bother setting up the tent; we just rolled out our sleeping bags on the floor of the helicopter and went to bed at night –what there was of it.

I had one engine failure and they had to come looking for me. No radio–the radio didn't work; usual thing in those days. I'd gone out and I had a magneto pack up on me. I tried to fly back to camp, but the engine got rougher and rougher; then she started missing on one cylinder, so I thought I'd better put her down because I still had some 60 miles [100 km] of muskeg to go over. We were working out of Fort Norman at the time. It was rather odd; I put down on a river called the Redstone, on a sand-bar which was composed of red and cream sandstone. The helicopter was painted cream and red. I had the best camouflaged helicopter you ever saw; and when I landed, there was thunderstorm activity and there were fires burning–little plumes of smoke all over the country.

I did the usual thing: I laid out a square on the sand bar with a W in it–meaning "I need an engineer." Then I gathered a big pile of brush to make smoke to compete with all the other smokes. Airplanes flew right over the top of me and never saw me. The fellow who finally found me was flying over a ridge 10 miles [16 km] away, and he saw the sun glint on the plexiglass. Even then, he had trouble seeing exactly where I was. It wasn't a big deal. I was only out one night. The engineer came in and changed the mag–the drive had sheered–and we flew back to camp.

Notwithstanding Bill's laconic description, it was a tough life. To prove that the helicopter really was a practical proposition, helicopter crews took considerable risks, worked very hard and, when they returned from the bush, they played hard. The products of the grape vine and the barley field were not unfamiliar to them.

As an obvious reaction to the disciplines of life in the bush, most of the early Okanagan company crews were given to practical jokes; Carl Agar, perhaps because he was so popular with his employees, was a favourite target. They delighted in jacking up the rear wheels of his car until they were just off the ground–then, when Carl jumped into the car to go home at the end of the day, and spun his wheels futilely, he would look around to see a row of grinning faces at the windows along the side of the hangar.

Once, when the amber had flowed to celebrate Carl's McKee trophy, someone sneaked out to the parking lot and chained the bumper of his car to one of the down-spouts on the hangar wall. Fortunately, the downspout tore loose before the bumper. On another occasion he nearly lost a valuable contract. He had gone up to do a quick test

As an obvious reaction to the disciplines of life in the bush, most of the early Okanagan company crews were given to practical jokes; Carl Agar, perhaps because he was so popular with his employees, was a favourite target. They delighted in jacking up the rear wheels of his car until they were just off the ground–then, when Carl jumped into the car to go home at the end of the day, and spun his wheels futilely, he would look around to see a row of grinning faces at the windows along the side of the hangar.

flight on one of the helicopters before driving down-town to meet a potential customer—a mining promoter who was considering using helicopters for a large exploration operation. While Carl was out flying, his crews were busy stuffing a deflated rubber helicopter float into his car. Then they inflated it. The problem for Carl was a difficult one: there was no way he could get into his car; he was in a hurry; but helicopter floats are very expensive and he didn't want to puncture the float with a knife to deflate it. Thus he spent the next 15 minutes, surrounded by fascinated onlookers, desperately trying to worm his way far enough into the car to reach the valve and deflate the float.

As Carl became a celebrity (by the early fifties the media had taken to calling him "Mr. Helicopter"), his crews made sure that he retained his sense of proportion. He happened to be a short man, and he was constantly reminded of the fact. One day he had a new lawnmower delivered to the hangar, intending to assemble it there, where all the tools were available, before taking it home in the trunk of his car. The mower arrived in his absence and one of the engineers decided to open up the carton and have a look at it. As he did so, an idea occurred to him. He cut some 18 inches (46 cm) off the mower handle, carefully buffed the edges to conceal the hacksaw marks and repacked the mower in its carton.

When Carl returned and assembled the mower, everyone in the hangar at the time (and there seemed to be more than usual for some reason) was bending over his work with unusual dedication. They intervened only when Carl went storming back to his office to phone the supplier. He was told that his loyal staff were merely trying to accommodate the mower to his size.

Apart from the practical jokes, though, both Alf Stringer and Carl Agar were individuals who tended to stand out in a crowd. Alf had a semi-military repartee which survived all the crises and occasional tragedies of a bush flying operation. When somebody's wife phoned and Alf answered the call, he would inform the husband that the "control tower" was on the blower. Peter Corley-Smith worked for him for nearly 15 years. He was always puzzled by Alf's insistence on calling everyone "Colonel." When asked why, Alf would pass it off by changing the subject. It was only when we came to interview his wife, Lynn Stringer, that we discovered the reason for this idiosyncrasy. Alf had an indifferent memory for names. By calling everyone "Colonel" he avoided the difficulty so many of us face.

Another of the penalties Carl had to accept when he became a celebrity was that he had to attend an increasing number of conventions and conferences at which speeches, sometimes almost interminable speeches, were delivered. On one occasion, at a

Alf had a semi-military repartee which survived all the crises and occasional tragedies of a bush flying operation. When somebody's wife phoned and Alf answered the call, he would inform the husband that the "control tower" was on the blower. Peter Corley-Smith worked for him for nearly 15 years. He was always puzzled by Alf's insistence on calling everyone "Colonel." When asked why, Alf would pass it off by changing the subject. It was only when we came to interview his wife, Lynn Stringer, that we discovered the reason for this idiosyncrasy. Alf had an indifferent memory for names. By calling everyone "Colonel" he avoided the difficulty so many of us face.

convention of the Helicopter Association of America in Los Angeles, a speaker grew fonder of his own voice as time went on. He waxed philosophical about the advent of helicopters at inordinate length; he rehearsed the technical achievements up to date and the infinite potential the future offered. He went on and on and on. Carl, who was seated at the head table, two seats away from the speaker, had a bowl of daffodils in front of him. He picked one up (even though daffodils are mildly poisonous) and began to eat it slowly. When he had finished the last mouthful, he picked up a second and started on that. By now, everyone in the room was watching him. He had consumed three daffodils before the speaker, jolted from his euphoria, realized that he had entirely lost the attention of his audience. When he turned to see what was happening, he closed his speech with a few brisk words and sat down.

At all future conventions of the Helicopter Association of America, someone always made sure that Carl Agar had a bowl of daffodils in front of him when he took his place.

A replica of Okanagan's CF-FZX, assembled with genuine Bell parts from a variety of sources, at the Royal BC Museum. The authors initiated this restoration, with generous volunteer help from helicopter engineers Chuck Roberts, Eric Cowden, Ian Duncan and the late Art Johnson.

ROYAL BRITISH COLUMBIA MUSEUM

CHAPTER FOUR

Vancouver Island Helicopters: Competition

We went through eight pilots on that job. Some of them would take one look at it and catch the next PGE *train out.*

BOB TAYLOR

The first hints of competition for Okanagan Helicopters appeared in 1950. An aerial survey company in Ottawa, Spartan Air Services Limited, had started to use helicopters to provide the ground control–the surveyed heights and bench marks–it needed for mapping projects. Spartan, like Okanagan, expanded rapidly. By 1955 it had a fleet of more than 20 Bell 47s; in another two years it had a base in Calgary and was operating across the country.

Closer to home, on Vancouver Island, a young man named Ted Henson was watching the success story across the Strait of Georgia with increasing interest. Ted had been in the RCAF, hoping to become a pilot, but joined too late in the Second World War to achieve this ambition. Returning to Victoria after his discharge, he began work as an automobile mechanic. Then he suffered a bout of pleurisy, and while being treated in the Royal Jubilee Hospital met and fell in love with Lynn, a trainee nurse. Lynn abandoned her nursing career to marry Ted and went to work as a dental assistant, while Ted, with the help of a friend, Ron Page, managed to finance the purchase of a small Ercoupe monoplane in which he learned to fly and eventually earned his commercial pilot's licence. As it turned out, Ted did very little commercial flying in fixed-wing aircraft.

Times were hard for Ted, just as they had been for Carl Agar and Alf Stringer when they were trying to get back into aviation after the war. When he conceived the idea of getting into the helicopter business the problems of financing seemed insurmountable.

He began by writing the Bell Helicopter people to tell them about his ambitions. Bell responded by putting him in touch with their western representative in Los Angeles, Art Fornoff. Fornoff came up to Victoria to see Ted. Apparently satisfied that Ted was both sincere and capable, he arranged for an interview in Seattle between Ted and Bill Boeing Jr., son of the founder of one of the largest aircraft manufacturers in the world, who was forming his own helicopter company, Aero-Copters Incorporated.

Fortunately Ted and Bill Boeing hit it off and the immediate outcome was the formation of a partnership. At the time–this was in 1953–an American could hold only a 40 per cent interest in a Canadian company. Boeing's share of the company was to pay for Ted's helicopter pilot training and finance the purchase of the first machine, a Bell 47-G, with a down payment of $18,000. It was registered CF-IDX. Ted named the company Vancouver Island Helicopters Limited.

All this had been accomplished with relative ease. Now began the hard part–acquiring a licence to operate from the Department of Transport and the first revenue contracts. Lynn Henson (later Lynn Stringer) describes the problems:

It was the biggest battle of our whole life; it was so hard. You have to appreciate that we had no money. In September [1954] Ted had to quit his job as a mechanic because he had all this work with the business. The Liberals were in then and it was very difficult to get a license. You had to prove that the traffic was there and that there was a public need for a helicopter service–which we did because we had done our homework. Then, when he put his application in, Ted made the mistake of asking for a protected base. This meant that no other operator could come within a 25-mile [40-km] radius –and Okanagan fought that; they fought it very, very hard. Things were really tough for us. Ted had quit his job and my pay was very small. There we were in a little tiny house, 700 square feet [65 m²], but with a big garden that kept us going.

Okanagan's objection to the founding of VIH had come as an unpleasant surprise, and while they waited with growing anxiety to see what the outcome of the objection at the Air Transport Board hearing would be, Ted was busy trying to raise capital to run the company. He went practically from door to door, urging people to invest–usually with indifferent success. The first principals, apart from Ted and Bill Boeing, were Ron Grant, a lawyer, and Dave Turnbull, a businessman whom Ted had met at the Victoria Flying Club.

At the same time, Ted was busy trying to find prospective customers. The B.C. Forest Service and B.C. Power Commission were his main targets. They appeared interested but they would not commit themselves. He received some encouragement from the newspapers, which followed his story with considerable coverage.

Okanagan's objections were carefully phrased. There simply wasn't enough business to justify another helicopter company; it was bound to fail. "We are not," they assured the Board of Transport Commissioners, "apprehensive of competition. Actually we welcome competition if it is shown to be in the public interest."

To which Ron Grant, Vancouver Island Helicopter's lawyer, responded dryly: "It is unusual for a business concern to set itself up as an economic watchdog."

The newspapers also referred to a mysterious American partner in the business (Bill Boeing, presumably), hinting at a threat to economic nationalism. At the same time they ran photographs of Ted and the brand new machine, CF-IDX, reporting that he was operating out of a field on Shelbourne Street. In fact, as Lynn points out, such operating as Ted was doing at the time was from the Howroyd strip in central Saanich. Joe Howroyd, always active in Victoria flying circles, was a friend and the landing strip was a very convenient base, at least for the moment.

In April of 1955, the long-awaited letter arrived from the Department of Transport informing them that their application for an operating licence had been successful. Now Ted had to move from the casual phase of parking the helicopter on a friend's landing strip into some sort of hangar where proper maintenance could be performed. Lynn describes this move: "Ted was looking for a suitable place, with some room for an office, and he went out to the airport and here was this war-surplus hangar, packed high with old windows. They were using it as a warehouse. Every window on the hangar itself was broken. Just to look at it was so disheartening; but what else was there. So he said he'd take it. I think he paid $132 a month. He had to replace all the broken windows; then he cut a hole in the front of the hangar for a door so the helicopter could get in. There was just room for one helicopter and a little office."

Nevertheless, they were in business and Ted left in May, with his mere 25 hours of helicopter flying experience, to work for the B.C. Power Commission on the Homathko River, one of the roughest sections of terrain on the West Coast.

Nevertheless, they were in business and Ted left in May, with his mere 25 hours of helicopter flying experience, to work for the B.C. Power Commission on the Homathko River, one of the roughest sections of terrain on the West Coast. Although the Power Commission was examining the potential for a dam and a generating plant on the Homathko, the actual work with the helicopter that first year was done for them by the Surveys and Mapping Branch of the provincial government. The engineering and environmental problems apparently could not be solved and no dam or generating plant was ever constructed, but the exploratory work continued for three years.

Ted was accompanied on this operation by Ted Protheroe, a fixed-wing engineer who had just earned his helicopter endorsement after a six-week course with Bell. Then, only a month or so later, Ted Henson suffered an accident, just as Carl Agar had on his first revenue operation, an accident which seriously damaged the machine.

Ted's accident was even more discouraging than Carl's encounter with the power transmission lines. He had a partial engine failure with two passengers on board. The only clearing within reach was a small, grass-covered sandbank on the edge of the river. He put the machine down parallel to the river. There was just room for his skids on the bank, and no more. The passengers got out while Ted ran the engine down. He switched it off and joined them for a moment to wait for the rotors to stop turning before he pulled some spark plugs to see if they had been the cause of the problem. As he stood there, the sandbank suddenly crumbled into the shallow water and the helicopter fell sideways with the blades still turning. The machine was a virtual write-off. It was a remarkable piece of ill fortune.

Ted and his passengers then had to endure a three-day walk down the rugged Homathko River to the head of Bute Inlet, where they were picked up by a fish boat. The wreck was soon salvaged with the help of an Okanagan helicopter, and Ted spent most of the remainder of that first year helping Ted Protheroe rebuild it.

The new company's second year of operation, 1956, was a more encouraging one. Ted went out again to the Homathko, to work with the rebuilt CF-IDX; in addition, he leased two machines, together with pilots, from Aero-Copters. The two leased machines were flown by Don Scholberg and John Watson. Meanwhile Ted hired a second engineer, Harvey Jones. They had a successful season and the future began to look rosy enough that Ted began to look for pilots to train for the following year's work.

He chose two people from different backgrounds. Robert P. Taylor was an ex-RCAF officer who had learned to fly late in the war and became an instructor. After the war he attempted to make a living as an artist, but in spite of his talent he was only just managing to survive. Early in the Korean War, he decided to rejoin the Air Force and spent the next five years training NATO students on Harvards at a training school in Calgary. By the end of five years he was becoming bored with the routine and decided he would like to fly helicopters. There were no openings in the service, so he went to see Ted Henson. Bob Taylor remembers that it was not an easy task:

A lot of civilian operators didn't jump up and down with enthusiasm at the prospect of hiring a military pilot in those days–didn't think they would prove too useful in the bush, I guess; so we more or less had to prove otherwise. And the conversion from fixed-wing to helicopters was much harder than I had expected. For a while I didn't think I was going to make it. The training was comprehensive: we did 50 hours of basic and then another 25 hours of mountain training. Earl Thompson of Aero-Copters had already done more than 4,000 hours of helicopter flying time by 1956, and in February of the next year he trained me up in Strathcona Park–Great Central Mountain and Golden Hinde were my initiation into mountain flying. It was hairy of course. You never landed far from the edge of a drop-off. You just had to hop, skip, get over the edge and clear your tail rotor and get some rpm on the way down. Terrifying.

The other pilot Ted chose was Bruce Payne. Bruce had worked in the bush, spending a summer with the B.C. Forest Service on the Hart Highway between Prince George and Dawson Creek, and another with the provincial Topographic Survey in northeastern British Columbia, building towers for triangulation grids. In the winters he had taken flying lessons at his own expense at the Victoria Flying Club. Ted decided to ask the

"In February of the next year he [Earl Thompson] trained me up in Strathcona Park– Great Central Mountain and Golden Hinde were my initiation into mountain flying. It was hairy of course. You never landed far from the edge of a drop-off. You just had to hop, skip, get over the edge and clear your tail rotor and get some rpm on the way down. Terrifying."

BOB TAYLOR

65

Ted Henson (*left*) and engineer Ted Protheroe.

Ted Henson (*right*) with Harvey Jones
the day before Henson's fatal crash.

Engineer Howie Goodall (*left*) and pilot Des O'Halloran freshen up KNC, north end of Stuart Lake, 1960.

Most things could be tied to a helicopter, as long as they weren't too heavy. This operation in 1961 was for Noranda Mines on the west coast of Vancouver Island. H. Vernon, Noranda party chief, stands by.

DES O'HALLORAN PHOTOS

After Ted Henson's death, Bruce Payne, chief pilot; Lynn Henson, president; Bob Taylor, operations manager; Harvey Jones, chief engineer, were left to carry on.

VANCOUVER ISLAND HELICOPTERS COLLECTION

club for a recommendation. Bruce, who had just turned 20, was chosen and he began his training at the same time as Bob Taylor.

In May 1957 both had completed training and were signed on as employees. An agreement had been reached that they would start at a salary of $450 a month, working up to $600 after three years, at which point their training would be considered paid for. Bob Taylor went with Ted Protheroe to the Power Commission job on the Homathko and Bruce's first revenue job was to fly people from the Department of Transport and Trans-Canada Air Lines up Mount Slesse southeast of Abbotsford, where a North Star had crashed, killing all on board.

For the rest of that season, Bruce worked on a number of jobs–some mineral exploration for Falconbridge Mining at Buggaboo Creek in the east Kootenays; powerline patrols out of Campbell River, on Vancouver Island; and a stint with the provincial Topographic Survey–before travelling all the way across to Ontario to fly a short contract with the Department of National Defence.

Meanwhile, Bob Taylor found the Homathko region an eye-opener on his first revenue flying job. He was mostly moving survey crews in preparation for dam construction. He had his first experience of slinging when he moved a big Kootenay wood-burning stove into a camp on the river. Kootenay ranges were substantial cast-iron units with double heating ovens. They were too heavy to be carried on one rack, so Bob flew his engineer to the landing site, then returned to tie the stove onto a cross-tube under the helicopter with a 10-foot length of half-inch rope.

When he reached the landing site and lowered the stove gently to the ground, the engineer, armed with a sharp knife, cut the load loose. It was an illegal and, of course, dangerous procedure. Any sort of mechanical problem en route could have been disastrous. Fortunately it was this experience that motivated Ted Protheroe to fit up part of a bomb rack from a Canso amphibian as a cargo hook, so that the load could be jettisoned in an emergency.

The third season, 1957, started out successfully for the new company. Ted Henson was quoted in an article in Canadian Aviation: "I started this business because I liked to fly. I've only been in it a year and yet this will have to be my last year of flying. We'll be getting a lot bigger, and managing the firm–mainly lining up work to keep the 'copters busy–will be a full-time job."

Ted spent only one short summer "flying" that managerial desk. Bruce Payne returned from his job in Ontario early in October, just as one of the Seattle pilots, whose six-month Canadian work permit had expired, was obliged to return home from the

When Bob Taylor had to move a heavy Kootenay range (stove) on the Homathko operation, it was too heavy to go on one rack, so he tied it under the mainframe with rope–which was cut by somebody on the ground to release the range at its destination.

TED PROTHEROE PHOTOS

Don Scholberg slinging a fuel drum, using part of a war-surplus Canso bomb hook that allowed the load to be released from the cockpit—a big step up in safety. Engineer Ted Protheroe designed and constructed it. "Fortunately," he commented, "no approval was required from the DOT in those days: we just did it."

Power Commission job on the Homathko. Ted didn't have the heart to send Bruce right back out again; instead he went himself to finish the few days of work left. He was flown by floatplane into Tatlayoko Lake, a narrow body of water which stretches for some 14 miles (22 km) between steep, rocky shores. The following morning, October 17, 1957, Ted took off in his helicopter for a five-minute flight along the lake to another camp. He was never seen again. The people in the camp he had just left reported hearing a heavy thud. The only remains ever found were a seat cushion and an oil can.

The loss of their president so early in the company's existence was a crushing blow. To Lynn Henson it seemed the end of so many dreams:

The sad part was that we had to go on. I can't remember now, but I think it was two weeks before the search was called off, everything was finished and he was declared dead. But in that two-week period, every time the phone rang I thought maybe he'd walked out after all and here he was phoning. But because I'd been on the lake in the summer, and knew how treacherous it was, I couldn't really believe that. Even if he had been able to swim ashore, there was no place for him to hang on–it was just straight down and there were no little beaches for him to lie on or anything.

The crisis was one of management and finances. The financial problem was eased by an unexpected bonus. Lynn recalls:

When Ted and I were sitting at home, waiting for our operating licence–when Ted was still working on cars in the evenings to bring in some money–Fred McGregor, of Mutual Life, came along and sold him a $30,000 life insurance policy. Ted never told me about this. He was paying about $25 a month in premiums; and because we had so little money, he fell behind on the premiums. That was how I found out. Ted was away flying when a letter from Mutual arrived. I opened it and it said that if you don't pay by such and such a date, your insurance will no longer be in effect.

I was pretty angry because Ted hadn't told me anything about this. I phoned Fred McGregor and told him so. I was looking after the bills and we couldn't afford it. I would find the policy and tear it up. I said, "Thank you very much" and "Goodbye," and I thought that was the end of it. This was in April '57. I wasn't very nice to him. Then came October '57 and Ted was dead. And you know what happened? Mr. McGregor had been paying those premiums himself for all those months. That's what saved the company–Mr. McGregor's generosity. Without that $30,000 I would have had to sell the company to pay succession duties.

So the financial crisis was solved, but there remained the problem of management. Lynn, who had been doing all the bookkeeping and paper work, was the only person who knew the day-to-day details of the operation. Bill Boeing called a meeting of the shareholders and the decision was reached that Lynn should be the president to run the administration of the company and that an operations manager and a chief engineer should be appointed. As the company's first employee, Ted Protheroe was obviously a candidate for the position as operations manager; but in the end Boeing recommended Bob Taylor for the job and Protheroe became chief engineer.

For Lynn, the next two years were devoted almost entirely to work in the hangar. Since she had a son who was seven and a daughter who was two, the problems were very real. She remembers the period with mixed emotions:

That was a hard time but I had a very good baby sitter. Danny went to school and we worked things out – even though I was out at the hangar 12 hours a day every day. At the time, though, I came in for a lot of criticism from my close friends, as well as from my family. They seemed to think I should stay at home and look after my children even if that meant going on welfare.

Also, I found out how very quick people are to take advantage of you. One day in a grocery store I met a man who was a friend of Ted's and mine, and he wanted to buy the company. He was into another fixed-wing operation and he wanted to buy our company to amalgamate with his. I said no. He said, "Just name your price. Every man has his price." When I refused again he said, "I'll give you six months to run that company into the ground!" I'm proud to think that every day that goes by makes him more wrong.

On the other side of the coin, there were considerable satisfactions for Lynn:

My office and a little room where we kept the spare parts were all we had, and my office was also the pilot and engineer crew room. That's where we all met and I tried to do my bookwork. Mind you, I loved being among them and listening to their talk about their experiences, but I was getting desperate because it was almost impossible to get any work done in that atmosphere. Then one day I remembered the story of Glenn McPherson. His wife wanted a new kitchen and she kept after him and kept after him and one day she took an axe and chopped down all her cupboards. He came home from work and there was this pile of rubble in the middle of the kitchen and she was just sitting there, and she said, "I'm not doing any cooking until I get a new kitchen." So the next day Glenn got started and had the kitchen rebuilt.

My own solution wasn't quite so drastic. I just picked up my desk and my typewriter, went into the parts room, plunked down in the middle of the parts and said, "I don't care what you people do; this is where I am going to work from now on!" The next day they started building a new parts room down at the back of the hangar, where it is now. The truth is I loved the work I was doing. I was determined to keep our company going for Ted's sake.

With Bob Taylor running the flying and Ted Protheroe the maintenance, business began to flourish. These were still boom years. The Power Commission work on the Homathko continued until 1959; meanwhile, Vancouver Island Helicopters was very active in mining exploration along the Stikine River in northwestern British Columbia. In January 1958, the company had on its books Bob Taylor and Bruce Payne as pilots, and Ted Protheroe, Ron Adams, Howie Goodall and Harvey Jones as engineers. In February, Des O'Halloran, an ex-RCAF officer, became the company's third full-time pilot. A young Australian, Noel Dodwell, was working as a volunteer in the stock-room. In June

Lynn Stringer, the young president of Vancouver Island Helicopters, in her hangar office at Pat Bay airport, 1958.

ALF STRINGER

1959 he became an employee at a salary of $200 a month. His perseverance paid off; eventually Bob Taylor trained him as a pilot and he became a very successful one.

This was the year, too, when Bob Taylor landed the company's first B.C. Forest Service contract. Bob recalls that it was a big step forward:

It was the inventory contract, and for us it was a winner from the start. You flew nearly all the time with one passenger, so it was easy on the machine and on the pilot. You had one man on board with a tape recorder and he called what were known as plots–areas of trees perhaps half a mile long marked on aerial photographs–and the "classifier" recorded the species, estimated heights and ages of the trees in each plot as you flew about 50 feet [15 m] above them. Then, after an hour or so, we would land beside a plot right after it had been recorded and the classifier would go in and check his estimates to make sure they weren't too far out.

What made the contract really worthwhile was that it was a big project; the inventory was to cover the whole province over a 10-year span. We had it for five years. And the good thing about it was that the forestry people would let us put a brand new pilot for the job. I'd train him in the winter, and this was an excellent job for him to build up his time without having to try anything too hairy.

Despite Bob Taylor's optimism, the inventory job could be "hairy." At least Noel Dodwell in his second year as a pilot found it so. One of the aspects of the program that Bob did not mention was the use of two-man sampling crews. These crews, almost invariably summer students, were put out by helicopter to sample random plots of trees. They would work out of a fly-camp for several days at a time, using a chain and compass to reach the randomly selected plots, and then physically measure the trees and record the data.

On this occasion, Noel had dropped the crew's food and camping gear in a clearing on the bank of a creek. Then he took off to drop the two students three or four thousand feet (915-1 215 m) up the mountain, near the tree line, so that they could put in two samples before walking back down to set up their fly-camp. He couldn't find a landing site where they wanted one and decided to prop one skid on a steep bank of scree, holding the helicopter in a semi-hover while they jumped off.

Before doing this, he explained to them the importance of leaving the helicopter one at a time, and of not lingering on the cargo rack before jumping because he could not hold the helicopter level for more than a few seconds in this unbalanced condition. Satisfied that they understood, he settled the skid on his side of the machine firmly on the scree and nodded to the student on the outside to go. Unfortunately the student was still wearing sneakers; he had tied the laces of his boots together and he was carrying them in his hand. When he got out on the rack and looked down at the jagged scree, four

A newspaper headline in the Victoria Daily Colonist, October 18, 1957. The "indestructible" refers to Ted Henson's previous episode on the Homathko River, when he was missing for four days before walking out to the head of Bute Inlet and being picked up by a fishing boat.

DAILY COLONIST

or five feet beneath him, it occurred to him that he should be wearing his boots before he jumped, and he calmly sat down on the cargo rack to change into them.

Noel shouted to the student still sitting beside him to tell his companion to get the hell off the rack (or words to that effect). As the second student moved over to do so, Noel finally lost control and the helicopter rolled down the slope, thrashing itself to pieces as it did so. Astonishingly, no one suffered anything worse than minor scratches and bruises; but people in main camp, more than 10 miles (16 km) away, claimed afterwards that they heard profanities couched in an Australian accent echoing among the mountain tops for several minutes.

But this happened later, and the problems they encountered during the first three seasons were usually the result of over-eagerness to take every job that became available. As an example, in 1958 a mining exploration consulting company called J. C. Sproule and Associates, through a series of mishaps, ran out of helicopters up the Mackenzie River in the Norman Wells area. Sproule's crew were stranded in the bush for six weeks without a machine. Bob Taylor finally went up at the end of the season which, as he said, "Spread the company a little thin, stretching our logistical supply line all the way from Pat Bay to Norman Wells."

Sproule had a reputation for running very economical operations, Bob recalls: "There were six of us in camp and he'd come off the plane with six steaks and six beer. That was a big, hearty surprise treat for the boys. It was at least a change from the eternal Chuckwagon stew." (A remarkable number of the people we interviewed spoke disparagingly of Chuckwagon Dinners. Presumably the producers dealt only with exploration company purchasing agents, people who never had to go out in the bush and sample the product.)

By 1960 the operation had settled down to five machines, supplemented by as many as six leased from Aero-Copters. Most work by this time was within the province. The Stikine River was being extensively explored–there were several large drilling projects in progress–and both provincial forestry and topographical survey contracts had been renewed. Bob Taylor became involved with experimental projects with the Forest Service:

They wanted to be able to drop food packages to people who were too far from a lake or a clearing to be reached. These packages weighed about 30 or 40 pounds [15-20 kg] each. We tried free-dropping them, but that didn't work very well–too many of them ended up smashed on the rocks. So we came up with the idea of attaching small parachutes to the packages, hooking them on to a bomb rack–we must have cornered the market on surplus Canso bomb racks–and tying the static lines to the cargo racks. Then all we had to do was to punch off the packages and the parachute

On this B.C. Forest Service contract, the VIH 47-G3B-1 was operated off a scow towed by the Forestry launch, *Forest Surveyor*, in the Bella Coola, Bentink Arm area.

PETER CORLEY-SMITH

would be yanked open automatically by the static cord. Trouble was, we had the packages on a short cord, hooked onto the bomb rack, and we hadn't figured out that the airstream would twist the loads round and round.

The first time I tried it, I had two of these packages hooked up. They obviously began to twist as soon as we took off. Just before I reached the drop area, one of the 'chutes opened by itself–the package had twisted until the static line tightened up enough to open it. So there we were all of a sudden, with the nose going down and when I looked back the 'chute was open and oscillating right by the tail rotor. I was afraid to punch it off in case it wrapped itself around the tail rotor. And I didn't want to let down too quickly for the same reason. The problem was to keep the nose up; I had the cyclic [stick] right back in my stomach. I tell you, there were two guys compressing their backs against the firewall. In the end, I sort of sideslipped and punched off both packages. The guys on the ground thought it was a big joke. They thanked me for waiting until I got close enough for them to retrieve the packages.

This was one of several experiments conducted by the Forest Service with helicopters. Another successful one in which Bob Taylor was involved was the use of a camera boom for stereoscopic aerial photography. At first the boom was attached under the frame of the helicopter; later it was slung from the cargo hook. The boom, which was about 12 feet (3.5 m) long, had two cameras mounted on it, one at either end. The cameras were operated electrically, by remote control, from inside the helicopter. This made it possible to cover the ground with overlapping photographs which, when fed into a stereoscopic plotting machine, made it possible to measure the heights of the trees very accurately. Using colour photography, the species and ages of the trees could also be estimated with some precision. In the end, this system permitted forest inventory to be conducted without the need for a classifier in the helicopter–a saving, both in time and manpower.

Some years later Bruce Payne took off with the test version of the camera boom slung on the cargo hook. He was flying a turbine-powered Alouette, a much faster machine than the Bell, and the purpose was to test the boom for high-altitude photography at 115 knots (215 km/h). As it turned out, this was fast enough to induce the camera to fly on its own. The boom came up and thumped the bottom of the helicopter; fortunately no serious damage was done and the boom was then modified so that it could be clamped to the bottom of the helicopter.

Another, more conventional job Bob remembers with a faint shudder was the installation of a Pacific Great Eastern (B.C. Railway) microwave tower:

If you look up the side of Lillooet Mountain, you'll see that it was pretty hairy. The side-hill is just about vertical. They blasted a little 14-foot by 14-foot pad off the top of a shoulder and it was a straight drop of 3,000 feet [900 m] down to the valley floor–I mean straight down. They lost a couple of pack horses getting up there to blast the pad.

When you landed there, you had to be careful about stepping out because there was practically no place to stand. And the winds you'd get were unreal; you'd toss a piece of plywood or something over the side and it would come spitting back up at you. The pad was on the northeast side, so you nearly always had subsiding air. You hardly ever got an updraft to help you get the tower steel up there; you had to dog it all the way up. And sometimes, when you got there, you'd get all set up on your approach and then at the last minute suddenly lose 200 feet [60 m] and have to start all over again. We went through eight pilots on that job. Some of them would just take one look at it and catch the next PGE train out.

While these things were happening, a meeting which had taken place shortly after Ted Henson's death was to have a good deal of influence on the future of Vancouver Island Helicopters. The company had carried insurance on the lost helicopter and the life insurance policy on Ted and when they were paid, they were used as the premium to purchase a new helicopter in 1958–a Bell 47-G2, registered CF-KNC. By the time the machine arrived in Victoria, however, it was so late in the season that Lynn could not place it on a contract. Rather than leave it sitting in the hangar for the rest of the summer, Lynn offered it on lease to Okanagan. She and Bob Taylor went across to Vancouver to discuss the details with Alf Stringer, Okanagan's operations manager.

It was a very business-like meeting [Lynn recalls]. We made the necessary arrangements for the lease and then left. But later, in 1959, there was a celebration of 50 years of flight in Canada, and I received an invitation to attend the banquet at a Vancouver hotel with Alf Stringer. I was very flattered that this important man from Okanagan would invite me, and it was an exciting evening: Igor Sikorsky was there as one of the guest speakers, so I met him, too. Anyway, the eventual result of that meeting was that Alf and I were married the next year and I went to live in Vancouver for the next three years.

Six months after her second marriage, and just before the move to Vancouver, Lynn suffered another tragedy. Her 10-year-old son was struck down and killed by a truck in Victoria. However, life had to go on and she moved to a large house which she and Alf had had built in the Oak Ridge area of Vancouver.

For the next three years, she ran VIH largely by phone. Then, because Carl Agar's health had broken down and he had retired from Okanagan, and because Alf was finding himself increasingly at odds with management, Alf decided to resign. "It was," as Lynn observes, "an awful wrench for him. He had built up this little company until it was one of the biggest helicopter companies in the world. So it was quite a letdown for him to come and operate five helicopters after being operations manager for Okanagan."

Alf Stringer became president of VIH and Lynn, as she puts it, "stepped out of the picture and stayed home and had children." As it turned out, Alf's first few years with VIH were not easy. The early and middle sixties were recession years and profits were scant. But gradually he built the company up to a 12-machine operation, and his heli-

"I received an invitation to attend the banquet at a Vancouver hotel with Alf Stringer. I was very flattered that this important man from Okanagan would invite me, and it was an exciting evening: Igor Sikorsky was there as one of the guest speakers, so I met him, too. Anyway, the eventual result of that meeting was that Alf and I were married the next year and I went to live in Vancouver for the next three years."

LYNN STRINGER

Alf Stringer in 1984.

D. N. PARKER

copters were so meticulously maintained that they were always a source of pride to their crews. After an experiment with an Alouette III, which turned out to be uneconomical for the small jobs and too small for the heavy-lift work, the company was equipped with turbine-powered Bell 206 Jet Rangers. More than 40 years later, it still operates from the same hangar at Victoria International Airport.

Forty years later, in the mid-1990s, even though by then the whole hangar had been taken over, Vancouver Island Helicopters had to utilize every inch of space for maintenance.

R. D. TURNER

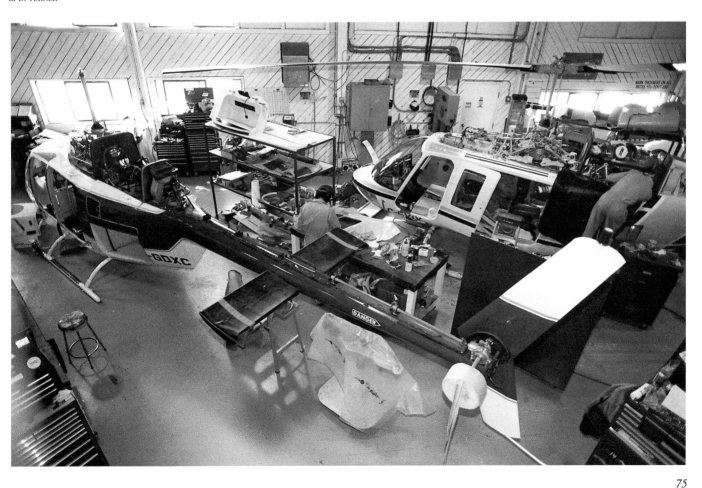

CHAPTER FIVE

Okanagan: One of the Largest Helicopter Operators in the World

A number of us decided that, instead of sitting at home, licking our wounds, we should bloody well do something. So we said to the company, "give us a machine and we'll go out and try to get some work for it."

DON MACKENZIE

For Okanagan Helicopters, 1952 marked the change from individual management to the corporate mode. Not only did bookkeeper Frances Heron move down from Kelowna to join Ada Carlson as the second woman employee, but there was a significant change in the structure of management. The board of directors resolved that Carl Agar was carrying too heavy a burden of administrative and executive responsibility. Consequently, Glenn McPherson was appointed executive vice-president and treasurer, to assume responsibility for marketing and finance, leaving Carl Agar free to look after the operational and training functions of the business.

The move was necessary because the number of enquiries for technical assistance and advice the company was having to deal with, particularly from the military, was becoming unmanageable. As an example, a major from the United States Marines was more or less seconded to the company, sitting in at virtually all of its meetings except Board meetings. The new administration began what was to become an era of amalgamations and the formation of numerous subsidiaries to deal with the growing complexity of their operations.

The first of these subsidiaries was called Sintilopter Surveys Limited. Formed in conjunction with Warmac Exploration Limited, its purpose was to provide airborne geiger and scintillometer surveys for geological exploration companies searching for radioactive minerals. At the same time, Agar Helicopter Consultants Limited was set up as another subsidiary to deal with the ever-increasing volume of enquiries about helicopter operations. Carl, in effect, became an advisor to both the Canadian and the United States military–but now the company was getting paid for his services.

By 1953, the company was beginning to get its financial head well above the water, and it took up its option to purchase one of the two ALCAN S-55s for $115,000. Operating profits had risen to $93,000 and towards the end of the year the company formed a much larger subsidiary. J. C. Charleson of Ottawa, who had worked both for the federal government and in private industry in the field of aviation, and who was one of Canada's first licenced helicopter pilots, became president of a new company called United Helicopters Limited, formed to serve eastern Canada. One of its first tasks was to provide helicopter services to the federal government and to the provincial fisheries department in Newfoundland.

In 1954, there were concrete signs of prosperity, or at least healthy growth. A contract was awarded to Dominion Construction Limited to build a new 10,000 square-foot (930 m^2) hangar, together with 5,000 square feet (465 m^2) of office space at Vancouver International Airport. But 1955 was the year of expansion. To begin with, Okanagan took over and incorporated into its eastern subsidiary, United Helicopters, the major part of the flying assets of Kenting Helicopters Limited and Smart Aviation Limited, most of which had previously been owned by the Abitibi Power and Paper Company. Alf Stringer was appointed general manager of this new and enlarged subsidiary and moved to Toronto to take up his responsibilities.

As well, one of the first and largest of the Geological Survey of Canada helicopter operations took place in that year. Called Project Franklin, it was to be "a broad geological survey of the Arctic Islands, of the Franklin District, Northwest Territories, the major part of Queen Elizabeth Islands and northern parts of Somerset and Prince of Wales Islands, plus the northwest part of Baffin Island."

This was an ambitious project, lasting from June to September. Two of Okanagan's S-55s, HHU and HVR, were outfitted with improved radio equipment and directional gyro-compasses. Then they were flown from Toronto's Malton Airport to Resolute Bay, Northwest Territories, in an RCAF C-119 freighter. Fred Snell was in charge of the Okanagan crew, George Chamberlain the supervising engineer. Orr, Iverson and Hazell were the other pilots; Kelly, Grover and Bryant the engineers. The party chief was Dr. Y. O. Foutier and Dr. E. F. Roots was controller of aircraft movements. In addition, there were nine geologists, each with an assistant, and two cooks. A successful enterprise, this was the forerunner of many Geological Survey of Canada helicopter operations to come.

There was much else going on in 1955. The company worked on a forest inventory survey between Kitimat and Prince Rupert; a Shell Oil geological survey in the Fort Simpson area and the Mackenzie Basin; and an extensive aerial survey for Northwest Explorations Limited in the Watson Lake area, on the British Columbia-Yukon border. All of this was in addition to many smaller prospecting, freighting and power-line patrol operations, as well as an emergency two-machine operation in Kildala Pass, where ALCAN's power transmission line had been knocked out by a snowslide.

By the end of 1955, the company had a staff of 90 people, its helicopters had logged 12,000 hours of revenue flying and gross revenue had grown from $740,000 the previous year to $1,555,000–for a profit of $127,000. But perhaps the most significant news was that negotiations with the federal government for a contract to provide helicopter construction and maintenance services on the Mid-Canada Line were progressing encouragingly. At the time, the government was considering the purchase of 20 S-55s by the RCAF–all of which would be turned over to Okanagan to operate on a cost-plus basis.

The Mid-Canada Line was an aircraft surveillance radar line stretching from Dawson Creek in British Columbia to Hopedale in Labrador. The helicopters were to be based at seven locations: Dawson Creek, Fort McMurray, Cranberry Portage, Bird, Winisk, Great Whale River and Knob Lake (Schefferville). Once construction of the line was completed in 1956, three helicopters were stationed at each of these bases to carry out maintenance and re-supply of the intermediate sites, with the exception of Dawson Creek, which had two.

The majority of the construction of the Line was being carried out by the RCAF, using S-55s and the newer and considerably more powerful S-58s. In fact, Okanagan began work with two S-55s on the Line to help with construction before it was completed. Eric Cowden recalls arriving in Fort McMurray with his pilot, Murray Couch, in 1956. When they stepped out of the helicopter, the people on the ground asked when the rest of their crew would be joining them. They registered disbelief when Eric replied that he and Murray were the crew. Apparently the RCAF had worked with at least six or seven crew members for each helicopter.

The Mid-Canada Line contract promised the same benefits as had the ALCAN contract–it would be a year-round operation and it would be possible to plan for several years ahead. However, by the time the maintenance contract was finally awarded, competitors were in the field. Okanagan's hopes of winning the entire contract faded when Spartan Air Services Limited of Ottawa was given the eastern section of the Line between James Bay and Labrador. Spartan was equipped with RCAF Vertol 42s and 44s–the large, twin-rotor helicopters popularly referred to as "Flying Bananas."

Although the Mid-Canada was a very desirable operation for management, for the crews working on it there were some singular disadvantages. Their responsibility was to provide each of the sites with food, mail, supplies and fuel oil for the electrical generators, as well as the electronic and mechanical maintenance technicians when they were required. The radar sites were located some 20 miles (32 km) apart, and flying

Carl Agar, by now generally referred to by the media as "Mr. Helicopter."

DOROTHY AGAR

along the line from one to the other became very much like truck driving. Each site had a prepared landing pad and after the initial familiarization, there were few challenges involved.

The main challenge, as it turned out, was posed by the realization that the line was obsolescent before construction was completed. This meant that few people were inclined to take their jobs seriously; an attitude of indifference prevailed amongst the crews whose responsibility it was to maintain the equipment on each site. For example, each site had a small Petter diesel engine running the generator, which in turn ran the electrically operated avgas pumps. In the winter, Okanagan's crews spent more time working on these diesels than they did on the helicopters.

But what seems to have frustrated everyone more than anything else was the failure of the ground crews to prepare a load in time for an early morning take-off during the winter. If the helicopter crew could get away at a reasonable hour in the morning, say 8:30, they could fly to the end of the Line and back before darkness fell at about four o'clock in the afternoon. When in base, the helicopters were stored in a heated hangar overnight. If they had to stay out on one of the sites, the problems of starting in the morning were compounded by the lack of ongoing maintenance. The Herman-Nelson gas-driven heaters would seldom start, and when they did, it took a long time to warm things up sufficiently to start the helicopter and clean the accumulated ice and snow off the machine. All the crews appreciated the inevitability of these disagreeable exigencies in winter operations. However, when they were unnecessary, and could easily have been avoided, they caused a good deal of friction.

The results for the company, though, were far from inconsequential. By the end of 1956, Okanagan was operating three S-58s, 13 S-55s (10 RCAF; three their own) and 22 Bell 47s—nearly all of them by now converted to G-2s with the more powerful Lycoming engine—for a total of 35 machines. The staff had increased to 108 and they were close to becoming the largest helicopter company in the world.

But there were a number of disconcerting clouds on the horizon. To begin with, the competition was increasing. In 1954, as we have seen, Vancouver Island Helicopters was granted an operating licence in spite of strenuous opposition from Okanagan. Then, towards the end of 1955, Pacific Western Airlines, a company run by one of the old-time bush pilots, Russ Baker, decided to get into the helicopter business. Bill McLeod was invited to run it for them. Bill recalls that it was not difficult for him to make the decision to move from Okanagan: "Not only did it offer more money, but it was an opportunity to sort of create something myself. Back in the days when I had first come over to the

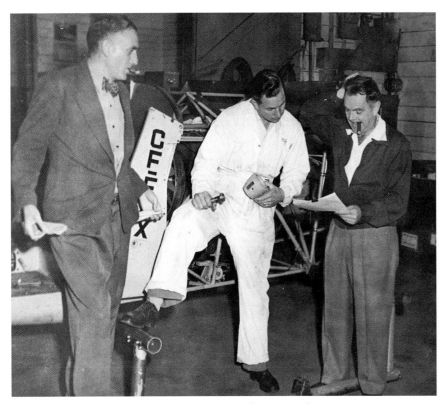

In 1952 Okanagan underwent profound changes in personnel, corporate structure and, before long, aircraft. Central to these changes was Glenn McPherson (*left*) shown with Alf Stringer and Carl Agar. Presumably, Stringer and Agar were demanding more operational funds and McPherson responded with the empty-pockets gesture.

GORDY ASKIN

Eric Cowden, like many in the helicopter industry in British Columbia, got his start in aviation with Queen Charlotte Airlines.

ERIC COWDEN

Okanagan S-55s used on Project Franklin were
flown north to Resolute in RCAF C-119s.
Operating conditions required the addition of
improved radio equipment and gyro-compasses to
the helicopters; magnetic compasses would have
been useless so close to the north magnetic pole.

ALF STRINGER PHOTOS

The Bell 47-B3s in the Okanagan fleet were kept in
operation long after introduction of later models.
The original Okanagan B3, CF-FZX, in noticeably
altered form, is shown here receiving floats.

Pacific Western Helicopter Division operated this Bell model 47-H, one of the few helicopters of the type used in British Columbia. It was a "tarted up" version of the Bell 47-G2 for the executive market.

A helicopter service connecting Victoria and Vancouver, the major population centres of British Columbia, has often been proposed since 1954. One of the most ambitious plans was for the introduction of the Fairey Rotodyne, a British design combining features of both fixed-wing and rotary-wing aircraft. Carl Agar and Alf Stringer went to the UK to view the prototype. The Rotodyne was unsuccessful and never got beyond the experimental stage. Proposals to build the aircraft in the Victoria Fairey plant likewise fell through.

Bud Tillotson (*left*) ran Okanagan's mountain training programme, a demanding task that greatly enhanced the reputation of the company. Students from all over the world learned how, in the lyrical prose of a Bell publication, to read the "subtle, quiet (and potentially treacherous) language of mountain air, feeling the subtleties of its 'bad air' (downdrafts) and 'good air' (power for free, upmoving)."

BELL HELICOPTERS TEXTRON

The late Don MacKenzie (*right*) and an employee of the Kootenay Power Commission near the Lower Arrow Dam, Castlegar, circa 1963. MacKenzie, later Okanagan's chief pilot, earned the Helicopter Association of America's "Pilot of the Year Award" in 1971. He landed a badly disabled S-61 on an oil rig off Nova Scotia, saving the lives of the 16 passengers and crew. In 1983, he was involved in the development of Emergency Multi-Person Rescue Apparatus (EMPRA) which will, if adopted, greatly increase the speed with which hoist rescues can be accomplished.

OKANAGAN COLLECTION

mainland from Vancouver Island and I was going through ground school with the Brisbane company, I shared a room with a guy called Laidman–Dick Laidman. He was with PWA. He got hold of me and said they wanted to form a helicopter division–would I be interested in setting it up and managing it? They made me an offer I just couldn't refuse and I joined them."

PWA's helicopter division started with one Bell 47-G. By the end of the year it had bought five more. At its peak it was operating 12 machines–six of its own and six leased. It succeeded in winning all the forestry contracts available, and did all the helicopter work on the Bennett dam project on the Peace River. But PWA as a whole had overextended itself. It had bought and leased a number of large fixed-wing aircraft for work on the construction of the DEW-Line (the effective corollary to the Mid-Canada Line on the Arctic coast) and, because it was funded to a large extent by the Federal Development Bank, it was obliged to rationalize its operations. The bank gave PWA an ultimatum: either it had to become an airline or it had to return to being a bush operator. It decided to become an airline and sold all its fixed-wing bush operations as well as the helicopter division.

The helicopter operation was bought by a group headed by Jim Storey, an ex-Trans-Canada Airlines captain, and the name was simply changed to Pacific Helicopters Limited. Under its new management, the company continued to compete with Okanagan until 1959, when Okanagan bought all its assets and equipment. But, although buying out the opposition was an effective solution, it was an option not always available. When John Diefenbaker's Conservative government came into power in 1957, the newly appointed Minister of Transport, George Hees, adopted a policy of laissez faire in commercial aviation, and Okanagan complained, with considerable justification, that it was now possible for newly formed companies to bid on government contracts, and often win them, before they had even bought any machines or hired any crews.

What Okanagan was complaining about was, of course, the ultimate in free enterprise, but it had some singular disadvantages, both for the customer and the operator. One-machine companies did sometimes succeed in giving good service, but more often they suffered an accident and, without any back-up of spares or expertise, they often folded and disappeared for good. There was also an obvious question of safety involved. The most expensive part of a helicopter operation is the maintenance and it was an ever-present temptation for a small company to skimp on maintenance, to try to operate with marginally qualified crews. For an established company like Okanagan it was bound to be galling to find themselves deprived of business by people with virtually no operating experience, and by 1959 the strain was beginning to show. During that year it suffered its first retrenchment, selling its subsidiary, United Helicopters Limited, to Eastern Provincial Airlines. Brief statistics for the years 1957 to 1959 give some indication of the problems. Although the size of the fleet was increasing, profits were not:

YEAR	REVENUE	NET PROFIT	AIRCRAFT	HOURS
1957	$2,888.115	$312,568	47	22,000
1958	$3,188,382	$254,412	54	24,000
1959	$3,044,004	$282,659	57	26,000

As well, several new companies sprang up to provide competition in British Columbia in the 1950s. In addition to Vancouver Island and PWA, Highland Helicopters, Haida Helicopters and two or three one-machine companies began operating. On top of this there was some incursion from companies based in Alberta, particularly Foothills Helicopters and Alpine Helicopters. Okanagan naturally would have preferred not to have this competition, but its principal complaint was that at least some of the new companies had an unfair advantage. They pointed out that because these companies had virtually no staff and little or no back-up equipment–which meant low overhead–they could afford to underbid an established company like Okanagan. There was some merit in the argument but unfortunately both private industry and government alike were very much inclined to accept the lowest bid without question.

But by the end of the decade a more serious problem seemed to be the growing tension between individuals in management. The most contentious issue was diversification of the fleet. Until then, the company had operated only Bell 47s for their light machines and Sikorsky S-55s and 58s for the heavier work. Now, decisions were made to start operating the Hiller 12E, a machine comparable to the Bell 47-G2. Those who disagreed with this decision claimed there were two potential disadvantages: first, it would mean two sets of spare parts and special tools; second, whereas the Bell had proved itself operationally with Okanagan, the Hiller hadn't; it was still a relatively untried machine. The result, the dissenters were quick to point out, proved to be an expensive mistake. There was a problem with the balancing of the crankshaft and the engine mounts in the 12E. This led to what were described as harmonic vibrations–a condition that caused long-term maintenance problems, and cost the company a good deal of lost revenue flying time.

A similar problem arose in connection with a contract awarded by the United States government to operate two large machines out of Goose Bay, Labrador. In addition to

A Bell 206 of Highland Helicopters Limited water bombing. This company, formed in 1959 and based in Vancouver, has become a major player. Now, in 1998, it operates 40 helicopters out of 10 bases in British Columbia, nine in Alberta and one in Saskatchewan.

HIGHLAND HELICOPTERS

an S-58, management decided to buy a Sikorsky S-62, a machine that turned out to be unsuitable for the operation, just as some directors had claimed it would when the decision was made. Other controversial projects were initiated at this time: announcements were made in the media that Okanagan had placed an option on the British Fairey Rotodyne, a composite helicopter/fixed-wing aircraft with a capacity for 70 passengers and a top speed of 200 mph (320 km/h). It was to be used for a scheduled service between Vancouver and Victoria. In fact, it was an experimental aircraft still in the prototype stage and it never did fly commercially. This was followed by the setting up of another subsidiary, Copter Cabs, which was to provide a commuter service for the Greater Vancouver area, using three-passenger Bell 47-Js. This venture was an undeniable failure financially.

In the meantime, however, the company continued to grow during the last years of the decade. A constant stream of Canadian, U.S. and overseas trainees passed through Bud Tillotson's mountain training school in Penticton. Then, in 1958, the company was awarded a contract by the Southern California Edison Company to construct a power transmission line through the Soledad Canyon, northeast of Los Angeles. Concrete bases were poured by the helicopter, an S-58, and then pre-rigged wooden poles were dropped into the prepared sockets in the concrete. The operation was a notable success and it was widely reported in North America.

At about this time, too, one of the directors decided it was time to have the story of the company written for publication in book form. As Barney Bent describes it: "The Board agreed to have an acquaintance of one of the directors carry out this work on a retainer fee of $400 a month, plus expenses, to a maximum of $4000. After the financial and time limits had been exceeded (the writer had moved in with the Agars to be close to detailed information, and refreshment), he gave up and left for parts unknown."

By now the company's story had entered a chapter of serious dissension. In 1960, Carl Agar's health had begun to deteriorate; he had emphysema, and unfortunately this illness coincided with the growing conflict between some of the directors. The following year, disaffected but no longer strong enough to put up a fight, Carl submitted a letter of resignation to the board. At a special meeting called by the directors, which must have been an unusually tense occasion, Alf Stringer presented a forthright criticism of a number of managerial decisions to which both he and Carl Agar had been opposed. Glenn McPherson, the president, offered to resign. However, further discussion produced a compromise. Carl Agar would take a three-month leave of absence; both Glenn McPherson and Alf Stringer, who had been also been contemplating resignation,

At about this time, too, one of the directors decided it was time to have the story of the company written for publication in book form. As Barney Bent describes it: "The Board agreed to have an acquaintance of one of the directors carry out this work on a retainer fee of $400 a month, plus expenses, to a maximum of $4,000. After the financial and time limits had been exceeded (the writer had moved in with the Agars to be close to detailed information, and refreshment), he gave up and left for parts unknown."

It was a sad day for Okanagan Helicopters and, because these two pioneers were so highly respected, it sent shock waves throughout the industry.

would stay on while a firm of management consultants, Douglas Dewar's old company, Peat, Marwick, Mitchell, conducted a management study and made recommendations for the future.

In the end, the consultants' report had little effect and both Carl and Alf resigned in 1963. Carl went into retirement until 1966, when he rejoined Okanagan as a Board member and consultant until his death in 1968, and Alf took over the management of Vancouver Island Helicopters from his wife, Lynn. It was a sad day for Okanagan Helicopters and, because these two pioneers were so highly respected, it sent shock waves throughout the industry. It was an unhappy time in other respects, too. The economy had swung from the boom of the 1950s to the relatively severe recession of the early 1960s. The company recorded an operating loss of $171,000 in 1962, and in that same year, for the first time, operational crews were laid off during the winter months.

Don MacKenzie, later chief pilot for the company, recalls those difficult years. He had been a co-pilot with Canadian Pacific Airlines, before joining Okanagan in 1960. Ironically, he had left the airline because he was looking for more security:

As a co-pilot in CPA I started out at $300 a month and worked up to $700. In fact, the captain's deductions were bigger than my pay cheque. That was the rule of thumb then. I joined Okanagan because a number of my very close friends were with them at the time, fellows like Don Poole and Jim Grady, and they persuaded me that helicopters had only been around a few years and they were obviously the coming thing. That, plus the insecurity in the airlines at the time–there were a lot of lay-offs, a lot of moves back and forth–made me think this would be the right move.

As it transpired, Don experienced a classic case of "out of the frying pan into the fire." Two years later he was faced with the lay-off problem again: "That was a tough year, 1962. We had our very first lay-offs. And the first guys in from the bush at the end of the summer got laid off. We all tried to jockey for position. I think it was the only year in memory when people actually tried to stay out in the bush."

Curiously, it was the pilots themselves rather than management who proposed a solution and pointed the way to the future. In spite of the anxiety, Don remembers it as a challenging and, in many ways, a satisfying period:

A number of us decided that, instead of sitting at home, licking our wounds, we should bloody well do something. So we said to the company, "give us a machine and we'll go out and try to get some work for it." Glenn McPherson, the president, was apprehensive at first, but eventually he agreed and I took a machine and went up to Squamish and worked out of a resort called Paradise Valley, flying skiers to Diamond Head and Whistler, doing a little hydro work, an occasional trip for Highways and B.C. Rail–that sort of thing. It tided us over the winter months. Then the next year I joined Jim Grady who had started a base in Nelson the year before.

The idea of bases caught on quickly and before long Okanagan had them spotted right across British Columbia. Even though the winter months were inevitably slow, nearly all the bases became self-supporting during the winter and made money during the rest of the year. By 1968, management had changed. Ian Kennedy became president for two years and, in 1970, John Pitts replaced him. The company moved into much larger machines, Sikorsky S-61s, and began to expand into overseas markets. The first of these operations was a short-lived contract to provide two S-61s to service offshore oil rigs in the North Sea.

Because of time constraints, the decision was made to fly the first machine to Britain rather than ship it by sea, as had been the case with previous overseas contracts. This was a genuinely historic flight, the first unescorted crossing of the Atlantic by a helicopter. The machine was flown by Russ Lennox, a Sikorsky company pilot, and Okanagan's Tommy Scheer. Keith Rutledge travelled with them as engineer. The route followed was from the Sikorsky plant in Bridgeport, Connecticut, up through Quebec to Baffin Island. From there they crossed Davis Strait from Cape Dyer to Sondrestrom in Greenland, over the ice cap and across Denmark Strait to Reykjavik in Iceland, then down through the Faroes to the British Isles. It was a route they were to follow a number of times in the future. In 1973, chief pilot Don Jacques and his crew flew an S-61 all the way from Canada to Britain, across Europe, the Middle-East and most of Asia to Songkhla in Thailand–a distance of 12,650 miles (20,358 km). The S-61 was a remarkable improvement over the little Bell 47-B3 Carl Agar had flown only 25 years before.

But we are moving a long way ahead of the early days of helicopter flying, and it is time to go back and see what conditions were like for the crews working out in the bush in those early days.

CHAPTER SIX

*No bread, no vegetables, no
meat. I didn't have scurvy, but
I was awfully close to it. My gums
were all sore and I had lost
30 pounds.*

IAN DUNCAN

Life in the Bush I

Perhaps because people needed relief from the starkness of the industrial revolution, society invested flying with an aura of glamour and romance from its very beginnings. The First World War helped entrench the profession with an almost mediaeval romanticism: pilots became individual knights, jousting in chargers of wood and doped fabric. The words chivalry and gallantry became unavoidable in any description of the war in the air. Canadians had more than their fair share of heroes: Billy Bishop, Raymond Collishaw, Billy Barker, Don MacLaren; indeed, the great Red Baron himself—Manfred von Richthofen—was finally shot down by a Canadian: Roy Brown.

This romanticism carried into the bush flying era. Canadian bush pilots became a symbol of individual bravery. Alone, they challenged what have been described as the "magnificent distances." As fixed-wing flying became more organized and moved into the realm of large corporations, some of the glamour began to fade. It was somewhat revived when helicopter pilots appeared on the scene, challenging nature in their frail, fluttering machines. For the helicopter pilots, though, as for the earlier generation of bush pilots, the supposed glamour and romance carried a penalty. It provided the businessmen who employed pilots with a neat rationalization: Since pilots were enjoying intangible benefits not available to others, they did not need the reward of appropriate financial benefits.

This fact became very obvious in Kemano, when a little ripple of scandal was provoked by the discovery that the helicopter crews were earning, by a considerable margin, the lowest salaries on the project. Even the most unskilled ditch-digger received a larger pay cheque. It left a bad taste in the mouth—but not bad enough to provoke any immediate remedies.

At least on the Kemano project the helicopter crews were well fed and housed. When they began to move out into other projects—mining exploration and survey operations in the bush—they were to discover another drawback to their newly adopted profession. It revolved around what Alvin Toffler a few years later was to describe as "future shock." Customers who hired a helicopter on contract were literally shocked at the cost. Although they realized that they were now able to cover ten times the area and accomplish in one season what would have taken at least five seasons by the conventional means–pack horses and back-packing–still they were appalled by the $100-per-hour rate for a helicopter. So they quickly persuaded themselves that they would have to compensate by cutting their food, accommodation and supplies budget to the bare bones.

For the crews, this meant tiny, worn-out tents and little or no fresh food. Fixed-wing re-supply trips were kept to a minimum, which meant that crews seldom received mail or news of the outside. Ironically, the technical progress represented by the helicopter had pushed the bush crews back at least 50 years. Nowhere did these economies manifest themselves more clearly than in the provisions made for the helicopter crews. They were, almost invariably, the last people to arrive in a bush camp. As they flew over it for the first time, they would usually see one tattered pup-tent pitched some distance from the other tents, and they would say to each other, "I bet that's ours!" Alas, they were usually right.

Eric Cowden, an engineer with Okanagan Helicopters (later with Vancouver Island Helicopters), describes what it was like to go out on an operation in those early days. He too had made the transition from Queen Charlotte Airlines to helicopters; in fact, he had just completed his training period under Alf Stringer. His pilot was Don Poole, and they set off from Vancouver for Stewart in the spring of 1953. Before they reached the bush camp, however, and faced the discouraging conditions, they had other problems. Fuel caches were few and far between along the coast, so they always carried at least four five-gallon cans of avgas on the racks. On this occasion, the leg from Prince Rupert to Stewart was a critical one, as a stiff northwest wind was blowing:

We got into Rupert and overnighted there [Eric recalls]. Next morning we headed up to Stewart. There was a terrific outflow [wind] that day. We'd already landed on the American side, which we weren't supposed to do–but you had to gas up somewhere. After we'd put the four fives into the tank, we set off up the Portland Canal. We were going nowhere–you know what it's like on floats: about 20 miles an hour [30 km/h]. And it was one of those days–a low overcast, so you couldn't climb out of the Canal and land up top somewhere. There wasn't even a boat around–nothing.

Finally Don said to me, "What do you think?" I said, "Well, Don, my watch says we're not going to make it. "You know what?" he replied. "So does mine."

Anyway, there was no place to land, so we just had to keep on chugging up the Canal, doing a little praying. Finally, we turned a corner and got some shelter from the wind. When we reached Stewart, I drained the tank. We had two gallons left–enough for about six or seven more minutes of flying.

The job Don Poole and Eric Cowden were to do in Stewart was supposed to last 10 days, after which they were to return to Vancouver; instead, they stayed out for five and a half months. To begin with, they were flying between Stewart and the Granduc Glacier. This was the site of the Granduc Copper Mine, which has suffered various reversals of fortune, closing down and then re-opening several times over the years. When they had finished there, they were sent to another mining exploration job, and, as Eric recalls, things started to go downhill.

From Stewart we went to Bobquin Lake with two geologists–McKenzie and Warren were their names, two guys who believed in living on bacon, bannock and beans. With a little tea and sugar, that's about all they had in their so-called camp. For several weeks we worked out of a little island in the middle of Bobquin. We stayed there about five weeks, and I'll never laugh again when people make jokes about beans.

From there we moved to Hottah Lake and then to Chukachida, more or less in the middle of the province. We were with some hot-shot mining promoter now–I remember this guy very well; I guess he was worth lots of money and behaved accordingly. The first day we were there he came into the camp in a beat-up old Travelair flown by Doug Chapelle, and the next morning the weather was socked in tight, right down on the deck. I hear him say to the party chief, George Radisics, "What's the weather like, George?" And George said, "It's socked in tight, but I think it'll clear up by noon." The promoter said, "That's not good enough. I want it clear now!" I guess he thought he could buy the weather, too.

This was just the beginning. Eric had other problems. The fixed-wing aircraft used on that operation, a venerable Travelair, was in sad condition. The company operating it had not provided a licensed engineer, so Eric found that he was expected to inspect it and sign the log book when it was due for a 100-hour maintenance check. Every time the Travelair, which of course was on floats, had been pulled up onto the beach to be loaded or unloaded, Eric had heard what he described as a funny noise. When the time came for the inspection and signature, he got somebody to grab the tail section and rock the machine up and down.

Sure enough, one of the mounts on the struts that connected the floats to the fuselage was just about ready to fall off. Eric refused to sign the log until the aircraft had been repaired–something that could not be done in the bush–and was exposed to ferocious recriminations from the mining promoter. In the end, everybody took off in the Travelair for Prince George, leaving Don and Eric sitting alone in camp for three days.

Their next move was to Yehinika Lake, a little to the southwest of Telegraph Creek. This was still Eric's first season in the bush, and his helicopter, CF-ETQ, even though it was a brand new Bell 47-D1, gave trouble.

"From Stewart we went to Bobquin Lake with two geologists–McKenzie and Warren were their names, two guys who believed in living on bacon, bannock and beans. With a little tea and sugar, that's about all they had in their so-called camp. For several weeks we worked out of a little island in the middle of Bobquin. We stayed there about five weeks, and I'll never laugh again when people make jokes about beans."

ERIC COWDEN

We'd been having the usual snags with those Franklin engines. They were very hard on plugs–we were constantly having to change plugs and dig the lead out of the electrodes, and the fan belts kept letting go. When they did, they'd smack into the back of the firewall, scaring hell out of the pilot . . . and then he'd have to get down on the ground within a couple of minutes and shut down or the engine would over-heat.

Those were routine problems, but this engine began to give me much more than that—nothing but grief. I thought the timing of the magnetos was out. Trouble was, I didn't have a manual with me on that trip; and this was a 200-horsepower engine. I'd been working on a 170-horsepower one, so I didn't really know what the timing should be. I thought I remembered Sig [Hubenig] say it was 36 degrees–so I retimed the whole thing. It didn't do a damned bit of good. Yehinika Lake was well up in the mountains and we still had a very rough engine. I checked the plugs and the points–re-set the gap–and everything was as it should be. Had me baffled there for a while; then, when I was shutting down–I shut down with the mixture control–and just before the engine quit, it suddenly smoothed out.

So I fired up again and played with the mixture–we had a manual mixture control in those days. It would run fine just before it quit. I came to the conclusion it just had to be the carburetor. Trouble was I had never taken one apart before. I pulled the carb off the intake and split it–and out fell a little ball check-valve. It was a bad scene because I hadn't the faintest idea where it had come from. I thought, "Oh my God! Here we are, way out in the tules and our only way to get out is in that damned helicopter."

Anyway, I found the float level was way out–way beyond limits, so I set that all up. Now I really had to decide where this little ball had to go. In the end, the only place that looked likely was the accelerator pump, so I popped it in there, clamped the carburetor together and bolted it back onto the manifold. When I fired up the engine, it ran like a charm. I didn't bother telling Don about the worry-session with the check valve. When he got back from a quick test flight and thanked me because the engine was running good, I just shrugged and said, "That's what I'm here for."

In truth, the helicopter engineer did a good deal of worrying at that time. Confidence in both machine and pilot was to come with experience. Few of the bush camps had radio, and in any case, geologists were always secretive; they did not want people to know where they were. Thus Don Poole would leave camp early in the morning with a couple of geologists, cheerfully advising Eric that he would be back in three or four hours. Then began the long wait. Geologists, if they think they may be on to something significant, lose all track of time. Eric remembers this only too clearly: "Noon would go by; supper time would go by, and still no helicopter; and I'm pacing up and down–I tell you, I had a trail worn down along that shoreline that was knee-deep, pacing up and down, worrying; what am I going to do? I'm in camp all alone, no radio in those days, or anything. And then, just as it was beginning to get dark, you'd hear it. I could hear a helicopter 30 miles [50 km] away. Talk about worry; man alive!"

This same theme of anxiety was reflected by Ian Duncan, another pioneer Okanagan engineer, later with the Canadian Coast Guard. He remembers when they were working

Before the advent of hydraulically assisted controls, irreversibles helped to damp feedback from the rotor system.

R. D. TURNER

for the Canadian Army, doing barometer surveys out of Puntzi Lake, some 50 miles (80 km) west of the town of Williams Lake:

About a week after we'd arrived there, the pilot, Mike (McDonagh), took off with this lieutenant and his barometer and all his instruments and away they went. "Be gone four hours, Duncan," he said. I said, "Okay, fine." So four hours went by, and then five hours, and I started to get up off my cot in the tent; I started to walk around the tent. By the time it got dark, I had worn a trench about two feet deep around the tent–just walking around. Believe me, you worry a lot when you don't know what's happened. Finally, just after breakfast next morning, in comes the pilot, back to camp. He'd walked all night, and you could see the blisters on his feet; his feet were bleeding.

Apparently Mike had tried to pull up too sharply after taking off from a little sand beach. He lost his revs and, since his machine was not on floats, it just settled into the water. Ian Duncan got hold of a 4-wheel-drive Dodge Powerwagon from the Army and made good use of the winch on the front of it, hauling himself through several swamps and fording at least three rivers to get to the damaged helicopter. Then he used it to get the semi-submerged helicopter back up onto the beach. Another pilot brought in replacements, including an engine, and they rebuilt the helicopter on the spot before flying it out. As a precaution, they installed floats instead of skids this time.

About a month later, they moved from Puntzi Lake right up to Satigi Lake, just south of Aklavik, at the estuary of the Mackenzie River. A week after that, Ian recalls, the helicopter disappeared again: "Mike went off on another of these barometer trips. He said he'd be back by 4 o'clock, but he wasn't, and I wore another trench around my tent. It took us four or five hours to get through to Aklavik [on the radio], where we could get some help to go and look for him."

Eventually a Beaver, belonging to B.C.-Yukon Air Services and flown by company owner Bill Dalzell, was sent from Aklavik into Satigi Lake to start a search. The Beaver's condition shocked Ian Duncan: "He had the most beat-up old Beaver you ever saw in your life. The rudder cables on the floats were so loose, he'd tied knots in them to bring them up to proper tension. You couldn't see the front of the engine for bugs and oil and stuff. You've never seen such a shambles in your life."

Nevertheless they took off in the Beaver to begin the search, and fortunately they quickly found where the helicopter was. Ian Duncan spotted some smoke coming up from a point of land. The first reaction was relief: somebody must be alive. As they circled the point, all they could see were the bottoms of two helicopter floats protruding from the water. When they landed and taxied ashore, they found Mike and his passenger both unhurt, but so badly bitten by mosquitoes that they were in sad shape. This time Mike had fallen victim to glassy water–a condition that makes it impossible to see the

Apparently Mike [McDonagh] had tried to pull up too sharply after taking off from a little sand beach. He lost his revs and, since his machine was not on floats, it just settled into the water.

A "fly camp" wasn't luxurious, as this 1959 Ted Protheroe photograph
illustrates. Such camps did provide shelter when a minimum of equipment
was carried on the helicopter, generally the case on short operations.

TED PROTHEROE

The cook is to many the most important person in a bush camp. His skill or lack of it can have considerable influence on the quality of work produced on a job.

PETER CORLEY-SMITH

Okanagan's first helicopter, the Bell 47-B3, CF-FZX, coming in for a landing at a lakeside Forestry camp in the Kitimat area, 1949.

OKANAGAN COLLECTION

An Okanagan Helicopters Bell 47-G2, which first brought in the materials to
construct the pad, and then the materials to construct a Forestry fire-lookout tower
on Mount Artaban, May 1961. Trees have been topped to permit a safe approach
to this pad.

BC MINISTRY OF FORESTS

Not quite up to Will Tompson's standards but a serviceable shower, nevertheless, and pilot Noel Dodwell is enjoying the amenity.

ERIC COWDEN

In cold, frosty weather, as much of the helicopter as possible was covered at night. Here the engine and transmission are still enclosed and the nylon covers are being removed from the blades of the main rotor.   BOB TAYLOR

Maintenance in the bush often meant making use of materials readily at hand. Trees would be cut, stripped of their branches and rigged into an A-frame for a hoist to remove a rotor or engine.

OKANAGAN COLLECTION

surface of the water. He had dug one float in and the machine had flipped on its side. Mike and his passenger had been able to scramble out before the machine turned over and sank.

Everyone was flown back to camp in the Beaver. Another pilot, Eddy Amman, brought a replacement machine up from Vancouver. Meanwhile, Ian returned to the accident site in the Beaver and after a struggle with "come-alongs" (manually operated ratchet winches) they managed to get the submerged helicopter ashore, where they dismantled it, loaded the pieces into the Beaver and flew them back to camp to start the rebuild. Mike McDonagh was "given a rest" after this second accident and replaced by Bud Tillotson. It was merely a temporary setback for Mike; he went on to a distinguished career as a helicopter pilot.

By 1954, some other operators had begun to use helicopters, and Jock Graham's first job in his new capacity as a technical representative for Pratt and Whitney was with one of them: Hudson Bay Mining. He spent six weeks in a camp some 250 miles (400 km) north of Teslin Lake in the Yukon. He describes an unnerving maintenance problem which occurred there:

The pilot, Russ Lennox, kept having the engine almost fail. It looked like fuel starvation. He would land, shut down and then start the engine again and everything would be good. He'd come back to camp and the other engineer and I would just about tear the whole fuel system apart and we couldn't find anything wrong. I was baffled. Then one day we were sitting around with all the screens [filters] out of the fuel system. One of them was a finger screen – a hollow tube with a fine mesh screen like a thimble on top of it. The mechanic from the Otter we were using picked it up and tried to poke a piece of grass up through the bottom hole. The grass wouldn't go. When I had a good look, I found there was another very fine screen in the hole, where it certainly shouldn't have been. The people who had made the filters for Pratt and Whitney had misread the drawings and this extra screen was causing the fuel starvation. So we had to ground every S-55 in North America until the second screen had been punched out. That was quite a worry session.

Anxiety, therefore, was one of the things a helicopter engineer had to live with; boredom was another. The days were long and usually uneventful; the evenings were spent, all too often, in the company of mosquitoes and blackflies, doing routine maintenance.

"You found some things to do," Eric Cowden remembers. "You could usually fish and walk around the shore of the lake, learning something about the vegetation and the animals; but most of the time it was sheer boredom. You had nobody to talk to during the day but the cook, and he was nearly always a cranky old bastard. I tell you, I've read thousands – and I mean thousands – of pocket books. In fact, I can pick one up even today and probably go through the first paragraph and say, 'Dammit, I've read that one!'"

Anxiety, therefore, was one of the things a helicopter engineer had to live with; boredom was another. The days were long and usually uneventful; the evenings were spent, all too often, in the company of mosquitoes and blackflies, doing routine maintenance.

While it would be an exaggeration to suggest that cases of incipient scurvy were commonplace, they were not unheard of; and many a helicopter crew in the fifties returned to base in the fall looking gaunt, if not emaciated.

As well as the anxiety and the boredom, there were the living conditions. To go back to Eric's and Don Poole's first operation, after their stint at Yehinika Lake and another spell back at Chukachida Lake, they were sent up to Paddy's Lake, some 60 miles (95 km) south of Atlin, to work with a provincial topographic survey crew. By now they were well into the summer, and living conditions, according to Eric, still had not improved:

Well, when you were at this camp at Chukachida, you were lucky to get a can of sardines thrown at you. And when we were ferrying from there up to Paddy's Lake, near Atlin–incidentally, by now the old girl was perking along fine; no plug misses or twitches or anything–Don suddenly made like he was going to land. And I thought, "I wonder what that old bugger heard that I didn't hear."

Anyway, we landed in a moose patch and I said to Don, "What the hell did we land here for?" "Well," he replied, "you and I have been out a long time; we're going to take ourselves a couple of days off. We're going up to Atlin." So we poured in our spare gas and when we took off again Don flew much higher than I'd ever seen him fly before, and we went right over Paddy's Lake. Of course, there's a brand new crew down there, all excited, all ready to go to work. They were waving frantically. We pretended we didn't even see them. Old Don was a good 5,000 feet [1 500 m] and we just chuga-chugged right up into Atlin.

The first thing we did in Atlin was to go to the cafe and order lunch; and the first thing I ordered was a salad. "Aren't you going to have a steak?" Don asked. "Yes, later; but I need to start with this. I think I'm getting scurvy; my gums are all sore. Me, too," said Don. "That's why we're here!"

We lived like peasants out there in those days. It was expected of you–part of the job, so you accepted it. Changed days now; nobody'll do it anymore.

While it would be an exaggeration to suggest that cases of incipient scurvy were commonplace, they were not unheard of, and many a helicopter crew in the fifties returned to base in the fall looking gaunt, if not emaciated. Ian Duncan talked of two incidents: "That first survey job we did for the Army, we lived on Burns Chuckwagon Dinners–in the can. That's all we had for the whole season. But that was nothing compared to the second season. That year I was working for an outfit called Fort Reliance Minerals, and I'll never forget that operation. The whole season consisted of dehydrated foods–no bread, no vegetables, no meat. I didn't quite have scurvy, but I was awfully close to it. My gums were all sore and I had lost 36 pounds (16 kg). At the end of the season I came home and I remember my wife was in tears. I guess I looked some scrawny."

Sometimes these conditions were rationalized by companies with head offices in New York or elsewhere which claimed to believe that Canadians were accustomed to living off the land. Sometimes it was the fault of Canadians themselves, caught up in the ageless syndrome of "You guys just don't know what it was like to live rough." And they would go on to elevate subsistence living to the level of virtue and virility–ignoring the fact that their unfortunate predecessors had usually died young, their health hopelessly impaired by cold, dampness and malnutrition.

It was a passing phase, but a long one for the helicopter crews. They accepted it for a few years, when they were still inexperienced, still a little insecure, trying to "sell" the merits of the helicopter; but as soon as they gained the confidence born of experience, more and more of them began to do what Don and Eric had done. They would jump into the helicopter and fly to the nearest town or settlement for what American servicemen call R-and-R. With clothes clean and fresh from the laundromat, a few tolerably good meals under their belts, and perhaps a hangover, they would return to camp to face the wrath of the party chief with some equanimity. By the end of the 1950s, the helicopter business was enjoying an unmistakable boom, so there was little fear of termination. The worst that could happen would be a change of location; a swap with some other crew who were in similar disfavour with their party chief.

The people hiring helicopters for bush exploration soon began to appreciate that if crews became genuinely dissatisfied with their living conditions, no amount of attempted coercion could make them productive. A pilot could find a dozen reasons not to fly, ranging from mechanical problems to weather conditions. An engineer could ground the machine for extensive safety checks. It made more sense to improve morale by housing people in weatherproof tents, feeding them properly, and providing sufficient fixed-wing supply runs to get mail to them at reasonable intervals.

This in turn led to a further problem. Once the customer had decided to provide a reasonable supply of fresh food, it was difficult to find someone who could turn it into a decent meal. Nearly all bush cooks were men who had descended, because of too many losing battles with John Barleycorn, to a state of physical deterioration which left them no option but to become cooks. One day they would find themselves unable to go out and cut line, or drag a chain through the heavy undergrowth to lay out a baseline. They would have to be left in camp to help the cook. From then on, with neither training, talent nor vocation, they would become cooks.

Geologist Will Tompson, party chief for bush operations over the years, recalls that this was his biggest headache. Will believed from his earliest days as a party chief in trying to provide good food and accommodation in a bush camp. He would invariably send in a crew, before the operations began, to build frames of plywood and two-by-fours for the tents. For each two people he provided a 12 by 14 foot (3.6 × 4.2 m) canvas tent, with wooden floor (one of those luxuries it is so easy for us to forget), a covering fly and an airtight stove.

Two people, given this sort of accommodation, could live very comfortably in the most extreme temperatures. The fly kept the tent cool when the sun was shining and weather-proof when it was raining. With only a little experience, you could keep an air-tight heater smouldering at just the right temperature for indefinite periods. All you needed now to make this resemble the comforts of home was a shower, and this, as Will points out, was neither difficult nor unduly expensive: "You don't need to spend a lot of time rigging up showers with 45-gallon drums. You can buy them from any hardware store. The ones I've used are made from steel and come in a square box. Then all you need is a hot water tank, some propane and a few lengths of plastic hose. What the hell, you've got lots of water around, and propane is pretty cheap."

But when it came to cooks, Will had no such easy solutions: "The biggest problem in camp, the most serious problem in exploration, is cooks! The years that Peter Corley-Smith and I worked together we had three bad cooks and one good one. I'd say that's probably about normal. My experience has been that cooks cause more problems than anybody else in the exploration hierarchy."

So this too was one of the disadvantages of the helicopter engineer's lot: he often had to spend his entire day with no other company but the cook. However, like all such generalizations, this one does grave injustice to the one out of four who was a good cook. Theirs was a thankless task, preparing and then cleaning up after three meals a day, seven days a week, for months at a time. If anyone contributed to a successful operation in the bush, it was a good cook.

The ideal combination for an air survey operation: here, at Dumbell Lake, near Mosely Creek on the Homathko operation, a de Havilland Beaver brings in food and supplies, and the helicopter shuttles them out to camps inaccessible by water.

DES O'HALLORAN

CHAPTER SEVEN

Life in the Bush II

So I shut down the engine and got out to have a look. Son of a bitch, there was wire wrapped around that helicopter like you never saw.

BRUCE PAYNE

While life for the helicopter engineer often seems to have been drab and tedious, for the pilot there were some compensations. First, there was the satisfaction of knowing that, practically without exception, everyone in a bush camp would have liked to be able to fly the helicopter. They seldom admitted it, of course, but they were all a trifle envious. The pilot was the pivotal figure. It was he who put them all up in those inaccessible mountains or down in the tiny moose pasture in the middle of the tall forest. There was still a touch of magic to it all.

There was also the satisfaction of developing new methods to improve the efficiency of the operation and the value of the helicopter. It was a constant challenge in those first years to work out some method of moving difficult loads. Bruce Payne flew his first season in the bush for Vancouver Island Helicopters in 1956. He speaks now of these events as though they were mere logical extensions of the helicopter's versatility, but at the time they had never been tried, and to try them required some courage:

I worked for Topo Survey for a couple of years, and then flew for the B.C. Power Commission up in the Homathko River. They were really active in there–a lot of drilling. We had to move the drill rigs–they were the BBS-1 rigs; the engine weighed, oh, about 300-350 pounds [135-160 kg] and the frame weighed a little more.

To begin with we had a heck of a time; we used outriggers to move them. We'd put the engine or the frame on the right-hand side, opposite the pilot, and we'd stick a board out the other side about 10 feet [3 m] long and hang a bag of cement on it to balance the load. It was pretty hairy.

Then Harvey Jones, or one of the old engineers in VIH, came up with the idea of fixing up part of an old Canso bomb rack and bolting it to the frame under the helicopter so that you could hook on a sling load and jettison it when you needed to. That was a heck of a lot easier than outriggers.

The drilling jobs were interesting because you were always running into something new; you had to watch yourself, though, or you'd get sucked in. I remember up in the Homathko there, before we started slinging, there was a fellow working for Boyle Brothers, the drilling outfit, a French-Canadian called Paul Roche who'd been up in Kemano before that. We had just finished drilling in this canyon–the landing pad was right in the canyon–and this guy Paul had three tripod poles that he was really fond of. They were 35 feet [10 m] long, but dry because he'd used them for a couple of months. He wanted me to move them up into Mosely Creek.

I looked at them and said, "Heck, there's no way we can move those." "Well," he says, "we used to move them up in Kemano all the time." "How the dickens did you do that?" I asked. "Show me." "Well," he says, "we put them on the sides; strapped them right beside the helicopter, on the racks."

So we strapped two of these things on, one on either side. They weren't that heavy; they only weighed about 150 pounds [70 kg] apiece. But here we were with these damn things sticking way out in front and way back at the back end. I took off kind of gingerly; but they were okay and I moved them up to Mosely Creek. When I got back, Paul says, "How did it go?" I says, "Jesus, it went good; it went good that way." "Well," he says, laughing, "that's the first time I ever saw that done."

That sort of thing happened quite often in those days. You had to be pretty careful. The trouble was, you wanted so badly to sell the helicopter you'd try near anything.

Another problem load before slinging came into practice was handling reflector dishes for microwave repeater stations. The dishes always had to be flown to the highest peak. They were about 18 inches deep, 5 feet wide and 12 feet long (45 cm × 1.5 m × 3.6 m). Bruce would remove both doors, then climb in and wait while the ground crew tied a dish on either rack. Once this was done, there was no way for the pilot to get out until the dishes had been untied. It was an uncomfortable feeling. The noise, reflected back at him from the exhaust stacks, was deafening.

No sooner had one load been mastered than another more difficult one would appear. Bruce recalls that the microwave dishes grew larger:

One reflector in particular, I remember. I had to fly it up the mountain from Little Prairie, which is Chetwynd now. It was a great big one; I think it was 22 feet [7 m] long, but it was the same depth and width. I couldn't put this one on the side because it was too heavy, so I tied it underneath the helicopter. I started off down this strip–there was a little old grass strip there–and when I got up to about 20 miles an hour [32 km/h], the cyclic [control column] was well back in my stomach, yet the nose kept on going down. The wind was hitting the front of the dish and driving the nose down. Well, I had just enough control left to slow down again and get the nose up. Then I hovered up the side of that mountain at 15 miles an hour [25 km/h]. It was a slow climb.

For Bruce, the next innovations came when helicopters began to be used for hydro power-line construction. Once the survey had been completed and the tower sites located, landing pads were built at each site. Ground crews would then be flown in to construct the forms for the concrete tower footings. Then the concrete, already mixed at a central point, would be flown in. Bruce describes the method:

Most of the buckets at that time were 45-gallon [205-l] drums. We'd just put a ring on the bottom of them. Then you'd lay the drum onto the edge of the form, a guy on the ground would transfer your lanyard clip onto this ring and you'd lift up and dump it for them. Later on we got the self-dumping

Doing what only a helicopter could do: slinging a complete section of a hydro-transmission tower onto its sidehill location. When it is lowered, the men on the tower pin the section in place and then replace the pins with bolts after the pilot has punched off the lanyard.

CAE JOURNAL

buckets. You'd just hover over the form, a guy on the ground would pull a lever and it would dump itself.

Once the footings were poured, the helicopter would start to sling in the steel for the tower. Sometimes, with the smaller helicopters, they would actually hang the tower steel, length by length, while the ground crew bolted them into place. Later, with the advent of the larger helicopters, the Sikorsky S-58s and the Bell 204Bs, whole sections of the tower would be dropped into place.

The next stage would be the installation of the cables. Once again the helicopter could speed things up enormously. The process began with the stringing of what is called a sock line–a thin steel cable, perhaps a quarter of an inch in diameter, which would later be used to pull the actual power cables into position.

This sock line would be on a large drum, mounted on the back of a flat-bed truck. The drum had a brake on it, operated manually, to allow the line to be paid out at a steady tension. A metal ball weighing 150 to 200 pounds (60-90 kg) would be slung below the helicopter. Bruce describes the procedure: "The ball hung about 20 feet [6 m] below the helicopter and they'd hook the line onto that. Then I'd just move out and pull it off the ground. I've pulled out as much as 42,000 feet [eight miles-12 km] with a Bell 47. It would take up to five minutes to get it moving."

On at least one occasion, it took longer than that. After pulling maximum climb power for some 10 minutes, Bruce finally gave up, dropped the ball and flew the mile or so back to the drum truck to find out what was wrong. When he got there, he found the operator sound asleep, with the brake firmly set.

When he had got the sock line moving, the pilot would pass each tower and then back up to give the ground crew enough slack to run the line through a "traveller" or pulley, which would then be pulled up and secured to the cross-arms on top of the tower. Once the length for that particular section had been run out, another truck with a winch would hook onto the sock line and pull the actual power cable, which was attached to the tail end of it, through the travellers.

"It wasn't a bad job," according to Bruce, "but some of the guys couldn't take it. They could pull sock line on the flat ground, or the not-so hilly stuff–but when they got over one of those big valleys, with a thousand feet of nothing underneath them, and they're sitting there at, oh, maybe three or four miles an hour for 20 maybe 30 minutes, pulling it across, then they'd get vertigo pretty bad and have a real problem."

Most of the power-line construction was done by private companies under contract to B.C. Hydro. The final task, after construction was completed, was for the helicopter

The Bell 47 series rotor head, which used a stabilizer bar to provide a measure of stability.

R. D. TURNER

pilot to take out the Hydro inspectors. As a rule he would land them on the pad near the base of each tower and they would climb the tower to make sure that all the bolts were in place and secure and that the insulators and cables were correctly installed. However, if the weather was calm and the pilot feeling intrepid, he could balance on the cross-arms on the top of the tower, drop his passengers and then pick them up on the pad below when they had completed their inspection. It was a popular pilot who was willing to do this.

These developments were stimulating and satisfying when they worked. When they did not, the result could be an accident. Those involved had to learn to be philosophical about accidents; they were part of the learning process, and few pilots went very long without one. The tail rotor, hanging out of sight some 20 feet (6 m) behind the pilot's back was an Achilles Heel. It was so easy, when landing in a bush clearing, to poke it into the stump of a rotted tree or a clump of willow. In the early days, all loads had to be carried on the external racks. It was often hard to estimate how much weight was on board, and once one was committed to take off, all that was needed to start trouble was a plug choking up—something not uncommon with the Franklin engine.

Fortunately the advent of the cargo hook relieved this problem. You could punch off the load if needed. Apart from the machine itself, perhaps the biggest hazard was posed by wires which stretched, usually unmarked, across rivers and valleys. Bruce Payne describes an encounter with wires early in his career:

I had been on fisheries patrols, counting fish, with a biologist called Mac Chapman. I'd been doing this job on and off for a couple of years, up and down the river—it was in connection with the dam work on the Fraser and its tributaries.

The wires we hit were thick ones, almost as thick as your finger. They crossed the Fraser just below Tejeune. I still can't figure how I didn't see them. We'd been up and down this stretch of river two years before—in fact, we'd been up and down it earlier the same day, and neither of us saw those wires.

I guess I just got low enough that run. I ran right into them. I saw them just about the time we flew into them. They hit the bubble about eye-level. They didn't break the bubble; they went up over it and into the mast. Then the blades caught them and they made an awful racket. That slowed the blades down and we just dropped right into the river bed; we landed in the water. It was only three or four inches deep, but it was muddy and we were settling into this stuff.

So I shut down the engine and got out to have a look. Son of a bitch, there was wire wrapped round that helicopter like you never saw. You know the scissors levers [two control arms running up on either side of the mast to alter the pitch of the rotor blades], they were just strapped right into the mast, tight.

The option to give up and wade ashore was not available: they were on a mud bank in the middle of the river, with deep water on either side. So Bruce and his passenger set

The Hiller 12E used paddles, once again to provide a measure of stability.

OKANAGAN COLLECTION

The installation of microwave dishes on towers was exacting work, requiring capable people both in the helicopter and on the tower. Cockpit visibility from the S-55 was less than ideal.

In the late 1960s, Okanagan Helicopters invested in a number of Hiller 1100s, that manufacturer's answer to the Bell 206 and Hughes 500. These machines proved to have serious teething problems and disappeared from the scene for several years, reappearing as Fairchild-Hillers. Here an 1100 is about to hook up to the sockline on a hydro construction project.

Pacific Helicopters Limited, a subsidiary of Pacific Western Airlines, operated for several years in the 1960s. Here, one of its Hiller 12Es is at the Banner Forestry Ranger Station, June 1960.

BC MINISTRY OF FORESTS

Returning from the Liard-Mattu rivers area where they had been doing seismic testing for Shell Oil, this Okanagan crew of (*l. to r.*) Bill Legge, Ian Duncan, Rod Fraser and Fred "Tweedy" Eilertson stopped at Ashcroft. Legge and Eilertson were pilots, Duncan and Fraser engineers. The Sikorsky S-55, CF-GHV, was purchased from ALCAN by Okanagan after the Kemano project.

IAN BURRARD

A. Y. Jackson (*centre*), one of the celebrated Group of Seven artists, travelled in this Bell 47-G2 on one of his trips north in the early 1960s.

PETER CORLEY-SMITH PHOTOS

A pilot would occasionally be able to take his family along. Bell 47-G3B-1, CF-VIH, was the pride of the Vancouver Island Helicopter fleet when this photo was taken at Alice Arm in the 1960s.

So Bruce and his passenger set about unravelling the wire. It took them more than half-an-hour. The wooden rotor blades were damaged, but Bruce replaced the shards of wood which had come off the leading edges and taped them into place with the black friction tape pilots always carried in a helicopter. Next he climbed up and pulled out the scissors levers until they were more or less straight and parallel with the mast. By this time the machine had sunk almost a foot into the mud.

about unravelling the wire. It took them more than half-an-hour. The wooden rotor blades were damaged, but Bruce replaced the shards of wood which had come off the leading edges and taped them into place with the black friction tape pilots always carried in a helicopter. Next he climbed up and pulled out the scissors levers until they were more or less straight and parallel with the mast. By this time the machine had sunk almost a foot into the mud.

So we got back in, and I fired up. It was pretty rough–things were out of balance –but I managed to move her up onto a little bench on the bank of the river, where I shut down again so that I could take a really good look at the blades. I thought, gee, maybe I can balance those things out. There was no radio, and nowhere we could've walked to from there, so I started wrapping tape on those blades. I started up and shut down several times, and in the end I got it so it wasn't too bad. Then we had a real good look, the two of us. There were quite a few nicks and creases from that flaming wire, but they didn't look too bad. So in the end we climbed in and flew back to Prince George–about an hour-and-a-half. It was rough as hell, but the tape held okay and we made it.

Helicopters even from their earliest days were generally reliable, but there were occasional bad "runs" when mechanical problems caused many a fast pulse. There was a period with the Bells in the middle fifties when some flaw in the manufacturing process caused many fan-belt failures. The Franklin engines were cooled by a large fan, belt-driven from the engine. The fan sat no more than six or eight inches behind the pilot's back, separated only by what was rather euphemistically called a firewall–a thin and remarkably resonant sheet of metal. When a fan belt let go, it invariably flailed into the firewall with a report like a rifle shot–a noise that would jerk even the coolest pilot hard up against his seat belt. He had to find a landing within two or three minutes or the engine would overheat and seize up. Over densely forested country, this could be a long and sometimes breathless time.

Another of these "runs" occurred with the advent of the Hiller 12E in the late fifties. This was Bell's competition in the light helicopter category; it was a very responsive machine, giving the impression of increased power and load capacity. But those who used it ran into teething troubles. Bruce describes the problems he had in the early sixties: "I was working on a seismic survey for an outfit called General Geophysical–a Texas company on contract to Shell Oil. We were working along the Redstone Dehadinni River, just to the west of the Mackenzie, between Wrigley and Norman Wells. That was a bad, bad one, that job."

When asked what was so bad about it, Bruce hesitated. "I don't think people will believe it now if you tell what conditions were like in those days." Apparently this had been one of the first big seismic surveys by helicopter. Lines had to be cut and surveyed, and drills and compressors had to be carried, as well as the dynamite for the seismic shots. The bidding for the contract had been very competitive, and General Geophysical had to pare expenses to the bone in order to make a profit. Some 75 to 80 men were employed, four to a pup tent. Packs and suitcases had to be stored outside, under a ground sheet. They were working two shifts, and each man had to share his sleeping bag with his opposite number on the other shift–four of them could not have fitted into the tent at once. The helicopter crews considered themselves lucky. At least they had their own sleeping bags.

But the more serious problem was food. The company had decided they could not afford to fly in fresh food, so the food all had to be trucked up the Mackenzie Highway to Hay River, then transferred to barges to be towed up and dropped on the river bank about 30 miles (50 km) from their main camp. Unfortunately communications were so poor they seldom heard that a load of food had been dropped until a week or 10 days later. By the time they did hear, the bears had usually got to it first–and most of it had gone bad. "The cooks used to ask you, 'Do you want one egg this week, or two next week?' It was that sort of deal."

Heli-logging with a 47-G3B-1, John King at the controls.

JOHN KING

Anyway, [Bruce went on], we had three engine failures in 19 days. They were all on Hillers. I was flying along one night and picked up a couple of guys about two o'clock in the morning–it was light almost 24 hours a day. Every half-mile there was an opening in the trees. I was going right down this cut line, heading for camp with these guys–they'd had some problems–and the first thing I saw was some oil splattering on the bubble above me. Then there was a terrific noise and a rod let go; it came right out the side of the crankcase, and that was it; we were going down.

Right about then there was this opening, and I just flared the helicopter and we went down into it and landed. A second either way and it wouldn't have worked. It was just there. I had to wait until next morning, though, before anyone came and found me.

The next one I had was at night again, but this time there was a fixed-wing following me. We'd moved a crew and we were going back into camp; it was a [Cessna] 185 and he saw me go down, so they knew where I was. I had a passenger with me and a drill compressor slung on the hook underneath when the engine started running rough. It got rougher and rougher and then it just went brrrmmmhh–that was it. But this time I was over muskeg. I punched off the compressor and landed without bending anything. The engineer came out, put new mags on and we flew her out.

The next incident, unfortunately for Bruce, was more serious, and it occurred only a few days later:

I'd moved a crew of Indians–line cutters–and had lunch with them. After lunch the foreman and I got into the machine to go back to camp. We used to run through the old preamble with those Hillers. Start the engine and then let it run for a few minutes to warm everything up. We were in an old burn on top of a knob. They'd just cut out a little landing for me; they were going to clear out a bigger area later.

So I got ready to take off, opened the throttle up to rpm and lifted off. There were dead trees, about 50 or 60 feet [15-18 m] tall all around, and I'd just got over them when the engine quit, just like that. Down we went into the trees–there was wood flying all over the place. Without power, I lost tail-rotor control and the machine turned sideways to the slope. We hit the ground so hard that the legs on the skids were snapped right off and we tipped on our side and caught fire.

Up to then it hadn't been too bad. Neither of us was hurt, but the fellow with me was above me now. There were flames shooting up behind us pretty high, and he got scared. He sure messed up my face getting out of there; his old feet started to flail. Anyways, we got out all right, and I put the fire out with the extinguisher.

I should have let it burn. We had a hell of a time getting it out of there. We took it out to the river, put it on a barge and it went up to Norman Wells. Then they found they couldn't get it into a DC-6. So it went back on the barge and all the way down to Hay River to be trucked down to Vancouver. They never got it home until wintertime. Heck, I should've let it burn.

To a pilot, accidents were a source of constant concern. Even though he might be blameless, the company's insurance premiums would rise. The Department of Transport, normally the overseer of flight safety in the bush, in reality played little part in the enforcement of regulations. It was the insurance companies that kept watch. In the eyes of the actuaries, the pilot could never win. If he had a number of accidents, he became a high risk. If he had none, the argument was that all helicopter pilots had accidents; he was due for one and was a high risk!

On the whole, life for helicopter crews in the bush was a mixture of much discomfort and occasional satisfaction; of considerable boredom punctuated by flurries of excitement. The long spells of isolation and in some cases deprivation were usually followed by parties which, in their eyes, became memorable. Ian Duncan describes the celebrations at the end of one season:

We all ended up in Aklavik. Dayton Reid and his pilot Snuffy Foster, Bud Tillotson and myself—the two crews had both landed there at the same time; we were both ready to ferry out at the end of the season. So you have to have a party. We went down to the liquor store and got all the booze we could and had a horrendous flipping party, just marvellous. I can remember going bblllmmmmmmbb in front of the old hotel. Must've been something I ate.

Anyway, we all went to this North Star hotel. It was a tiny little place, but they had a partition you could fold aside to make one room if you wanted to have a dance. There was one on that night, run by the Eskimo girls. So of course we all had to go to the dance and we were somewhat into our cups when we arrived. There was a young Mountie standing at the door, being very officious. We were dancing around and I paused when I got near this fellow–I was feeling very happy, fatuously happy, I suppose–and I said, "Look, Constable," I said, "if there's going to be any shooting, let's have it outside–outside the building." He wasn't amused. In fact, he was incensed, and I moved on smartly.

I had seen Bud dancing with a little Eskimo girl and he was having a great time. I saw him pass by and he said something to the Mountie, too. Next time I looked round, Bud was gone. The girl he had been dancing with was standing alone. I went up to her. "Where's my friend?" I asked.

When no suitable clearing was available for a landing, helicopters were occasionally refuelled from a boat—in this case a B.C. Forest Service boat.

BOB TAYLOR

She said, "The policeman just took him to jail there. I seen him put him in the car and took him away there and put him in jail." "Well, I'm going to get him out," I told her. "You much better not," she replied. "They put you in jail there too."

I had just enough sense left to realize she was right. But the next morning Snuffy Foster went down to bail Bud out. The magistrate was the CO of the Navy Communications Centre at Aklavik. Snuffy got nowhere with him. "Look buddy," he said, "there are two Eskimo boys involved in this too. They've been charged and you don't get any different treatment than they do." So Snuffy came back to tell us the bad news and we all went down to court, which was the church. We all sat in the back pew, and there's the constable sitting there and the magistrate.

The two Eskimos were tried first. They both pleaded guilty. They were fined 10 dollars, and four dollars court costs. The magistrate asked them if they could pay. They both asked for a couple of days, and the magistrate agreed.

Then came Bud's turn. Bud had a hearing problem. When he didn't hear what was said, and he was a bit rattled, he used to say "Ehhh?" in a loud voice. And sure enough, when he gets on the stand and the judge asks, "Do you plead guilty or not guilty?" Bud says, "Ehhh?" and we started to break up in the back pew. "Order in court!" He asks him again and Bud hears him this time and pleads guilty.

The magistrate says, "Ten dollars and four dollars costs. Do you have that, Mr. Tillotson?"

Bud takes out his wallet and gazes into it with a look of dismay. You don't carry much cash in the bush, and he'd spent all his on booze the night before. He looked so funny, gazing sadly into his empty wallet. This time we really broke up; we were just about falling out of the pew, and I think the magistrate was having a little trouble keeping his face straight.

Anyway, in the end we managed to come up with the 14 dollars between us and they let Bud go.

Asked what Bud had said to the Mountie to get himself arrested, Ian chuckled. "He just asked him if could have the next dance, and this little turkey took umbrage and ran him in for drunk and disorderly. Hell, we were all drunk and disorderly. Who wouldn't be after a long season in the bush?"

The celebrations were uncomplicated and the humour unsophisticated. The incidents remembered usually depended on the personalities involved. In this case, the victim, Bud Tillotson, was such an amiable and unaggressive person that it made people who knew him burst out laughing to hear that he had been arrested for disorderly conduct. For many years Bud ran the mountain training course for Okanagan Helicopters from Penticton. He is always spoken of with respect and affection.

Another pilot spoken of fondly is Fred Eilertson. Wherever he happened to be, flying in the bush or attending to business in the city, Fred was always dressed in a tweed jacket and a floppy tweed hat. Not surprisingly, he became known as Tweedy. So firmly did this nickname become attached to him that some people have trouble remembering his actual name, but they never have trouble remembering the man.

Tweedy had a slight hesitation in his speech and this, combined with his unconventional bush clothes, led many an unwary bush worker to think he was a little slow-witted.

"Bud takes out his wallet and gazes into it with a look of dismay. You don't carry much cash in the bush, and he'd spent all his on booze the night before. He looked so funny, gazing sadly into his empty wallet. This time we really broke up; we were just about falling out of the pew, and I think the magistrate was having a little trouble keeping his face straight."

IAN DUNCAN

Tweedy could handle this sort of thing. Given an aggressive party chief who would jump into the helicopter and order the pilot to take him somewhere, Tweedy would look around at the instruments and switches vaguely, then open the door, lean out and say to the engineer in a loud voice, "H-H-How do you start this thing?"

Ian Duncan recalls an incident early in their careers, when he and Tweedy went to Laidlaw to move a crew into the Reco Copper Mine. They had to move nine men into the mine at the 6,300-foot (1 920-m) level, in one of the early Bell 47-D1s. Tweedy was taking them in one at a time, and after a while Ian noticed that one individual kept going to the end of the line. It was obvious he was nervous and he didn't want to fly in the helicopter. So when his time came and he had to climb into the passenger seat, Ian opened the door on Tweedy's side and advised him that he had a very nervous passenger.

"Thanks for telling me. I appreciate it."

When Tweedy returned 20 minutes later, Ian asked, "How did it go?" "Well, p-p-pretty interesting," he replied. Apparently the passenger had begun by jamming himself into the seat, his feet pressed hard against the stubs into which the rudder pedals were inserted when dual controls were needed for instruction.

"If you don't take your f-f-feet off those I can't steer and we'll crash," Tweedy advised him. The passenger moved his feet and after a few minutes began to relax a little and study the instrument panel. He asked about one instrument and Tweedy told him it was the altimeter. He asked about another and Tweedy explained that it was the tachometer. Finally, the passenger's eye fell on the fuel gauge. The fuel gauges in the early models were notoriously unreliable: the needle invariably hovered around the empty mark, and pilots had long since taken to using a dip stick to measure the fuel in the tank. However, when Tweedy told him what the gauge was for, his passenger's eyes widened. "But it's on the E," he protested. "Don't that mean empty?"

"Yeah," Tweedy agreed, "but with a b-b-bit of luck, I think we'll make it."

When Tweedy landed up on the mine site and his passenger was getting out, he said to him, "I'll be back in a couple of weeks to p-p-pick you up."

"No you won't," replied the passenger. "I'm going to walk down!"

CHAPTER EIGHT

Helicopters in Forestry

*Sometimes a pilot would spot a
chokerman's lunch sitting on
a stump and would very precisely
drop the 60-pound [30-kg] hook
on it with inevitable results.*

WALTER PALUBISKI

Possibly the most eloquent demonstration of the helicopter's versatility is in forestry, where tasks include basic transportation, pest control, logging and fire suppression.

One of the earliest contracts awarded to the newly organized Okanagan Air Services in July 1948 was to spray forests in the Windermere Valley in the Kootenays to counter an infestation of the hemlock looper. While the helicopter had proven less than successful for spraying small orchards in the Okanagan, it proved ideal in this instance. The downwash from the rotor blades spread the insecticide over large stands of trees, both rapidly and efficiently.

Other innovations came quickly. In November 1951, the Forestry Division of MacMillan Bloedel undertook the first aerial re-seeding of logged-off areas in British Columbia. Two sites were chosen for the experiment: Alberni Pacific Camp One and the Chemainus Division Copper Canyon logging operations. The work began using a Hiller 360 owned and flown by Dean Johnson of McMinnville, Oregon. Initially Johnson laid rodent bait on 1,760 acres (712 ha) of logged-off land at Camp One. If the poisoned bait had not been laid, forest mice might have quickly disposed of tree seeds (evidently there was little concern for biodiversity at the time). The helicopter, flying at 60 mph (95 km/h) could cover 24 acres (10 ha) a minute laying bait in 200-foot-wide (60-m) swathes. A week after dropping the bait, the helicopter repeated the process over the same territory, this time sowing Douglas-fir and hemlock seeds. The process of laying bait was subsequently repeated over 2,500 acres (1 000 ha) in the Copper Canyon area. The helicopter laid the bait and seed from two side-mounted hoppers, the devices being set to spread 25,000 seeds per acre. The helicopter allowed reforestation to be carried out more quickly than was otherwise possible. Easily accessible timber resources could be renewed.

Helicopters were also considered for actual logging operations. A considerable proportion of British Columbia's high-value first-growth timber resources–most estimates are in the vicinity of 15 per cent of the total–have until recently been inaccessible to loggers because of rough terrain and constant, steep sidehills. Conventional methods are inadequate in such circumstances, being uneconomical and often physically impossible. One proposed solution to the problem was to use captive balloons to bring logs out–the ultimate high-lead yarding. A number of experiments were carried out by the Skegs Forsknings Institutein in Sweden in 1956-57 and in British Columbia in 1963, 1968 and 1971 at Vancouver, Sproat Lake and Hope respectively. While the system worked to a degree, a major disadvantage with balloons, and one that virtually negates their feasibility in many areas of the province, became apparent: they could not be used when winds climbed to 25 mph (40 km/h) or more. The helicopter, which is not as subject to winds, appeared to offer much better potential.

By the late 1950s, the size and payload of helicopters were increasing and they were establishing themselves in the "skyhook" role. Indications were that they could be the means of harvesting inaccessible stands of timber. They could be safer in the woods during fire season because the chokers on the logs would not be dragged along the ground, sending sparks into the dry underbrush as they hit rocks. In addition, there would be less environmental impact because there would be no need to construct logging roads or rail lines. This feature was to assume greater importance from the mid-1990s when logging, particularly in environmentally sensitive areas, was subject to the Forest Practices Code, which imposed far more stringent (and expensive) regulations for the construction of logging roads to minimize slides and soil and stream degradation. Theoretically, the advantages and capabilities for heli-logging were there, but it would require considerable experimentation with aircraft and equipment before operations could be undertaken economically and successfully.

The first significant experiment with heli-logging in British Columbia was carried out in 1971. OK Lifts Limited, a subsidiary of Okanagan Helicopters (now, in 1998, following the absorption of Okanagan into Canadian Helicopters, Canadian Heli-logging), logged experimentally on the Richmond Plywood quota of timber on Redonda Island, 27 miles (45 km) east of Campbell River. Between June 3 and June 24, 1971, Grant Soutar of Okanagan flew an S-58T, often carrying up to three logs, or approximately 750 board feet, at a time. This load used the helicopter's 5,000-pound (2 200-kg) payload to its maximum. Logs were hauled two miles (3 km) from the side-hill on East Redonda to the drop zone in Pendrell Sound. There were three objectives in this experiment: to test the aircraft as a logging vehicle; to develop and try methods; and to see if the combination was economical. With an average of 5½ flying hours a day, 1,400 logs were hauled out during the three-week experiment. The only major problem was with the hook to which the cable used to lift the logs was attached. For both safety and speed, a quick-release mechanism was used. This had considerable spring-back tension and it was found that after the load was released, bolts in the mechanism were often sheared off and sometimes the hook itself was broken. This problem was solved by Okanagan, and another hurdle was overcome in making heli-logging feasible.

In March 1974, Okanagan was once again involved in heli-logging on Vancouver Island, this time in the Port Alberni region. Along with MacMillan Bloedel and the Tahsis Company, Okanagan was hoping to determine the economics of heli-logging by carrying out tests over a period of three to five weeks. According to Dave Turner, MacMillan Bloedel vice-president in charge of logging, there were two main goals for the tests. The first was to compare the merits of hauling logs from the logging site to water dumps versus hauling to dry sort areas. Environmentalists and fisheries biologists were becoming increasingly concerned about saltwater dumping since a large amount of debris inevitably remained in the water. The second was to try harvesting previously fallen logs from areas where second growth had taken over. The feasibility seemed to depend on the height of the second-growth trees, because ground crews could be obscured. When this was tried again some years later in the Prince Rupert region, it once again proved difficult for the helicopter crew to spot the chokerman below the canopy of second-growth trees, so various methods of locating the man on the ground were considered, such as using a powerful strobe light hand-held by the chokerman, using a balloon which would ascend above the canopy and serve as a marker, or simply having the chokerman direct the helicopter by radio. The last proved to be the only method that worked, according to Okanagan heli-logging manager Walter Palubiski.

In sharp contrast to the excellent relations today, difficulties with labour complicated the experiment. Ken Blackwood, who oversaw the operation for Okanagan, recalled:

The union more or less sabotaged the experiments – apparently didn't want to see the new technology come in. Initially everyone was enthusiastic since they were all eager to get their first helicopter ride but they still demanded three hours travel time; then the fallers apparently felt that they could help out the "troops" by not allowing us to haul according to plan. The scale cuts for bucking they cut were too light and too short or too long. Instead of falling timber in a parallel fashion the way they were requested, they started building big jackpots [piles], so it affected our production in such a way that it was not economical. The union failed to recognize that heli-logging was complementary to conventional methods, not in competition with them. No union jobs would be affected for different timber stands were involved. Moreover, the expense of heli-logging precluded its use where conventional methods worked.

The experiments were successful from Okanagan's standpoint because they proved that heli-logging was technically practical, but the logging companies were still not entirely convinced. They thought, as had nearly all customers when using helicopters for the first time, that the costs were too high to be acceptable. Experiments were again undertaken, this time on Cortes Island in the summer of 1977 with an Okanagan Bell 214. Although the 214 was too small to be economical in logging service and the job was very hard on the aircraft, this experiment was successful. Three companies, T. M. Thomson Associates, Trace-Mahood and Okanagan, had formed Heli Aero Logging Limited for this operation and by its end had logged 4,500 cunits.

Okanagan's Heavy Lift Division, despite the fact Okanagan was an aviation, not a logging company, decided that the best means of harvesting otherwise inaccessible timber would be to have their own ground crews. Walter Palubiski recalls that workers came from a somewhat surprising source:

Initially a high percentage of our ground crew came from Victoria. I guess word spread quickly among university students that we were looking for help. Later, people also came from communities near our operations such as Campbell River. Few, if any, of the university applicants had had any logging experience and so we had to train them ourselves. Despite their inexperience they proved to be very willing, hard workers who were enthusiastic about working with helicopters–there was a form of romanticism attached to it. It wasn't unusual for these people to come in at the end of a shift and enquire about the day's quota. Relations between ground and air crews were extremely good, a necessity in heli-logging.

As in any situation where morale is very high, there were practical jokes. It was necessary for a man on the ground to take out rain gear and food since he was going to be out for up to twelve hours at a stretch. Sometimes a pilot would spot a chokerman's lunch sitting on a stump and would very precisely drop the 60-pound (27-kg) hook on it with inevitable results. The air waves would usually be filled with comments that didn't bear repeating. We had to put a stop to that.

The heavy-lift helicopters available in the late 1970s, the S-61L, the S-64 "Skycrane" and Boeing Vertol 107, proved to be the most suitable helicopters for logging. The machines used by Okanagan, all of which were S-61Ls, came from two sources: on lease and then purchase from Boise-Cascade, and by purchase from New York Airways. The former were already configured as logging helicopters when acquired; the others were converted from passenger service. The ex-New York Airways aircraft had their interiors stripped down to the exposed airframe to reduce weight. Pressed into service on arrival in B.C., vestiges of their former liveries in some cases persisted into 1981 before being repainted in Okanagan colours. Those S-61s used exclusively in logging were not equipped for instrument flying, as were others used by Okanagan for resupplying drill rigs and other transportation duties. Moreover, a logging S-61 on the job carries only one hour's fuel, 150 gallons (680 *l*), because weight is a critical factor. The more the aircraft weighs, the less load it can sling.

Dean Johnson of Portland, Oregon, used this early Hiller, a model 360, in British Columbia's first attempt at aerial tree reseeding.

The Sikorsky S-58T, the turbine version of the S-58, was used in some of the earlier experiments in heli-logging in the 1970s and continues to be used in small numbers in the 1990s. This Okanagan S-58T is shown in the Fraser River Canyon.

Forests can be devastated by insects. In June 1962, this helicopter was pressed into service spraying pesticides, in this case phytoactin, to combat an outbreak of white pine blister rust.

This S-61L is shown before being repainted in Okanagan livery. It previously worked as a passenger aircraft for New York Airways, and on arrival at Vancouver, had had its "airliner" interior stripped out to reduce weight. The S-61 in various forms has been the workhorse of heli-logging in this province. In the late 1990s, a shortened version, termed the "Shortsky," was introduced.

D. N. PARKER

Many logging companies have their own helicopters. Williams Logging of Spuzzum in the Fraser Canyon used this Bell 47-J2 in the 1970s.

R. D. TURNER

Heli-logging operations are reasonably self-contained. This S-61 of Vancouver Island Heli-Logging has fuel and crew and basic maintenance facilities on site near Shawnigan Lake on Vancouver Island. A Bell 206 is used to carry crews and chokers.

D. N. PARKER

The Sikorsky S-64 was designed specifically as a flying crane for the US Army. A modification of an earlier piston-engined helicopter, the S-64 is powered by two turbines which, improved in the 1990s, have given it enough power to lift 28,000 pounds (12 700 kg) under ideal conditions. In the late 1990s, with the addition of a large detachable tank, a number of S-64s have been used in fighting forest fires.

BC MINISTRY OF FORESTS

Helicopters like this Bell 206, shown at Mica Creek, are used to drop water on fires–generally 'hot spots' as opposed to larger blazes. Various types and sizes of buckets are available and the amount of water to be dropped can be regulated easily, in some cases by removing or retaining plugs in the sides of the bucket.

BC MINISTRY OF FORESTS PHOTOS

Helicopters used for rapattack–not all are capable or certified–are equipped with connecting points for the lines, and they carry a crew member as a spotter. The bag situated above the firefighter contains necessary fire suppression equipment and supplies.

It normally takes two years in heli-logging for an S-61 captain to become thoroughly proficient at placing a hook quickly and precisely over the chokerman, who has attached a 26-foot (8-m) choker cable to the log, and to hoist the log out efficiently. The S-61 carries a two-man crew, both of whom are qualified to take command. The pilot, while at the controls, concerns himself exclusively with flying the aircraft and with the load. The other pilot monitors the instruments and records the weight of the load from a digital readout situated on the right-hand side of the instrument panel. This enables the crew to ensure that the load is within acceptable limits, and to keep track of the amount being hauled.

A fairly standard practice is for the pilots to fly for approximately an hour, then change places. Weather permitting, they aim to fly ten hours a day: five in the morning, with a break for lunch and maintenance, and five after the break. The load itself is attached to the helicopter by means of three hooks: one on the belly of the machine, a second attached to a shock absorber, and a third at the bottom end of a 250-foot (76-m) line. The choker or chokers, depending on the load, are attached to the third hook. If the load is too heavy, or if it is caught in the ground cover, it is possible to punch it off at any of the three connecting points. The pilot can do this simply by pressing a button on the cyclic control column. A more recent innovation is a double hook. In the case of the recently introduced Kamov KA-32, with a standard payload of 11,000 pounds (5 000 kg), the primary one is hooked onto a fairly heavy load, an estimated 9,000 pounds (4 010 kg). The secondary hook is loaded with about 2,000 pounds (910 kg). Thus, if the primary load is heavier than estimated, the secondary one can be punched off. The whole operation of picking up a load is controlled by the loadmaster who is in communication with the pilot by radio.

Up to two months before the heli-loggers move into an area, a crew of fallers go out to cut trees, falling them as much as possible in parallel to permit more efficient hoisting by the helicopters. The logs can be repositioned by the helicopters, but if this is necessary, time may be lost. Limbs are removed from trees at this time as well, except for those situated on the inaccessible side of the log. Loadmasters are trained to estimate weights of logs. A formula that has proven to be very accurate was worked out by Okanagan in 1978. This still requires a loadmaster to be proficient, since log weights can vary according to location, and the amount of moisture absorbed by the log can throw off the formula.

Meanwhile, other companies moved into the province, some initially inexperienced in heli-logging like Okanagan. Bow Helicopters of Calgary were among the earliest

A Columbia "107" photographed in Vancouver in 1981.

operators to experiment with logging when they moved into the Pitt Lake region in June 1972, working under contract to Higher Profit Research and Development of Vancouver. Experiments apparently proved successful since the latter company was soon talking about using S-61s in the Jervis Inlet area. This scheme did go ahead, but with another company.

Five years after the Pitt Lake experiment, an experienced American operator began working in British Columbia, initially employing few Canadians but increasing the numbers as work progressed. This firm, Columbia Helicopters Limited of Portland, Oregon, used the Kawasaki KV-107, a Japanese-built version of the Boeing Vertol 107. This was a medium-lift type very much like the CH-113A helicopters used by the Canadian Forces. Columbia worked both Drury and Seymour Inlets, the former on the quota of a wholly-owned subsidiary, Jewell Timber, and the latter under contract to MacDonald Cedar Products Limited, a firm that had earlier supported the idea of helicopter logging. The operation was successful, profits varying with the "show" and location. The MacDonald Cedar Products operation in 1978 involved an area of 150 acres (60 ha) from which it was hoped that close to 5.5 million board feet could be removed.

Whonnock Industries, as MacDonald Cedar Products became, formed INTERFOR (International Forest Products of Vancouver) and HELIFOR, the wholly-owned helicopter subsidiary. The single 107 was joined by a second aircraft of the type, also on lease. The following year saw the addition of a third 107, and, in 1994, a Boeing 234 Chinook, also from Columbia, was introduced on a trial basis. The latter has a lifting capacity of 28,000 pounds (12 700 kg) under ideal conditions.

Another American firm that has operated in British Columbia is Erickson Air-Cranes, which works the Silver Grizzly timber quota in the Prince Rupert region. This operation differs little from others except for the logging aircraft–a very large Sikorsky S-64 Skycrane, a heavy-lift machine carrying loads of up to 20,000 pounds (9 000 kg), twice that carried by the S-61 or KV-107. Two of these machines have been used by Silver Grizzly since 1977, but one crashed in 1981.

While the Okanagan, Columbia and Silver Grizzly operations are spectacular, they have not been the only helicopter logging companies in British Columbia. Skyhook of Courtenay logged on Vancouver Island using a Hiller 12E, and Transwest Helicopters of Pitt Meadows worked in the Pitt Lake area for several years using a Bell 204 and later a 214, which subsequently crashed at Bella Coola while fighting a forest fire. The 12E and 204 are classed as utility helicopters and are typical of others used in various aspects of logging such as general transportation and, in heli-logging, moving the ground crews and retrieving the chokers.

By the mid-1990s, steps were being taken to extend the use of older helicopters. Heavy lifting inevitably calls for ruggedly constructed machines and one problem experienced with both the S-58T and the S-61 was a structural one: the heavy twisting effect of the anti-torque tail rotors, combined with rear-end vibration, was causing skin damage to the tail end of the fuselage–damage that made for costly maintenance. In the case of the S-61s, Helipro International of Bellingham, Washington, which had started out in Langley, B.C., developed a partial solution to this problem. A 50-inch (130-cm) fuselage plug is removed from behind the cabin. When control cables, fluid tubing and wiring are shortened and connected again, a reduction in weight, and increase in payload, of 450 pounds (205 kg) is realized. Vancouver Island Heli-logging took delivery of the first conversion, nicknamed the "Shortsky," and it has proved to be reasonably successful.

Other companies have also operated the S-61. Hayes Heli-log had a "Shortsky" in service in the Franklin River area on Vancouver Island in 1996, and were unique in British Columbia because their pilots were trained on an S-61 flight simulator in Scotland. In 1995, Hayes had leased an S-64 but found that with parts coming from a single source in the U.S. it was difficult to operate the type efficiently. Coulson Aircrane, of Port Alberni, had been in heli-logging since 1987 and was, by 1996, operating a fleet of four S-61s. An interesting aspect of the Coulson operation is its use of a 300-foot (90-m) long vessel as a floating log sort which affords great flexibility in their operations. As well, to become as independent as possible, Coulson has undertaken overhaul of the CT85 engines "in house" and has carried out 9,000-hour major inspections on the S-61s.

By the mid-1990s, it was apparent that helicopters then employed in logging, with the exception of the much newer Boeing 234 and Eurocopter Super Puma, were in need of replacement. New aircraft were entering the field, such as the K-Max "Flying Truck" from Kaman, with that builder's characteristic two masts with intermeshing contra-rotating rotors. This configuration, designed to counter torque, did away with the necessity of a tail rotor and placed the main rotors over the centre of gravity, directing all power to lift. Midwest Helicopters of Winnipeg experimented with a single K-Max in heli-logging service in B.C., and the success of that operation led to plans to introduce a second.

When Vancouver Island Helicopters became interested in heli-logging and formed Vancouver Heli-logging in 1989, they investigated the Super Puma. They were proposing an arrangement with a company operating one in the Campbell River area; an arrangement whereby they could share the aircraft that wasn't being fully utilized.

The simple instrument pedestal of a Bell 47 D-1.

R. D. TURNER

The instrument panel of the Kamov was somewhat more complex.

When we first started flying it [the Kamov], all the other operators thought it was a joke that would be here for a little while then leave, but after the first couple of weeks, rumours started getting out from people in the logging industry about what it was actually doing, how much wood it was moving, and how it never broke down . . . and questions started to be asked as to why it had ever been allowed to come here in the first place.

KEN NORIE, PRESIDENT, VIH LOGGING

Unfortunately, the Super Puma crashed, evidently because of a structural failure. As a consequence, VIH abandoned the idea of using this type but were still faced with the problem of finding another heavy-lift machine to complete an existing contract. They were able to lease an S-61N from Chum Carley of Victoria. Though they subsequently purchased it, they had to dispose of it in 1991 because business was slow and it proved too difficult to integrate the S-61N into the VIH fleet for other than logging use.

Ken Norie and his father, Frank (who had long experience running his own logging company before his involvement with VIH), felt, along with Barry Hewko, then general manager, that it would be possible to make a go of the heli-logging if they harvested less accessible timber off their own stands. Having heard of the success of the Russian Kamov KA-32 helicopters in mining and exploration operations in New Guinea, Ken Norie and operations manager Bill Ross travelled to the South Pacific to have a look for themselves. They were impressed with the performance of the Kamovs, which featured a twin, co-axial rotor configuration, giving the same advantages as the much smaller K-Max, but with a payload of up to 11,000 pounds (5 000 kg). A further advantage of both types lay in the direction of the wind. With the more conventional tail rotor, it is difficult to hover accurately if the helicopter is not facing into wind (in a cross wind, considerably more power goes to the tail rotor to keep straight, and a down wind causes the machine to vacillate). Both the K-Max and the KA-32 are impervious to wind direction, which provides substantial operational benefits when working on a steep side-hill. VIH decided to try to acquire a Kamov.

After some negotiation, the Russians agreed to send a KA-32 over to the Abbotsford Air Show of 1991 in an Ilyushin transport plane. Vancouver Island Heli-logging obtained a permit to conduct logging tests with it, but these had to be done under Russian air regulations and under Russian supervision.

The tests were very successful, accomplishing up to 200 hours a month with very little maintenance. Moreover, the pilots were delighted with the Kamov. Jim Stone made this comparison: "We aimed for two shifts of five hours a day, with a break for lunch and maintenance. With other machines, you'd be just about beat at the end of the day; with the Kamov, it was no problem."

After long and often frustrating negotiations with two bureaucracies, VIH finally managed to purchase two of the Russian machines, suitably modified to meet Canadian air regulations. They were flown directly to Victoria in two trips by an Ilyushin transport in March 1997. However, they still did not have Canadian certification; they were under Russian air regulations, which meant that a Russian pilot had to be on site at all operations,

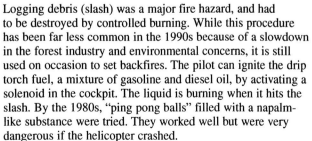

Logging debris (slash) was a major fire hazard, and had to be destroyed by controlled burning. While this procedure has been far less common in the 1990s because of a slowdown in the forest industry and environmental concerns, it is still used on occasion to set backfires. The pilot can ignite the drip torch fuel, a mixture of gasoline and diesel oil, by activating a solenoid in the cockpit. The liquid is burning when it hits the slash. By the 1980s, "ping pong balls" filled with a napalm-like substance were tried. They worked well but were very dangerous if the helicopter crashed.

BC MINISTRY OF FORESTS PHOTOS

Helicopters have been used to collect cuttings (or scions) for breeding. Shears, operating off the helicopter's hydraulic system, are used to remove the cuttings. Before this method came into use, foresters would shoot scions down, often using considerable amounts of ammunition and time in the process.

BC MINISTRY OF FORESTS PHOTOS

An important use of helicopters in the forest is aerial fertilization. This Bell 205 is having the bin of its dusting apparatus refilled. Time is an important consideration, so the helicopter simply hovers while the bin is filled.

B.C. Forest Service crews at work. In the top photos, a crew uses chain and compass to locate the sample plot, measures the heights of trees and logs the species; as well, the ages of the trees in the sample perimeter are determined with an increment borer (a device that removes a small core containing the annual growth rings without damaging the tree).

Bottom photo: The camp has always been an integral part of life in the bush. No matter how rudimentary, it still looks good at the end of the day.

BC MINISTRY OF FORESTS

The cameras in the boom are controlled from the cockpit with the switch box being held by Hugh Lyons, in the lower left-hand photo.

A number of attempts were made to determine the best method of mounting the camera boom. This Bell 47-G3B-2 is shown lifting off with one version that was suspended from the airframe in an effort to reduce vibration. Ultimately, rigid mounting of the boom to the helicopter proved most effective. The type of boom shown was designed specifically for use with the Bell 206 Jet Ranger, in this case a Vancouver Island Helicopters machine. By the late 1990s, camera booms were being used comparatively rarely because of budget constraints.

BC MINISTRY OF FORESTS PHOTOS

and maintenance followed a less than ideal schedule for heli-logging. Finally, in May 1998, Canadian certification was granted and by the end of the year the burden of two operational systems will be set aside.

However, not all logging has been carried out using heavy-lift helicopters. Smaller logs can be moved quite effectively using lighter utility machines. Skyhook of Courtenay logged on Vancouver Island using a Hiller 12E, and Transwest Helicopters of Pitt Meadows worked in the Pitt Lake area for several years using a Bell 204 and later a larger and more powerful 214, which crashed at Bella Coola while fighting a forest fire. The 12E and 204, like the Bell 206, Hughes 500 and Eurocopter Astars and Twin Stars, are classed as general purpose helicopters and are used for a wide variety of duties such as general transportation and, in heli-logging, moving the ground crews and retrieving the chokers.

In the end, though, if heli-logging is to continue, there must be trees to harvest, and here too helicopters have excelled by proving themselves extremely valuable in forest fire suppression: setting out lookout towers, transporting firefighters and their equipment, and water bombing. From its earliest use in forestry, the helicopter has carried fire-fighters directly to a blaze. Covering the same ground on foot is time-consuming and difficult when speed is so vital. The sooner a fire is caught the better.

While basic transportation is vital in fire suppression, and was initially the most important task for helicopters, it was not long before they were also used for observation. Fire bosses (those in charge of fighting the fire) used them to watch progress of the fire and plan strategy accordingly. They could decide in advance where to place crews and equipment and where to create fire breaks. If necessary, the helicopter could be used to quickly remove a threatened crew from the path of a fire that had changed direction. As well, prompt medical evacuation was now possible in the event of an accident, something that boosted crew morale.

The first use of a water-tanker helicopter in British Columbia was in 1958 when Okanagan converted an S-58. The cabin was fitted with a 225-gallon (1 000-*l*) tank and appropriate plumbing, and discharge "gates" were cut in the belly of the aircraft. The S-58 was used to extinguish a fire near the headwaters of the Ashlu and Squamish Rivers. Alf Stringer, when asked about the conversion, commented that it created a significant problem. With it, the S-58 ceased to be a general purpose machine and became exclusively a tanker. This was impractical and other solutions had to be found.

Jim Grady, Nelson base manager for Okanagan Helicopters, and Henry Stevenson, who ran his own machine shop, are generally credited, in British Columbia at least, with

A Soloy conversion on a Bell 47. Replacing the piston engine with a turbine dramatically increased the power available and the smoothness of operation.

D. N. PARKER

Jim Grady, shown at the time of the "Monzoon" experiments.

the invention in the early 1960s of the "Monzoon bucket." In its earliest form, it was simple: a 45-gallon (205-*l*) drum filled with water, with a basketball plugging a hole in the bottom. Hovering over a fire with the bucket suspended from the cargo hook, Grady would pull on a line attached to the ball to release the water–he must have had a strong right arm–but he soon complained that having to lean out of the helicopter while hauling on the sash cord almost caused him to fall out of the helicopter.

Clearly this was impractical for long days of water bombing, so they went back to the drawing board. Over the next year, they built and experimented with several other designs. Henry takes up the story:

Our next idea was what Jim described as "an upside-down toilet lid." We cast a circular aluminum plate with a hole in the centre (corresponding to the hole in the bottom of the drum) onto which we attached a lid that was hinged. The concept was reasonable, but we had problems because the seal was allowing the water to leak away too quickly. After experimenting with several seals, we found that machining a 45-degree angle groove in the plate with a neoprene ring inserted in the groove, the weight of the water on the angled ring would seal it perfectly.

Next came the mechanism to release the lid. They fitted a spring latch that could be released by an electric solenoid. This was energized through an electric cable running back up to the aircraft and connected to a button on the control column. They found that, when they tried to fill the bucket, the downwash from the rotor caused the bucket to rotate without tipping. A counterweight had to be attached to one side of the upper rim of the bucket to make it tip, sink and fill. A final necessity was to attach a block of wood to the lower side of the lid to push it up and close it under the sprung latch before the bucket tipped to fill.

A demonstration of their bucket over Kootenay Lake for forestry officials was received enthusiastically. Encouraged, they applied for a patent, which was granted in 1965. A further development was the production of a kit to convert any available empty 45-gallon drum into a Monzoon bucket. This sold well, especially on the west coast, but they also had sales as far away as Australia.

More recent versions bear little resemblance to the original. They are of lightweight plastic that can be rolled up and stored, and have various capacities; in some the capacity can be altered by the removal of plugs in the sides of the bucket.

The Monzoon bucket has several advantages over the early and extensive S-58 conversion. Any general utility helicopter can use one because all that is required is a belly hook and an electrical connection. The bucket can be readily attached or detached. It can be filled simply by hovering over water, or other fire retardant. Not having to land decreases turnaround time between loads. The bucket, when not in use for fire fighting, can be used to transport supplies and equipment without the helicopter's landing. The primary use of a Monzoon bucket is in extinguishing small flareups or "hotspots" after the main fire has been extinguished. They are unsuitable for use on large fires because they have limited impact.

A disadvantage of the Monzoon bucket is that it releases water slowly as compared to fixed-wing tankers like the Canadair CL-215, or Firecat. This increases the time the helicopter must remain over a blaze, which in turn may result in the fire being fanned by downwash and embers blown about to start other fires.

Another way of converting a helicopter into a tanker without compromising its other functions is used by Frontier Helicopters. A detachable belly tank of much greater capacity than the Monzoon buckets is used. This system has the advantage of having bomb-bay doors to regulate the quantity and pattern of the drop. Initially, a major disadvantage was the turnaround time necessary to refill the tank on the ground, but this has changed with the addition of a pump and suction hose that allows the tank to be refilled from the hover.

Among other methods of getting onto a fire quickly is rappelling, a technique used by the Canadian Forces and others to land infantry from a hovering helicopter. This technique has been adopted in forest fire suppression. Rappellers slide down to the ground on ropes, from above tree-top level if necessary. First used operationally in the summer of 1977, "rapattack," as it has been termed in British Columbia, has proven effective in placing crews in to fight fires set by lightning strikes. Frequently there are no suitable landing spots near a fire and rappelling is the only means of getting a crew in to deal with a blaze that can spread with frightening speed. Rapattack headquarters, which coordinates operations over the province, is situated in the Kamloops Forest Region in Salmon Arm, the training base for the program.

Only Frontier and Okanagan were initially approved by Transport Canada for rapattack, and only the Bell 206, 206L-1 and 205A were certified for use. These are equipped with connecting points for rappelling ropes. Their skids are useful for the rappellers as they can climb out onto them before beginning their descent. Three rappellers and a spotter are normally carried. The pilot must be qualified and experienced, particularly in vertical reference work (steady hovering at up to 200 feet [60 m]), a necessity when fire-fighters leave the helicopter.

Another forestry task, setting slash (logging debris) fires by helicopter, was also developed in British Columbia. In 1938 a serious fire broke out on Vancouver Island. The

Henry Stevenson with a replica of the prototype Monzoon bucket "toilet seat."

N. CORLEY-SMITH

outbreak advanced rapidly in accumulated logging debris near Campbell River and it spread out of control over a 20-square-mile (50-km^2) area, threatening Courtenay. Fortunately the town survived, and the danger posed by slash resulted in constructive action. The British Columbia Forest Act had a section added (section 116) to ensure that the forest service could require the destruction of debris, a practice that would help deprive a fire of fuel. Slash burning was normally carried out with hand-held Panoguns, devices similar to flame throwers, which were fuelled with diesel oil. This was a time-consuming process and often required large crews.

In 1973, John Muraro of the Canadian Forest Service at Prince George developed what has been termed a drip torch: a 45-gallon oil drum bolted to a metal frame and connected to a long spout which dispenses a 60/40 mixture of diesel oil and gasoline. This apparatus is suspended below a helicopter and the fuel is ignited electrically by means of a solenoid activated by the pilot. The flaming liquid then drops to the ground, setting fire to the slash. Using the drip torch, slash burning can be more selective; it isn't necessary to fire the whole setting as would often be the case with ground-based methods, a process which could result in an uncontrolled fire and even soil damage. With the drip-torch operation, the pilot is directed by radio, sometimes setting a number of fires simultaneously. Using ground methods it would have taken perhaps 10 people to achieve the same result. There was also some element of risk to the ground crew; there is virtually none for the helicopter pilot. However, slash burning has seldom been used in the 1990s because of environmental concerns.

While helicopters have proven so important in the harvesting and protection of British Columbia's timber resources, they have also been vital in a less exciting but equally important operation. Forest inventory, a laborious process to determine the nature and extent of timber resources, has been going on for many years. But the introduction of helicopters in the late 1940s made it possible to cover much larger tracts in the annual five-month inventory period. A helicopter could set out sample crews quickly. Usually, a crew consisted of two students who worked from a fly camp. They would hike from there to selected random samples marked on their aerial photographs. At their destination, they laid out circular plots about 60 feet (18 m) in diameter, marked them off with orange seismic tape, and measured and described all the trees within them: the species, diameters, heights and ages—the latter on the basis of core samples taken with an increment borer. In this instance, the helicopter provided quick and economic transportation into remote and rugged terrain.

The helicopter was also used for forest classification or forest-type description from the air. Before flying an area, a number of representative forest types would be selected from aerial photographs and connected to form a flight plan route. The route would then be followed, using the photographs to navigate from forest stand to forest stand, and the classifier, who was usually a graduate forester, would "call" the plots into a tape recorder, identifying the species and estimating the height, diameter and age of the trees. Classification was carried out just above tree-top level at about 40 mph (64 km/h). Data were checked from time to time by landing and allowing the classifier to compare his most recent "call" with actual measurements. If his estimates from the air were faulty, he could adjust them accordingly. Information from each flight plan would be transferred from tape to classification sheets and correlated with the observed stands on the photographs after the flight. At the end of a season, all the data were brought together to produce forest cover maps.

An advanced approach to forest inventory, the helicopter-mounted camera boom, was in use in British Columbia until the 1990s. Hugh Lyons of the Ministry of Forests Valuation Branch was the first in the province to propose this method. He recalls:

The idea of the camera boom goes back to an article I was reading in Photogrammetric Engineering Magazine by Eugene Avery. He was working in the southern States and had experimented with a hand-held boom with two cameras, and had succeeded in getting measurements by laying out plots on the ground; in other words, using ground control. I talked it over with Bill Hall, the head of Aerial Surveys. So Bill and I figured that if you could get the cameras far enough apart, and knowing that the same distance would always separate centres, we felt that we could dispense with ground control.

We then got hold of a couple of Fairchild F-24 cameras with five-inch [127-mm] film. Bob Taylor and I then put our heads together with Ron Adams who, like Bob, worked for Vancouver Island Helicopters. Ron built the first camera boom to my specifications. We mounted it on the helicopter by clipping it directly to the cross tubes below the cockpit and to the nose and tail by means of straps. This was necessary because there was a long cantilever.

There was an electrical firing mechanism; wires stretched from the cameras on the boom up through the door into the cockpit and a control box. The system worked very well; accuracy was excellent. I was still looking for even better results, however. The cameras weren't fast enough and vibration was a problem.

We then went to Linhof cameras to actually begin operation with the booms. Before this, all our efforts were purely experimental. There were still problems—the cameras wouldn't fire properly. If the rear camera fired too late or too early it would distort the base length. When things did work properly, it was possible to get accurate gross volume estimates of timber by species, and results were comparable with ground sampling methods. We checked this by flying a section with the boom and then checking the same area on the ground. We could get the same results for roughly 56 per cent of the costs experienced using ground methods.

134

A streamlined camera boom was developed specifically for use on the Bell 206 series of helicopters.

The camera boom was progressively improved by the Forest Service. After the initial experiments with a fixed boom, which had resulted in vibration problems, a new approach was tried. A boom was produced that was attached by two lanyards to a longitudinal bar clipped to the cargo hook and suspended beneath the helicopter. This helped resolve the vibration problem, but the boom required a specific airspeed before it would fly without oscillating. Eventually, in 1976, another boom was designed specifically for use on the Bell 206. This system was attached in a matter of minutes, by means of a semi-rigid mount to the helicopter.

By the late 1990s, however, camera booms were hardly being used for forest inventory, except by a number of consultants. When inventory information is needed, a forester, with the appropriate aerial photographs and maps, will carry out a 'fly by' of the stand concerned. The few camera booms that remain have been acquired by forest consultants who now use them sparingly. Satellite photography, which some hoped would prove ideal for this aspect of forestry, has proved to be too expensive and apparently is, at this stage, of less value than standard aerial photography.

For years, the forest service has been seeking what are called "plus trees"–trees that are as close to the ideal as possible–for each of the various species found in this province. By genetic engineering it hopes to produce a "super tree" for each type that can be cloned to produce higher quality timber. This genetic information is acquired from cuttings, or scions, taken from the tallest, straightest, generally closest-to-perfect tree in a stand. Foresters on the ground would search out such trees and, using a rifle, shoot down a cutting. With helicopters, cuttings could be removed directly from tree tops by means of a harnessed crewman hanging out of the cabin. Before long, shears were developed to clip cuttings from trees, and these devices worked off the helicopter's hydraulic system. Also, baskets were developed to harvest cones so that trees no longer had to be climbed by pickers or felled so they could harvest the cones on the ground.

Helicopters have largely overcome many of the forest industry's problems with topography and geography, making possible and practical the harvesting, protection and inventory of near-inaccessible timber, and reducing dramatically the time required for routine forest management.

CHAPTER NINE

Search and Rescue

I do not speak English so good, but I know brave men, any language, any country.

GREEK SEAMAN: SS *Glafkos* Rescue, January 1962

Danger, whether due to rugged topography, darkness, dense forests or changeable and sometimes violent weather conditions, is often characteristic of search and rescue operations in British Columbia. In many cases the capabilities of a helicopter have meant the difference between survival and tragedy.

As early as 1943, the RCAF had attempted to acquire helicopters for rescue work. With the military flying in Canada during World War II, improvements were needed in the Air Force's rescue capability. Accordingly, Air-Vice Marshall E. W. Stedman, Director of Technical Services, requisitioned six Sikorsky XR-6 helicopters. This attempt, however, was thwarted by the federal Treasury Board, which insisted that costs were too high. The Air Force was to wait four years for the arrival of its first helicopters.

A year later, Canada took part in creating an important United Nations agency, the International Civil Aviation Organization (ICAO), when it held its first meetings in Chicago in late 1944. Subsequently, Canada and other nations signed agreements committing themselves to set up standardized search and rescue facilities in areas where they exercised sovereignty. The organization of services in Canada was further refined on January 16, 1946, when the RCAF assumed chairmanship of an interdepartmental search and rescue committee to coordinate the efforts of all government facilities for search and rescue, including the Departments of National Defence, Fisheries, and Transport, and the Royal Canadian Mounted Police.

On April 5, 1947, the RCAF accepted its first Sikorsky H-5 helicopters, costs having been reduced by quantity production for the United States armed forces. The helicopter was to become part of a coordinated "team" of aircraft, ships and ground parties assigned to search and rescue.

When a search was necessary in these early days–a downed aircraft was among the most common incidents–fixed-wing aircraft such as Cansos, Norsemen and Lancasters would fly search patterns to locate the wreck and survivors. Para-rescue teams would then be dropped along with survival supplies, and ground parties, where feasible, would hike in. Survivors would then be prepared for removal to a point from which they could be evacuated. If it was a difficult situation, far removed from other forms of transportation, or one of great urgency, a helicopter would be used.

Ironically, perhaps, the first helicopter rescue in British Columbia did not involve the Air Force. In October 1947, an employee of the Greater Vancouver Water Board shattered his foot while working in the Rodgers Lake area of the North Shore. A North Vancouver doctor hiked up to the accident site. It was an arduous five-hour trek and, on assessing the problem, he recommended immediate evacuation. An attempt at removal using a Tiger Moth of Charter Flight Services failed. The topography immediately surrounding the headwaters of the Capilano River prevented it from landing. Sheer rock cliffs rose to a height of 1,600 feet (490 m) on three sides, and frequent mists reduced visibility at that time of the year.

Jim Sampson of Aero Surveys Ltd., a division of Skyways of Winnipeg, was working in the vicinity. A mercy flight was arranged using his Bell 47-B3. In spite of heavy mist, he was able to fly up the valley and land on a sand bar that had been cleared of debris by Water Board workers. The injured man was loaded into the two-seat helicopter and flown to North Vancouver. With the assistance of police, a city boulevard was turned into a helicopter landing pad, from which an ambulance took the victim to hospital. The 15-minute flight had made unnecessary an agonizing journey and a delay that might have had serious consequences.*

In February 1950, a USAF C-47 search and rescue plane crashed into a western Yukon mountain while looking for a C-54 transport with 44 people on board thought to be down in the area. The C-54 had disappeared while on a flight from Great Falls, Montana, to Fairbanks, Alaska, on January 26. Once the wreck of the C-47 search aircraft had been located, para-rescue teams, including a doctor, were dropped to care for the injured air crew. As soon as feasible, the survivors and rescuers were brought out to civilization by an Air Force helicopter. However, it had not been possible to evacuate them safely directly from the 7,300-foot (2 225-m) crash site, so the entire party made its way on foot to a place where a helicopter could land and load. While under most circumstances the H-5 could use its rescue hoist to evacuate victims, the presence of stretcher cases made this impossible. The H-5 had to make nine trips, but it certainly demonstrated its usefulness. The C-54 transport was never found.

Later that February, a B-36 Strategic Air Command (SAC) heavy bomber experienced problems while flying south along the British Columbia coast from Fairbanks en route to Fort Worth, Texas. Distress messages were received shortly before midnight on

* In Appendix I, we describe an even earlier civilian helicopter search and rescue attempt.

February 13, indicating that severe icing was being encountered at 16,000-17,000 feet (4 800-5 000 m) and that instruments were failing. Two of its six engines then caught fire and a third had to be feathered. The last message received suggested that ditching in Queen Charlotte Sound between the Queen Charlotte Islands and Vancouver Island was likely. Radioing from 90 miles (145 km) southwest of Prince Rupert and over water, the operator made a final plea that searchers watch for flares or wreckage at sea.

Weather in the search area was poor. The ceiling was a mere 500 feet (150 m), and winds up to 52 mph (80 km) were blowing, whipping up rough seas. Fortunately, surface visibility was better at three miles (5 km) in light rain. But life rafts, assuming there had been time to deploy them, and especially life jackets, would be hard to spot even under favourable conditions. They would be mere "pinpricks" on the surface of the sea, obscured by rising and falling swells.

Aircraft from 123 Search and Rescue Flight, RCAF Station Sea Island, near Vancouver, were making their way north as quickly as possible. RCAF search headquarters felt that the most critical search area would be along the last known flight path of the bomber, which led towards Vancouver Island over open water. The crew's chance of survival in the ice-cold water would be slim indeed and so time was vital. Hypothermia, or exposure, was the main worry, and it was possible that survivors in the water might drift apart. "Operation Brix," as the search was called, was to cover 25,000 square miles (64 700 km²).

One aircraft making its way to the search base was the Sikorsky H-5 from Sea Island. Secured to a barge towed behind an RCAF tug, it headed up the Strait of Georgia. Because it was dangerous to fly a helicopter at night without proper instruments and training, this method was used to get as close as possible to the search area by daybreak when it was possible to fly safely. The helicopter lifted off from the barge on the morning of February 14, stopping off en route at the RCAF Station at Comox to have a mechanical problem corrected. It then flew on to Port Hardy, the forward search base.

Older helicopters were not the ideal search aircraft when little was known about the crash location. They lacked the range to cover large areas. Once the wreck or survivors were located, however, helicopters often could be the only means of rescue. They could also assist in directing ground parties or surface vessels to the site.

As it turned out, the pilot of the B-36, after jettisoning his nuclear bomb (which was never recovered), had turned toward land to give the crew a better chance of rescue. Twelve of the 17 crewmen were found on Princess Royal Island. The remaining five were never seen again: they probably came down at sea. Two U.S. helicopters joined the

Survivors from the B-36 crew were taken to the rescue headquarters at Port Hardy shortly after their retrieval from Princess Royal Island. The highest priority when they were debriefed was to attempt to discover the fate of the five crew who were still missing. The five airmen were never found.

VANCOUVER PUBLIC LIBRARY 41228

Ground to air signals to allow crash survivors to communicate with aircraft using materials at hand.

CANADIAN FORCES

search and operated from the Surf Inlet area on the west coast of Princess Royal Island. After survivors had been located by ground rescue parties and some removed to the destroyer HMCS *Cayuga*, the Canadians were told politely but very firmly that it was now an American show. The presence of a nuclear weapon on board the bomber was undoubtedly the reason. When documents relating to the incident were declassified nearly 30 years later, it was learned that a "Broken Arrow," or nuclear accident, situation had been declared. The B-36 wreckage was not found until 1953, three years later, in the mountains south of Smithers, B.C.

In the rescue effort, the helicopters were hampered by winds, poor visibility and darkness. Their small payload and short range had also restricted their value in this situation. Ideal in other circumstances, they were less than effective in this one.

In June 1950, a Rescue Coordination Centre (RCC) was established at the Sea Island Headquarters for No. 12 Group. All calls for assistance would now be passed through this agency, greatly increasing the level of efficiency and decreasing response time.

The H-5 went into a well-earned retirement in British Columbia in the spring of 1955; its replacement, the Vertol H-21A, was introduced in March. The first of these large twin-rotor helicopters had been delivered to the RCAF in September 1954. Subsequently the H-21A was upgraded with gyroscopic stabilization, a feature that greatly reduced pilot fatigue. The H-21A had a medium-lift capability that made it much more useful than the H-5. It could carry greater loads internally and externally and do so over longer distances. These "flying bananas," so called because of their shape, were a great improvement.

H-21A 9613 had only been in service a short time when tragedy struck. On April 21, 1955, while on a routine flight from Vancouver to Cold Lake, in Alberta, it slammed into a mountain peak near Rossland. The pilot's vision had been obscured by blowing snow and fog while flying at low altitude, and he was unaware of the danger in his path. A witness related how the noise of an aircraft, followed by the sound of a crash, filled the cab of his truck. Only two of the five on board survived. The lost machine was replaced by one of six ordered for the Mid-Canada Line. The new helicopter arrived at Sea Island in late December 1955.

On December 9, 1956, a four-engined Trans-Canada Air Lines North Star left Vancouver for Calgary with a crew of three and 59 passengers on board. Cleared to climb to 19,000 feet (5 800 m), it was already two hours late when it left the terminal at six o'clock that evening; weather reports received earlier hadn't been encouraging, indicating turbulence and snow.

At 6:57 p.m., the pilot reported to Vancouver that he had just lost number 2 engine in icing and extreme turbulence. Rather than continuing to Calgary, the pilot decided to return to Vancouver and requested permission to descend to 8000 feet (2 400 m), perhaps hoping to reduce icing at a lower altitude. That was at 7:10. Ten minutes later, when the tower attempted to contact the North Star with landing instructions, there was no response.

There were three emergency airfields in the general vicinity of the plane's last reported position: Abbotsford, Penticton and Kimberley. When the plane was last heard from, it was, the pilot thought, just east of Hope, approximately 90 miles (145 km) from Vancouver on Airway Green, one of the Abbotsford Radio Range airways. The North Star had enough fuel to last until 11:00 p.m. even if the pilot dumped his reserves, something he may have done if anticipating an emergency landing. The estimated time of arrival at Vancouver was 7:40. When this passed and there was no indication that the plane had put down at an emergency field, it was obvious that something was terribly wrong. The Rescue Coordination Centre launched two Lancaster maritime patrol aircraft from Comox, sending them to the airliner's last reported position. They were instructed to watch for distress flares or other signs of the missing aircraft. It was later reported that the plane was not carrying flares or any other emergency equipment beyond extra blankets—those on board would stand little chance of survival in the bad weather that had spread across the southern interior of B.C.

At first light, search aircraft began scouring a path 30-miles (48-km) wide from the vicinity of Hope west to the Gulf of Georgia, a distance of about 100 miles (60 km). The search master, Squadron Leader George Sheehan, gave instructions that mountain peaks were to be checked closely and that aircraft should descend to even lower than 200 feet (60 m) if possible, a dangerous thing to do in this region in these conditions. Visibility was poor and turbulence so severe that many aircrew suffered airsickness.

The search master believed that the pilot may have become confused and gone off course, so numerous reports of flashes in the sky were checked out as were alleged sightings of wreckage. The Sea Island H-21A was kept busy but nothing was found. After 18 days the search was called off. Mountain peaks had been combed for wreckage by ground parties, especially Mount Cheam, 25 miles (40 km) west of Hope, and Silvertip Mountain, about 18 miles (29 km) southeast. The location of the crash site would remain a mystery for some time.

In mid-May 1957, two climbers were making their way up Mount Slesse, many miles from the other peaks searched in December, when they came across pieces of metal and clothing at the 7,500-foot (2 280-m) level. A metal part bearing a serial number was returned to TCA and subsequently identified as part of the doomed plane's fuel system. One of the reported flashes in the sky the night of the crash appeared to have been the North Star. An army corporal from Chilliwack had seen a pinkish-orange flash near Vedder Mountain.

The search master had been correct in assuming that the plane was off course: it was 30 miles (48 km) from where it should have been and 50 feet (15 m) too low. The plane had gone into the peak of Slesse and its wreckage was strewn over the saddle known to climbers as "The Circus." It was a difficult spot to reach, so helicopters were used to carry investigators and airline officials up the mountain.

The H-21A flew to the site to evaluate the situation after the discovery of the wreck, and other helicopters were on the scene as well. Bruce Payne, on his first job as a helicopter pilot, flew Bruce Young of the Vancouver Sun to the crash site. Young later wrote that "pilot Payne brought his craft onto the crash scene at exactly the same angle as the North Star must have taken in. It made my spine tingle to approach the spot even at 45 mph [42 km/h] in a highly manoeuvrable helicopter." Helicopters carried parties headed for the wreck to the 5,000-foot (1 525-m) level, from where they proceeded on foot. They then served as communication links between the radio-equipped parties on the ground and kept the curious from the site. There was an inducement for people to attempt the hazardous climb – rumours had circulated that a passenger from the Orient, bound for the eastern United States, was carrying a money belt with $80,000 in cash. A helicopter later had to rescue two amateur treasure-seeking climbers.

Hints began to emerge on the west coast in 1956 that the Royal Canadian Navy would soon be operating helicopters in British Columbia. The Navy had operated Bell HTLs (Bell 47s), Sikorsky HO4Ss (S-55s) and Vertol HUP-3s in eastern Canada off a platform-equipped frigate, the Buckingham, and off the icebreaker Labrador. The latter had made the difficult east-to-west voyage through the Northwest Passage in 1955, using its HUP-3 and HTL for ice patrol.

The Minister of National Defence, Ralph Campney, denied rumours that the RCN had plans to operate helicopters in British Columbia. It would, he felt, be redundant for that service to do so when the RCAF was already performing search and rescue as well as transport and communications duties with its helicopters. However, by 1958, VU-33 Squadron, RCN, based at Victoria's Patricia Bay Airport, was operating three of the HUP-3s. These machines were for utility work such as transportation and observation

When the wreckage of the North Star was discovered in May 1957, Mount Slesse became the focus of considerable activity. Officials from Trans-Canada Airlines, the RCAF and the Department of Transport swarmed over the crash site. Here a crew, including a commercial helicopter pilot, is being briefed by an RCAF officer. ERIC COWDEN

The Sikorsky H-5 (S-51) was the first helicopter used by the Royal Canadian Air Force in British Columbia. A machine of this type took part in Operation Brix, the search for a USAF B-36 bomber in February 1950. The H-5 was equipped with a rescue hoist.

CANADIAN FORCES

British Columbia's heavily forested terrain makes locating a downed aircraft difficult and sometimes impossible. This 442 Squadron CH-113 hovers over the remains of a crashed Bell 47.

CANADIAN FORCES

The Vertol H-21A and Grumman SA-16B were the mainstays of search and rescue operations until the introduction of amphibious CH-113 Labrador helicopters in the mid-1960s. British Columbia experiences a large number of marine incidents every year.

CANADIAN FORCES PHOTOS

The Vertol H-21A based at Sea Island was as impressive on the ground as in the air. Inflatable bags were attached to the landing gear for safety when operating over water. The cylinders attached to the folded bags contained the gas to inflate them.

The HUP-3 shown landing at the playing field of HMCS Naden was powered by a single engine despite having twin rotors. Three of these helicopters were used by VU-33 Squadron, RCN, on general duties and rescue missions when needed.

with the Navy's Pacific Command, but inevitably rescue became an important function as well.

The HUP-3, with twin rotors and single engine, was a design typical of Piasecki, the predecessor of Vertol and Boeing Vertol. It was very stable and, though small, was robust–a U.S. military pilot had executed a loop in an earlier HUP in 1948. The HUP-3 had been designed as a "plane guard" for aircraft carrier operation. If an aircraft went over the side of a carrier, the helicopter would retrieve its crew. It was not amphibious, so had to rescue a downed pilot while hovering. The RCN machines, while not used in this role, occasionally used the internally mounted rescue hoist. The sling in these aircraft passed through a hatch in the floor through which the victim was lifted.

The use of the rescue hoist and sling invariably makes a two-man crew, apart from the pilot, necessary: one to secure a victim into the rescue harness, the second to operate the hoist and transfer the victim from the sling into the helicopter. This could make an H-5 or HUP-3 very crowded indeed. It was not long before the Navy was flying rescue missions and the hoist proved valuable, particularly in one incident near Victoria. A young mountain climber had suffered a fall on Mount Finlayson. Help was summoned and a helicopter from VU-33 was soon on its way. To reach the injured climber, a crewman had to be lowered to the ground to direct the pilot so that he could manoeuvre between the trees on the mountainside. The hoist was situated well aft of the pilot making visibility awkward. The fact that the victim had a spinal injury complicated things; he had to be moved as little and as gently as possible. Moreover, had good airmanship not been exercised the helicopter and its crew might well have been lost. As it turned out all went well and the climber was flown to hospital in Victoria.

The HUP-3s, all of which had been struck off strength by January 1964, were the last naval shipboard helicopters used in B.C. until the transfer of 443 MH (Maritime Helicopter) Squadron and their Sea Kings to the west coast in the late 1980s.

In 1961, RCAF Station Sea Island was deactivated and 121 C & R (Composite and Rescue) Flight moved to Comox, the main RCAF base in British Columbia. Comox, 150 miles (240 km) north of Victoria, was home to most Air Force crews in B.C. including 409 Interceptor and 407 Maritime squadrons. It was more centrally located for coastal rescues, a factor that was to prove important in future operations.

In January 1962, a Greek bulk carrier, the SS *Glafkos*, was heading for Vancouver to take on a cargo of grain for Venezuela. Working its way along the west coast of Vancouver Island, it went off course, and high winds pushed it towards that rugged coast that had claimed so many ships over the years. Hard aground at Amphitrite Point south of Barkley Sound, the *Glafkos* presented one side to the shore, the other to the sea. It was too far from the shore for a rescue via breeches buoy – a lifesaving line – from shore. The wind was far too strong to permit an attempt from the weather side.

The Island Tug and Barge Company of Victoria dispatched salvage vessels to the scene and the Rescue Coordination Centre ordered the 121 C & R helicopter into the air. It was to land two salvage experts and their equipment on board and remove most of the crew. Several plates on the bottom of the ship's hull had been ripped off by the rocks holding the vessel fast, and it was taking on water. Without power, there was no hope of using the ship's own pumps. After rescuing crew members, the priority for the helicopter crew became to sling two portable pumps on board. This was soon accomplished.

A *Colonist* reporter, Ed Cosgrove, hired a Vancouver Island Helicopters' machine to see the *Glafkos* first hand. He arrived just as the big Vertol was moving in. In the Thursday, January 4, issue of his paper he recorded his impressions: "We watched breathless as the RCAF helicopter edged closer to the stern of the ship which lay broadside to the sea and wind. . . . Precise as a hummingbird the big twin rotor machine dropped to wave top level and eased its way up to the stern of the wallowing freighter. Man after man dangled for nerve tingling minutes over the tossing sea. The helicopter would flutter shoreward returning minutes later for another man."

With most of the crew safe on shore, the ship's anchor cables were cut and the *Glafkos* was pulled free under supervision of the salvage crew and towed to Victoria. Had a helicopter not been able to place the salvage crew on board and remove the seamen, the ship and several lives almost certainly would have been lost.

In late July 1963, Flight Lieutenant D. M. Campbell was involved in a rescue that earned him the Air Force Cross. A civilian aircraft had gone down on a Vancouver Island mountain slope. An attempt to winch the survivors out with the hoist failed as the line was too short. With daylight fading, Campbell allowed the helicopter to settle onto the tree tops. A rescue team climbed out of the Vertol down the trees to the ground and prepared the survivors for evacuation. Campbell later returned to lift the whole party out. Once again he was forced to execute the dangerous landing on the trees. Experience proved crucial and a difficult rescue was accomplished.

The Vertol H-21As performed their assigned roles very well for several years, but they too were replaced before long. In October 1963, search and rescue on the West Coast was upgraded by the introduction of the Boeing Vertol CH-113 Labrador helicopters. The new machines had twin-turbine rather than single-piston engines and were amphibious.

On occasion helicopters have been instrumental in evacuating people on a large scale. In January 1966, during one of the worst winters on record, slides in the Fraser Canyon cut rail traffic between the coast and points east. The eastbound *Panorama*, a Canadian National transcontinental passenger train, became stranded by slides at Stout, 20 miles (32 km) north of Hope. It could move neither forward nor back. An Okanagan crew in a Bell 204B airlifted food for the passengers and train crew, landing on a makeshift pad near the train. A second Okanagan machine, a two-seat Hiller 12E, was chartered to carry CN officials over the site to plan their strategy.

Plans to extricate the train by January 9, two days after it had been marooned, appeared unworkable. With fuel for the train's steam heaters running low, it became necessary to remove the passengers. The railway contacted the Rescue Coordination Centre and a Labrador was soon on the scene, working along with the Okanagan Bell 204B in the evacuation of 209 people. By the end of the operation, the Vertol, according to Air Force sources, had removed 184 people.

On July 8, 1968, in another reorganization, 121 C & R Flight became 442 Squadron.

By mid-1976, Ottawa was at last convinced that air-sea rescue should be improved. In November it was announced that four mothballed helicopters would be returned to service. They were Army Voyageurs which, having been built as tactical transports, required major conversion to upgrade them to rescue configuration. As a result, Comox was to have its complement increased from three to five machines.

The conversion program, Search and Rescue Capability Update Project (SARCUP), was still underway in the spring of 1982. Upgrading took place at the Boeing Vertol plant at Arnprior, Ontario. While an aircraft was at Arnprior for upgrade, it was replaced at Comox so that there were never fewer than four helicopters on hand at all times until the conversion and mid-life upgrade were complete. This was the first of what stretched to three major upgrades to extend the operational lives of the CH-113s and CH-113As in SAR service.

The hoist on the Voyageur, unlike that on the Labrador, was situated in the midship position and extended through the floor as in the HUP-3. Before long the hoist was moved to the door on the forward part of the starboard side. The pre-conversion position of the hoist created problems for pilots since visibility towards the rear was limited. According to Lieutenant Colonel Gordon Diamond, Commanding Officer of 442 Squadron in 1982, "It's like sitting at the front of a boxcar and attempting to watch what's happening behind and below you. Pilots must depend on mirrors mounted on each side below the nose and upon directions from crewmen to position the aircraft when making a hoist rescue. This situation was particularly difficult when a pick-up was being made from a vessel in heavy seas—the wildly gyrating masts can give the helicopter crew some bad moments since the hoist line can become fouled in the rigging or the helicopter itself may be struck."

The Voyageur was less sophisticated in its original configuration than the specially-built Labrador, which from the beginning had been intended for search and rescue. Most subsystems were hydraulic on the former aircraft, electrical on the latter. The two machines were almost totally incompatible in terms of parts—over 2,500 components are different—even though externally they look the same.

Pilots in 442 Transport and Rescue Squadron, the sole West Coast military SAR unit, are specialists either in fixed-wing or in rotary-wing aircraft; few fly both types. Their fixed-wing aircraft are Buffaloes. It takes a minimum of 500 hours helicopter time on type for a pilot to be considered for command of a Vertol, which carries a crew of six: two pilots, two Search and Rescue (SAR) technicians and two engineers. The Buffalo also carries a crew of six: two pilots, two SAR technicians, a flight engineer and a navigator. The SAR technicians, a fairly recent trade classification in the Canadian Forces, are trained paramedics, scuba divers, bushpersons, parachutists and mountaineers. These people have the satisfaction of being the ones who actually effect the rescue.

The Buffalo, with its superior instrument flight capability and a navigator, will often act as a "pathfinder" for the helicopter, particularly in the case of missions out to sea. The extension of Canada's territorial waters to 200 miles (320 km) expanded the area of responsibility for search and rescue as well. An important aspect of the Voyageur upgrading was the enhancement of its range by increased fuel capacity; the two sponsons at the rear of the machine were replaced by larger Kawasaki-built fuel tanks. When an incident occurs far out at sea, the helicopter, even with improved range, can waste little time on site. With the Buffalo providing navigational aid, the rescue can be made more efficiently and with greater safety.

The two types are therefore complementary in the search and rescue role. The Buffalo has superior range, speed and altitude, so it is more useful in medical evacuation (medevac) operations from distant locations, while the helicopter is the better machine for operating in a restricted space. Often both types fly together, particularly when little is known about the emergency; for example, when an Emergency Locator Transmitter (ELT) signal is received. An ELT is set to transmit a signal automatically by the impact of a crash, and aircraft with direction-finding equipment can pick up the signal. The Buffalo, when it has homed in on the signal, can drop flares if the incident

In January 1962, the 10,000-ton Greek cargo ship *Glafkos* lost power and ran aground on the west coast of Vancouver Island. High winds pushed the ship onto the rocks and made it dangerous to attempt a rescue with a lifeboat or a line from shore. An H-21A arrived from Comox, hoisted crew members to safety and transported salvage crews and their pumps out to the ship.

Responding to the *Prinsendam* distress call in
October 1980, Canadian and US helicopters and
fixed-wing aircraft operated in very poor weather
conditions. Here, a Labrador with its "Night Sun" in
operation has apparently just hoisted a survivor
from a lifeboat.

USCG PHOTOS

Survivors from the *Prinsendam* were taken by
helicopter to the USCG cutters *Boutwell* and *Mellon*,
and the tanker *Williamsburg*. A USCG HH-53 is shown
approaching the landing pad of the *Mellon*. Before
long the *Boutwell* had 87 on board, including the
occupants of a lifeboat that had gone missing in the
deteriorating weather.

On occasion, a rescuer needs to be rescued. This USCG HH-19G went down in white-out conditions. Too badly damaged to fly out but otherwise repairable, the Sea Island H-21A was brought in to transport it back to Port Angeles. This sort of cooperation is typical between American and Canadian rescue services.

USCG PHOTOS

Training and practice are necessary are therefore integral aspects of search and rescue. The HH-19G is hauling a "survivor" off this pleasure craft near Port Angeles.

Medical evacuations (medevacs) are frequent, if not routine, missions for SAR helicopters. This HH-19G from USCG Air Station Port Angeles, Washington, is shown waiting to load an accident victim for the trip to hospital.

USCG PHOTOS

The HH-52A replaced the HH-19G. The HH-52As were amphibious and on occasion would land on the water to effect a rescue.

occurs at night, lighting the search area, and the helicopter is equipped with "Night Sun," a searchlight mounted below the nose. The two-million-candlepower light is useful once the location of the victim is known more precisely.

The Rescue Coordination Centre at Canadian Forces Base Esquimalt, near Victoria, is responsible for 690,000 square miles (1 787 100 km^2) of ocean and 310,000 square miles (802 900 km^2) of land and water—for a total area of one million square miles (2.6 million km^2). The area extends north from the Canada/United States border, to cover all of British Columbia, the Yukon, and the Northwest Territories west of the Mackenzie River; out to sea for 200 miles (320 km); and east to the Alberta border. The nature of the territory covered creates problems. Mountains and valleys can make the accurate locating of an ELT signal difficult because the signal can bounce off the valley walls for a considerable distance. In one incident, a signal from an ELT was picked up in the Enderby region of the Okanagan. Following standard procedure, a Buffalo and a Vertol were quickly airborne to locate the aircraft and determine the problem. As it turned out, the signal had come from a plane at the Spokane, Washington, airport—the topography had carried the signal north. Weather conditions, too, can be and often are difficult, creating severe problems. Rescue aircraft are often called to operate in far less than ideal weather—in conditions which often have been a major contributing factor to the original problem. Regardless of the weather, certain procedures are always followed. Lt. Colonel Diamond describes a typical operation:

In the case of an aircraft being reported as overdue to the Rescue Coordination Centre, several things happen almost simultaneously. The Department of Transport undertakes a communications search to determine if any messages have been received from or concerning the aircraft. The RCMP or other available agencies will check airstrips along the last known flight path of the plane—by phone if possible, or in person if no phone is available. In the meantime, we usually launch both a Buffalo and a helicopter with full crews, which are in the air less than 30 minutes of the call from the RCC.

The first day is critical since there may well be injuries. We maintain a constant watch for signals over the next two days and nights, and comb hills along the flight path. When the RCC message is received, I'm informed and, along with the squadron operations officer, appoint a search master. This is usually a captain on the squadron who has been fully trained in this role, and an assistant. A search master has a big job, directing the operation of what can sometimes be 60 or 70 aircrew and spotters. During the winter months, he's usually up at 0600, in the summer 0500, preparing his search strategy, maps and briefing packages for crews. When the aircraft return to refuel, he will interrogate the crews and give them their assignments for the next phase of the search. Assisting the search master will be an accounts clerk with a "bag of money" to pay for hotels and food, and people to provide for the logistical end of the operation—fuel and maintenance for the aircraft, and communications. He must be left as free as possible to direct the search. One other complication is dealing with the press, relatives of the missing, and on occasion, politicians. A search can last any time from a few hours in some cases, to days or weeks in others. Some are successful; some are not–it's a matter of luck as well as skill.

One prolonged operation in which I was involved within the last year [1981], was the search for an Air B.C. Beaver that had gone missing on a flight from an Indian village at Klemtu to Ocean Falls with some federal government employees on board. We searched along the flight path normally taken by Air B.C. aircraft without success, but spotted an oil slick on the surface of a lake. Using a blotter, we took a sample of the oil–as you can appreciate, it was thin and difficult to collect. The first sample was insufficient but the second worked and we sent it to the RCMP crime lab for identification. The oil proved to be of a type similar to that used by Air B.C. in their aircraft.

The next step was to dive on the object releasing the oil to determine if in fact it was the Beaver or simply a piece of equipment that may have fallen off a barge at some point. Where there is some possibility of saving life, we would normally send in our SAR techs who are qualified scuba divers. Such was not the case in this instance and the object was in any case far too deep. We contacted CanDive who sent down a sonar device and determined that the object was metal, man-made and of an angular shape, not unlike that of a Beaver aircraft. In order to be certain, however, it would be necessary to dive using a small submersible. We were fairly certain that we had found the aircraft but had to be sure. Two Hercules transports were sent down to Houston, Texas, where the CanDive sub was working. We nevertheless continued the air search and, shortly before the C-130s were ready to return with the submarine, one of our spotters saw the wreck of the Beaver in an area we had flown near perhaps 15 times before. Hidden in high timber, it went in without having broken a twig. We were fortunate to have found it. Apparently the Beaver had run out of fuel a mere eight miles from its destination. Unhappily, the pilot and passengers were all dead.

Not all searches are as extensive as the one just described. In late August 1976, a Comox-based Labrador flew three separate missions in one day. The first was fairly routine, picking up an injured hiker in the Buttle Lake region of central Vancouver Island; the second was to Wolfe River, some 20 miles (32 km) into Strathcona Park. At this point things started to go wrong. While evacuating a woman from a heavily forested area using the hoist, everything went smoothly until the woman "became excited" and damaged the hoist. The account does not elaborate about how this occurred. Later that day, they were sent out for another evacuation to the Forbidden Plateau ski slopes near Comox. The helicopter developed a vibration which forced the pilot to land on an access road. A truck from base arrived with parts and maintenance personnel, and the helicopter was soon on its way again to pick up the injured skier and return to base. It had been a long day.

The duties of 442 Squadron are varied, including search and rescue, humanitarian missions such as emergency medical evacuations–though this type of mission has declined with the creation of a provincial air ambulance service–and "giving aid to the civil power," such as assisting in the control of penitentiary inmates, flood control and forest firefighting. Incidents involving lost or downed aircraft have been constant over the past decade, but those involving pleasure boats or larger vessels have increased dramatically. Most incidents are routine, but there are some that are spectacular. One of these involved the cruise ship *Prinsendam,* sailing in the frigid North Pacific.

At 2:25 a.m., October 4, 1980, Victoria Marine Radio monitored a distress signal from the Holland-Amerika Lines' *Prinsendam*, at sea 150 miles (240 km) west of Sitka, Alaska. Twenty minutes after the "mayday," the duty controller at RCC Victoria reported the situation to the duty operations officer at 442 Squadron, CFB Comox, in case any aircraft might be needed quickly. RCC Victoria had immediately offered assistance to its counterpart in Juneau and was asked by them to stand by; a Search and Rescue aircraft was on its way to the scene to look things over.

The first report from the ship had indicated that the engine room of the 430-foot (130-m) vessel was on fire. The fire spread rapidly and soon the ship, dead in the water without the use of its engines, had flames shooting high above the decks. The situation had become desperate. Two-and-a-half hours after the first mayday, the 329 passengers and all of the crew except those fighting the fire were ordered into the lifeboats. Some of these lifeboats, designed to carry 50 persons each, had as many as 80 crowded into them—a necessity since two others were unusable because of problems with the lowering gear. The passengers, virtually all of whom were dressed in sleepwear, had no protection from spray, wind and cold; what had started as a leisurely cruise from Vancouver to the Orient had turned into a nightmare.

RCC Juneau requested that the Canadian aircraft and crews be prepared to leave at one-and-a-half hours notice. Staff at Victoria RCC, by now certain that they would become involved in the rescue, recalled Labrador helicopter 11306 from a medical evacuation to Vancouver, and requested 442 Squadron to prepare additional aircraft and crews to assemble as soon as possible in support of RCC Juneau. The anticipated request came at 6:15 a.m. Helicopter assistance was required at the scene and fixed-wing aircraft were needed for transport duties. A rescue force was already converging on the stricken ship and her passengers.

An American supertanker, the *Williamsburg*, had responded to the *Prinsendam*'s call for assistance and was standing by, as was a US Coast Guard cutter, the *Boutwell*. No time was wasted; American helicopters were already transferring survivors from the boats to the *Williamsburg* and the pad-equipped *Boutwell* even before the arrival of the Canadians. The tanker, with a crew of only 29, quickly found itself overwhelmed. Two Labrador helicopters and two Buffaloes were dispatched from Comox as soon as they were fuelled and the crews briefed; an additional Buffalo left the following day. A main

442 (T & R) Squadron Report:

Special Report,
SAR Operation Prinsendam
Victoria Rescue
Coordination Centre
Maritime Forces Pacific
04 Oct 80

SAR Prinsendam
0245 The RCC Duty Controller advised 442 Duty Operations Officer of the Mayday from the MV Prinsendam. He and the Buffalo navigator came in and assessed the situation. . . .

0540 RCC Victoria requested that the Duty Operations Officer recall Labrador 306 from the Medevac in progress, arrange for maximum 442 response in support of RCC Juneau and launch all aircraft as soon as possible.

function of the fixed-wing support was to transport the considerable equipment and personnel related to both rescue and salvage operations to Yakutat and then on to the *Prinsendam.* Later, those passengers and crew of the ship who required hospital treatment would need to be moved from Yakutat to larger centres with more extensive facilities. An Argus maritime patrol aircraft of VP 407 Squadron also headed north from Comox to act, along with an American Hercules transport, as a communications link and rescue watch for the Canadian aircraft and US Coast Guard and Air Force helicopters from Sitka, Kodiak and Elmendorf.

The nearest point to the rescue with an airport, Yakutat was the logical base for receiving survivors. With the cooperation of the Alaska state authorities and the citizens of the town, the considerable preparation required was carried out successfully: a command post and reception centre were established in the airline terminal and a high-frequency radio was set up in the airport manager's office. Limited contact with search headquarters in Juneau was maintained by a landline. Aircraft operating between the ships and shore used Yakutat as the base. Major C. B. Fletcher, Acting Commanding Officer of 442 Squadron, was asked by Juneau to take charge there until a US Coast Guard replacement could arrive.

Canadian Forces medical personnel, as soon as possible after their arrival at Yakutat, were on their way to the *Williamsburg.* Master Corporal R. Holliston, Team Leader, reported later that "there were approximately 100 survivors on board, and we were the only medics available. We checked all the survivors, completed emergency treatment, and set up an area in the main mess deck to check and treat new survivors coming aboard."

Captain Gary Flath in Labrador 11303, which had taken off from Comox at 7:51 a.m., arrived at Sitka some 800 miles (1 300 km) to the north at 1:25 p.m. Nurse Captain Costello remained at Yakutat where she would be needed when evacuees began arriving in large numbers. The weather was beginning to worsen, and Captain Flath, after refuelling his helicopter, was bound 20 minutes later for the *Williamsburg* carrying six medical personnel: three Canadian SAR technicians; Molly Seifert and Anne Keinitz, both trained paramedics from the Alaska Civil Defence organization; and Major McLean, Base Surgeon at CFB Comox. The tanker proved difficult to locate and Flath requested that the ship transmit so he could home on it without visual contact. Seifert was on board Flath's Labrador for the trip to the ship. Recalling the incident, she wrote:

1:30 p.m. My first ride on one of these and am not sure how I'll react, but what a ride! The weather is getting worse all the time, with winds increasing and raining steadily, and I can't see where we're going.

2:30 p.m. We figure we'll be on the tanker within 45 minutes. Someone mentions a fire in a helicopter and I'm checking exits! Not to worry, the helo that left before us has an electrical fire and may have to ditch, so we circle a couple of times. The pilot gets word that another plane is escorting the first one to Yakutat.

We land on the tanker Williamsburg, which is doing quite a dance on those seas. We slip and slide over what seems like miles of pipes and ramps, etc., to get to shelter. Another discovery–the helo pilot hasn't landed on a ship before!

Survivors, with the help of Canadian Forces SAR TECHs (Search and Rescue specialists), were winched into the helicopters from lifeboats.

USCG

Meanwhile, Captain Ken Pettman, who had left Sitka in Labrador 11306 just as Flath in 11303 had arrived, was coping with technical problems. Everything had been functioning normally en route to Sitka and for the first portion of the trip out to sea, but before long, things began to go wrong and Pettman was forced to declare an emergency. Navigation systems had failed and attempts to have Argus 731 home in on the helicopter proved futile. The Emergency Location Transmitter (ELT) was turned on and Flath indicated that he could home on the signal if necessary. This proved unnecessary since a USAF C-130 was able to locate the helicopter and was in formation within two minutes of the declaration of the emergency. Captain Pettman, by this time feeling utterly frustrated at having come so far without problems, only to have to turn back, asked that the Hercules escort him the 120 nautical miles back to Yakutat, where they arrived safely at 4:50 p.m.

After unloading on *Williamsburg* and hearing that Ken Pettman was being escorted back to base, Flath headed for the *Prinsendam*, which he reached some five minutes after lifting off the tanker. A lifeboat was located, one with only 40 persons in it, and the decision was made to use the high line and the horse collar. This was the fastest method of recovery in such severe wind and sea conditions. Before long, passengers were being hoisted into the aircraft. A "Sky Genie," a rope normally used by an SAR technician when he descends from a hovering aircraft, proved to be an effective means of returning the horse-collar to the boat after a survivor had been hoisted into the air-craft. As Flath recalls:

The Sky Genie rope remained attached to the hook and collar, with Sergeant Williams holding onto the other end of the rope. This enabled me to move the aircraft off to one side to allow better reference on the boat during recovery, and to keep oscillations of survivors being hoisted to a minimum. When the hook and cable were being let out I could stay clear until I saw Sergeant Williams hook up another survivor. I would then move over the boat and, as the cable tension was tightened up, would lift up gently on the collective when directed by the hoist operator. This manoeuvre ensured that the survivors cleared the boat quickly to avoid getting wet or caught up on the lifeboat.

Fifteen people were removed from the first boat by Flath's helicopter and flown to the *Williamsburg*. A further 16 people were removed from a second boat with Master

Corporal Lang being lowered to the boat and Master Corporal Amadio working the hoist. Meanwhile, on board the *Williamsburg*, medical personnel and crew attempted to cope with exhausted, cold and frightened people. Tired and short of medication, clothing and space, the medics began to feel the strain. As Molly Seifert described the scene:

Into the night the paramedical personnel meet each other coming and going throughout the ship's living quarters. We all make rounds of all four decks, stopping to visit with people who can't sleep, carrying coffee, sandwiches, etc.

3 a.m. to 5:30 a.m.: We all sit and drink coffee with the two Canadian paramedics. If the lady rescuers look as bad as the guys, there'll be no contests won. I think I would kill for a shower and a Coke.

There were still more passengers to be removed from the boats. Flath, with his Labrador, continued hoisting people and at one point looked for a lifeboat that had gone missing. The cutter *Boutwell* requested that the helicopter attempt to find the boat so, very short of fuel, Captain Flath trimmed for endurance flying. "The weather was very poor at this time, with 100- to 200-foot (30-32 m) ceiling, and ½-mile (800 m) visibility and high winds which made it very difficult for rescuers to spot the white lifeboats hidden by large swells and whitecaps. When the cutter finally saw me I flew over the lifeboat and flashed my landing lights. Once he acknowledged that he had a visual on the lifeboat, I departed for Yakutat and arrived there 1.5 hours later, after dark, with about five minutes fuel remaining."

With the last survivors located and safely transferred, the rescue vessels headed for Valdez. For Molly Seifert it had been an exhausting but memorable experience:

It will take a good two weeks to get this out of our systems. After flying home on a Canadian Air Force Buffalo, Anne and I spent almost two hours mostly staring at each other. My family got the doubtful privilege of being sounding boards. My immediate reaction was to try to tell everything that happened and we both talked and laughed and related war stories until we were hoarse. Ironically, very few people in Sitka knew we were gone. It is difficult to come to the realization you are part of a history-making event, at best; and when no one knows you were there being a hero, it becomes impossible.

Attempts to salvage the *Prinsendam* and return it south for repairs failed when, under tow by the Vancouver-based tug *Commodore Straits*, the ship capsized and sank in 9,000 feet (275 m) of water. The rescue itself was extremely successful, more than proving the value and effectiveness of the search and rescue organizations involved. All the passengers and crew had been lifted off safely and remarkably quickly, considering the distance from shore. Without the helicopters and other aircraft, the rescue would have been far more difficult and lives might well have been lost. As ever, cooperation between Canadians and Americans involved was excellent.

The United States Coast Guard was a very early operator of helicopters; they were quick to appreciate their advantages in search and rescue work. In November 1943, the USCG set up a training base for helicopter aircrew at Floyd Bennett Field, New York, where pilots for that service, the Royal Navy and the US Navy were trained on Sikorsky R-4 helicopters. The first helicopter mercy mission flown by the Coast Guard took place in the first week of January 1944, when Commander Frank Erickson flew plasma to treat victims of a ship explosion. He had to fly the desperately needed supplies in bad weather from New York to Sandy Hook, New Jersey. While it was not a long flight, it did dramatically demonstrate the value of helicopters in such circumstances and began a long tradition of helicopter rescue work by the Coast Guard.

The US Coast Guard Air Station at Port Angeles, Washington, some 20 miles (32 km) south of Victoria on the Strait of Juan de Fuca, received its first helicopter in 1950. This was a Sikorsky H03S-lG like the H-5 used by the RCAF at Sea Island. Before this, the rescue service had employed a variety of fixed-wing aircraft such as lifeboat-equipped Boeing PB1G (B-17) Flying Fortresses from the Ediz Hook base, and even after the introduction of rotary-winged craft a number of flying boats and amphibians such as the Grumman Albatross continued to operate from the station. The helicopter was quickly pressed into service rescuing victims of marine and aircraft accidents and carrying out medical evacuation missions. The role of helicopters in search and rescue has changed little in terms of the type of operations flown, but their capability has increased dramatically due to advances in techniques and, obviously, technology.

The US Coast Guard, like the RCAF, replaced its aircraft when those of superior capability became available. Sikorsky HH-19G helicopters, the Coast Guard/Navy equivalent of the S-55 used by Okanagan, were introduced in the early 1950s. In October 1956, the USCG had occasion to call on the Canadian search and rescue service for assistance. Two USAF Northrop F-89D Scorpion jet interceptors had disappeared from radar over the rugged Olympic Mountains and it was vital that the aircrew be located as quickly as possible. It was feared the pilots might have come down high in the mountains where, at high altitude during winter conditions, exposure could prove fatal. That was assuming they had survived the crash. A very large area had to be searched.

The Rescue Coordination Centre at Sea Island responded immediately, sending an Otter fixed-wing search aircraft and a Vertol H-21A helicopter. Since it was possible that the airmen might have come down in the Strait, the RCC also sent four tugs from Island Tug and Barge Ltd. of Victoria to the scene. Apparently when one of the F-89Ds had developed technical problems, the second had moved in to have a look and the two aircraft had collided. Three of the four crewmen ejected successfully and parachuted from the aircraft, which crashed three miles (5 km) from each other on the west side of Humes Glacier. The *Vancouver Sun* reported on October 6, 1956, that two of the aircrew had been located by RCAF aircraft – one by the H-21A and the other by the Otter. The first survivor was rescued by the Vertol, and the second by a Coast Guard HH-19G helicopter, which had been directed to the site by the Otter pilot. The third survivor was able to walk 40 miles (64 km) out to safety.

One of the USCG helicopters crashed during the search operations when it encountered white-out conditions. Fortunately the crew were uninjured and the helicopter was not a write-off. It could not be flown out, however, because the damage was too severe for repairs to be carried out on site; weather conditions and logistics would have rendered this difficult in any case. The obvious solution was an airlift by a large helicopter. Fortunately the RCAF Vertol was nearby and it had the capacity to do the job. The downed HH-19G was stripped; the engine, cockpit and tail-boom were removed to reduce weight, and the H-21A airlifted all the pieces out for repair and reassembly.

In 1963, the Sikorsky HH-52A, a single-engined, amphibious helicopter, entered service with the US Coast Guard. It could operate off water and reduced the dependence on fixed-wing amphibious machines to deal with the large number of marine incidents characteristic of northern Washington and southern British Columbia. Ensign Jeff Vail, who has served as a co-pilot on the type, describes the duties of a copilot and other aircrew:

The commonly used Stokes litter with flotation devices attached for use in marine incidents.

When the SAR alarm goes off, you respond quickly: while the Aircraft Commander goes out to pre-flight the aircraft and run it up, the co-pilot gets all the details he can on the case and then runs to the helicopter. My job when airborne is to do a few checks and handle the radios, the onboard computer, and to navigate while the Aircraft Commander is doing the flying. He usually makes a decision, informs me and I pass it along to the base. If it's a particularly difficult mission, he'll fly the airplane, but sometimes we'll swap; otherwise you'd get no experience flying. I usually monitor the radios and the aircraft's in-flight performance. I'll also act as an observer.

On a standard SAR mission, we normally go with a three- or four-man crew: one man is a dedicated flight mechanic and it's his job to maintain the helo between missions. A lot of his training for rescue work centres around hoist operation. On a search, he acts as an observer. He may or may not have paramedical experience, and so we try, if possible, to take a duty corpsman along with us, particularly in the case of a heart attack. Any aviation "rate" – aviation mechanic, avionics tech or in fact anyone involved with the aircraft – can become qualified as a SAR aircrewman and go out on a mission. Anyone who works with the aircraft can qualify.

We seldom, if ever, drop an aircrewman to assist with a rescue, since both our aircraft and crew are too small for that. Perhaps it's the type of flying we do; we spend a minimum time on-site because the helicopter simply doesn't have the endurance to remain for any length of time. We no longer use the "horse collar," except in cases involving trained military personnel; the Coast Guard dropped that since too many people were slipping through–one of the astronauts almost drowned while being hoisted in one a few years ago after a mission. We use the basket and the Stokes litter.

Since they are in situations which often involve a high degree of risk in the normal course of operations, the rescuers can on occasion end up on the receiving end of rescue efforts. Just such a situation occurred in early 1976. Commander Paul Milligan of the US Coast Guard relates what happened:

It was February 29, 1976, a memorable day apart from being a leap year. It was sometime after midnight and I'd only just drifted off to sleep when the phone rang—one of our aircraft was down while responding to an emergency on the west coast of Vancouver Island. We didn't know a thing beyond this and the fact that the weather was extremely bad, with intermittent snow and heavy winds, which made the situation particularly difficult. Getting to the base in what must have been record time, we launched immediately and headed for Cape Beale where the incident occurred. Even from our side of the Strait, we could see that a Canadian SAR aircraft was dropping flares.

Lt. Commander Dennis Maclean, then a lieutenant, was flying as co-pilot on this mission and subsequently served on the board of enquiry. He relates details of the incident:

We soon learned by radio that a Canadian Coast Guard 44-footer [14-m, Bamfield Lifeboat, CG-104] had picked up our crew and two survivors of a fishing boat, and that all were well. Knowing this and having no desire to fly under flares while they were being dropped, we flew to Neah Bay where we stayed the night. The next morning, in beautiful clear weather, we headed for Cape Beale to pick up our crew and investigate the loss of the helicopter.

We learned that the H52 had been in the vicinity of the Cape Beale lighthouse the night before on another call–the Canadians would have normally handled it but couldn't get over the mountains separating Cape Beale and Comox in the weather–when the lighthouse keeper contacted them by radio. He had heard cries for help but couldn't locate their source. Our crew, from the air, spotted someone clinging to the reef in the vicinity of the lighthouse and were able to make a hoist rescue. Almost as soon as the survivor was on board the helicopter, there was a loud bang and the pilot instinctively pushed down on the collective to autorotate onto the water–probably on instruments under the circumstances.

Safely down, he still had to contend with heavy seas and snow, and winds of 30-40 knots (55-75 km/h). The helicopter was in immediate danger of being pushed onto the rocks and pounded to pieces. The water was too deep for an anchor to be effective and so he deployed a sea drogue, a device not unlike a small parachute. This became fouled around the sponson and was ineffective. By this time, the aircraft was rolling from side to side–it was a miracle that it was still afloat at all since it had not been designed to cope with seas of this magnitude. Half the length of each rotor blade was disappearing below the surface of the water with each roll. It was obvious that it was going to be necessary to leave the aircraft. The crew spent a nervous 20 minutes in the pitching, rolling helicopter edging towards the rocks, until a Zodiac boat, launched from the Canadian Coast Guard 44-footer, came alongside to take them off. Knowing what had happened, the lighthouse keeper had directed the Canadian 44-footer in through the reefs using a CB radio: "Go left, go right, back up"–that sort of thing. Once the drenched helicopter crew and the boat survivors were below and warming up, a crewman told them that they weren't safe yet–they still had to get out the way they had come in, once again using directions from the lighthouse keeper to clear the reefs. The bottom of the boat scraped over the reef at several points.

USCG pilots, Lieutenant-Commander Denny Maclean and Ensign Jeff Vail.

The HH-65A Dolphin, an Americanized, re-engined, mission-equipped version of the French Aerospatiale Dauphin, was introduced into Coast Guard Service in the mid-1980s as that service's new Short Range Rescue (SRR) helicopter. Very capable and well-liked by its crews, it replaced the HH-52A at Port Angeles.

When we looked at the remains of the H52 the next day, the largest piece that we could locate was the bottom of the hull; the fuselage above the level of the floor had been completely sheared off. The first part we went after was the engine. After investigating, the conclusion we came to was that snow had been ingested into the intake and the "fire" had gone out.

The crew of the Bamfield lifeboat, Coxswain David Christney and crewmen Martin Charles, Clifford Charles and Robert Amos, were presented with a Certificate of Commendation by the Commissioner of the Canadian Coast Guard in a ceremony on March 6, 1976. This was in recognition of an "outstanding rescue at sea under extremely dangerous conditions, demanding the utmost skill, courage and devotion to duty in the finest traditions of the sea." The US Coast Guard also presented an award to the lifeboat crew and lighthouse personnel.

Generally speaking, the presence of the amphibious HH-52A helicopters near Victoria has proven vital on numerous occasions but perhaps never more so than a foggy day in December 1976. An Air West Twin Otter, a twin-engined STOL aircraft equipped with floats, was approaching Victoria on a late-morning flight from Vancouver when it ran into heavy fog. The harbour, with its marine traffic, can be difficult even in good visibility, so the pilot elected to put down at sea and wait until the weather cleared enough to enter the harbour safely. The aircraft hit the water at 110 mph (180 km/h) and bounced 150 feet (46 m) into the air. The impact damaged a float and the plane began to settle to one side shortly after it landed.

A mayday distress call went out immediately. The Rescue Coordination Centre at Esquimalt responded quickly, requesting assistance from the US Coast Guard at Port Angeles, only 20 miles (32 km) from the crash site. Within 16 minutes of the distress call, an HH-52A landed beside the sinking plane. It was 11:34 a.m. All 16 passengers and the two aircrew of the Twin Otter were quickly taken on board the US helicopter. Then, without warning, the plane tilted and a wing moved up into the rotor arc of the HH-52A, shearing pieces off the rotor blades. The damaged helicopter had to be towed back to Port Angeles. Crash victims, all of whom were in good condition thanks to the fast action of the Americans, were transferred to a Canadian pilot launch for a quick trip into Victoria and waiting ambulances. Praise for the US helicopter crews was heartfelt. A CTV news cameraman, who was on board the Twin Otter, commented that if it had not been for the USCG he thought it unlikely that he'd have been around for Christmas, which was only eight days away. While this incident, like many others, had a happy ending, such has not always been the case.

In September 1980, a US Navy HH-46A from Whidbey Island Naval Air Station responded to a call from the Esquimalt RCC to rescue an injured hiker. By the time the

This platform attached to the side of the HH-52A makes the loading of a probably frightened survivor into the helicopter easier and safer. It is only used when the amphibious HH-52A has landed on water.

USCG

Lt. Richard Wall, USN

helicopter reached Perfect Pass, near Vedder Crossing, flying conditions were marginal, with scattered clouds below 8,000 feet (2 400 m) and a solid overcast. To complicate matters, it was only 30 minutes until sundown and they were still about 30 miles (48 km) south of their destination. Lt. Richard Wall, USN, the co-pilot, was doing the flying while the pilot and a sheriff were checking maps. A new heading was decided upon and control of the aircraft was transferred, the Aircraft Commander turning the helicopter to the new course. Suddenly, without warning, visibility was lost and the radio altimeter indicated that the ground was coming up fast. They had lost 1600 feet (490 m) in just four seconds, and just as the altimeter reached 400 feet (120 m) the helicopter crashed.

Lt. Wall was thrown clear of the wreck and 200 feet (60 m) down the side of the mountain. He was very fortunate; five of the seven on board the HC-46 had been killed; only the deputy sheriff and he survived. Late in the morning following the crash, two hikers arrived on the scene and, performing what first aid they could, made the crash survivors as comfortable as possible. Leaving their packs, water canteens and warm clothing, the hikers went for help. The next day, rescuers arrived. Richard Wall describes what happened:

At first light the next day I felt a wave of emotions like none before or since, as I heard the sound of an H-46 [CH-113] overhead. The clouds were in solid, but the Canadian HH-46A crew from 442 Rescue Squadron, Comox, British Columbia, gave it their all. Hovering IMC [Instrument Meteorological Conditions], with only a few rocks for reference, the Canadian crew commenced the rescue in weather worse than at the time of our crash. I recall thinking, "Lord I hope they know what they're doing!" and apparently they knew just that, as the rescue proceeded without a hitch and we were flown out to the nearest hospital.

Both Richard Wall and the deputy sheriff recovered from their injuries. This incident vividly demonstrates the dangers encountered in rescue missions by American and Canadian crews. Cooperation between the rescue services of both nations has always been excellent since they share the same traditions that have characterized individuals and organizations dedicated to the saving of life. The helicopter has proven to be all that its inventors could have hoped in this respect.

By the late 1980s, it was increasingly apparent that Canada's Search and Rescue helicopter fleet was ageing rapidly and replacements had to be found. Several manufacturers came forward responding to a Request for Proposals (RFP) and the one from EH Industries, a consortium of European manufacturers, was chosen. The Department of National Defence contracted for 50 EH-101s to replace both the Labradors and the CH-124 Sea Kings, the latter being in as urgent need for replacement as the former.

Responding to criticism about the expense, the Conservative government cut the order to 43 aircraft, and the Liberal administration that replaced them in 1993 cancelled the entire $4.8 billion project as it had promised to do during the election campaign. The cancellation cost taxpayers $478.6 million and set the replacement of the helicopters back indefinitely. The process began again but with a significant difference: the SAR helicopter and shipboard helicopter replacements were to be separate issues. Not surprisingly, the second round of the SAR competition had the same companies entering proposals: Eurocopter with the "Cougar Mk. 2," Sikorsky with the "Maplehawk," Boeing Vertol with the CH-47D "Chinook" and EH Industries with the "Cormorant." In January 1998, the government announced that the Cormorant, a civilian utility version of the EH 101, had been selected for SAR. Canadian companies are to play a major role in equipping this machine, which is due for delivery between 2000 and 2002. The same manufacturers, with the exception of Boeing-Vertol, will be bidding on the CH-124 replacement.

Helicopters continue to justify the faith placed in them in the role of search and rescue, and they continue as well to help protect those travelling by sea.

Labrador 113302 photographed in its original red, white and blue livery. High visibility chrome yellow and dayglo red soon identified Canadian Armed Forces SAR aircraft, both rotary and fixed wing.

R. D. TURNER

CHAPTER TEN

After some time, we spotted the boat
in a vast expanse of ice, looking like a
black speck on a white sheet.

BOB JONES

Canadian Coast Guard

Canadian Coast Guard experience with helicopters began in 1950, when a Sikorsky S-51, CF-DOY, was acquired by the Marine Service of the Department of Transport, the predecessor of the Coast Guard. Jack Charleson, Canada's first civilian to qualify as a helicopter pilot in 1945, suggested in 1949 that a helicopter operating from a deck rigged on the "fan tail" of a ship would prove useful in ship-to-shore transportation and ice patrol duties. Flying helicopters off ships had been tried before; in May 1943 two Sikorsky R-4s were successfully test flown off the tanker SS *Bunker Hill* in Long Island Sound. There had been proposals earlier to use ship-based rotary-winged craft in an anti-submarine role and with later developments they have excelled in this military role.

Charleson's suggestion was put to the test and, despite an accident which destroyed the S-51 – a tie-down cable from the deck of the vessel to one side of the aircraft had not been detached before take-off and the helicopter crashed – the Department of Transport was more than satisfied with helicopters. It purchased a number of Bell 47s over the years to service lighthouses and other marine navigation aids, and for use with East Coast icebreakers and buoy tenders.

Initially they were used almost exclusively from ships, their primary roles being ice patrol and personnel and light cargo transport. In the early years all the helicopters were based at the Air Services headquarters in Ottawa and were detached to the various marine agencies when requested. This worked reasonably well when only a few ships were equipped with flight decks. The success of helicopters in these roles tended to obscure their potential as land-based transport. It was in the latter role that helicopter operations began on the Pacific Coast in 1960 when two Bell 47-G2s were based at Vancouver and, a year later, a larger Sikorsky S-62 began flying out of Prince Rupert.

In British Columbia, as on the East Coast, the primary purpose of the Department of Transport Marine Services was the maintenance of coastal aids to navigation, still a vital task today on this treacherous coast. Ships had to be protected against such hazards as reefs and collisions with other vessels in narrow passages. Spare parts and technicians could be airlifted to sites where repairs were required on short notice, and the construction of helipads near navigation aids from 1961 onwards dramatically reduced the time required for resupply and maintenance. These functions previously had been carried out using ships, such as the lighthouse tender CGS *Estevan*. The introduction of the aircraft boosted the morale of personnel at lighthouses: they were less isolated. If an emergency occurred, if someone were sick or injured, it was possible to carry out an evacuation quickly. Though the value of the helicopters was proven beyond doubt, their efficient use was restricted to a degree by a bureaucratic complication.

The basing of the two Bell 47-G2s in Vancouver proved to be inefficient because the main Department of Transport Marine Services base in the province was then, as is that of the Coast Guard now, in Victoria. Both machines and aircrew were the responsibility of Air Services, and their use by Marine Services had to be formally requested – a cumbersome and illogical practice. For almost a decade the helicopters were exclusively land based in British Columbia. The inefficiency of this situation became apparent when operations from icebreakers recently equipped with landing-pads began in the late 1960s. When interviewed in the 1980s, Ivor Roberts, who had received his initial training on Sikorsky R-4 helicopters with the Royal Navy shortly after the Second World War, explained the situation:

We started out servicing the lighthouses – there are about 30 in this agency – from the Vancouver side. They would bring the helicopter over from the hangar there and work off two icebreakers; one was the Camsell, which we still have, and the other the Simon Fraser, which is now back in Quebec. There were no facilities here in Victoria until they got an office and space in one of the old Fairey hangars [Fairey Aircraft of Canada at Pat Bay] which we kept for some years. We then went to the VU-33 hangar when the military abandoned it and stayed there until we got our facility at Ogden Point. We were always divided in our loyalties between the Air Services and Maritime Services and this situation continues even to this day, since administration is by Air Services and, for operations, it's under control of Marine Services.

Administrative problems notwithstanding, the role of West Coast helicopters expanded dramatically with the construction of flight decks on two Victoria-based ice-breakers. These ships had been constructed in British Columbia yards to service Distant Early Warning Line radar sites in the western Arctic from the West Coast.

As had been the case in Eastern Canada for some years, the helicopters before long were being used for ice patrol during the annual northern re-supply cruises. Sailing from Victoria, usually during the first week of July, the ship proceeded west and north, passing through the Aleutians at Unimak Pass, and stopping at the US Navy base at Dutch

Harbour to refuel if the ship was not accompanied by a tanker. This base was one of the few locations in continental North America attacked by the Japanese during the Second World War. From there the ship passed into the Chukchi Sea and the Northwest Passage. Once through the Bering Strait, the ship passed Point Barrow into Cambridge Bay and finally into Spence Bay, the last point on its voyage.

The helicopter provided the "eyes" for the ship when it was making its way through the ice, an important job since it is all too easy for even an icebreaker to become trapped. The *Camsell* found itself in this situation in 1979 when its hull was holed by pack ice and the engine room flooded. Fortunately the ship did not sink and it was returned to Victoria for extensive repairs. Bob Jones, who has flown 10 seasons in the north with the Coast Guard, describes the procedure employed in ice patrol work:

The helicopter normally scouts 20-30 miles [32-48 km] ahead of the ship, carrying an ice observer who makes a detailed map of the ice field for the ship's captain. Nowadays they have a complete division of ice observers, and they put one on all the ships carrying helicopters. The ice observer's job is to give a picture of the ice amount and type; you have, say, 8/10 of ice of which 3/10 is polar and 5/10 pack ice. Polar ice is usually relatively easy to go through, unless you have some that is rafted (that is, new ice piled on top of old). Polar ice is refrozen year after year and there's no limit to its thickness—it can be anywhere from 5 to 150 feet [1.5-46 m] thick.

Single-year or winter ice normally poses little problem for the icebreaker, but multi-year or polar ice can, and often does. It can damage both icebreakers and other shipping. Sometimes when the ice is particularly bad, the helicopter will literally lead the ship through "weak spots" by hovering only 100 yards [90 m] ahead. Usually in these circumstances, a ship's deck officer accompanies the pilot, as he will be better able to decide on the ship's capability of penetrating the ice ahead.

The other major problem associated with the ice is determining whether or not it is under pressure—that is, pressure from wind. Any ice field under pressure can bring all but the most powerful icebreakers to a halt. Once the wind abates, however, normal navigation is resumed. Where ice fields are extensive, the helicopter would be on patrol at intervals of two or three hours. Knowing where the thicker, more difficult ice is allows the ship to take the "path of least resistance" through the field.

Weather conditions in the Arctic are generally good during the summer, with constant daylight or at least twilight. There is, however, occasional fog and the possibility of whiteout, when an overcast sky and the snow merge without any discernible horizon. This is extremely dangerous when flying without the appropriate instruments, and, according to Jones, particularly unpleasant because "once you lose your horizon and can't see the ground, vertigo tends to take over. So you do everything possible to avoid such circumstances."

On board ship, the helicopter is stored in a telescoping hangar extended by means of cables operating a rack and pinion on each side of the hangar. In other words, the hangar can be extended to cover the helicopter when it is on its landing area on the deck, then retracted for take-off. This is a tremendous improvement over working on an exposed flight deck as had been the case earlier. The structure provides an excellent working space for the engineer, as Ian Duncan recalls: "You've got steam heat in the hangar and we had our own compressed air system for cleaning parts or whatever you wanted to do. We also had our own facilities on board. When we first started all we had was barrels, 45-gallon [205-*l*] drums, which was a dangerous situation. With the addition of the hangar, there were always two seamen assigned to the engineer to help out on the flight deck – such as getting the machine in and out."

On occasion, though, the combination of a warm hangar and a machine in which vital components were exposed could result in potentially serious problems. Once again in Ian's words: "The only trouble we did have was going ashore to one of these bases. You'd take the aircraft out of this heated hangar, and if there was any water in any part of the lower cables, like your throttle, just as soon as you got airborne this water would freeze. On this occasion the throttle froze. We got ashore okay and we stayed at the base for about half an hour. But when we came out we still couldn't move the throttle. The only way I could thaw it out was to get a little propane torch and just lightly dust it over the cable."

The Bell helicopters used on board the ships were much like their commercial counterparts with an open latticework tail boom and exposed engine, fuel tanks and tail-rotor shaft. The main difference was the amount of radio equipment carried. Compared to most helicopters in use today, the G2 was less than sophisticated. According to Bob Jones, "The Bell 47-G2 was the last machine which you were literally flying by the seat of your pants – because there was no slip or drift indicator, your 'seat' told you if you were flying correctly. Fixed-wing instructors always said to keep your nose on the horizon. Try doing that while enclosed in a plastic bubble." Despite its limitations, the 47-G2 was for several years the Coast Guard workhorse.

A typical day for the helicopter crew would, in addition to the ice patrol, involve transporting personnel to shore – it was faster and less dangerous to do it with the helicopter. The icebreaker carried a doctor who would go ashore to visit facilities and settlements as part of the routine health service. He would even extract teeth if necessary. In addition to these routine duties, the helicopter crew would on occasion assist Inuit who had experienced difficulties. Bob Jones recalls one such incident:

Working among Eskimos for many years with the eastern and western Arctic Patrols, one finds that they have many distinctive characteristics. Generally a happy people, they rarely go into shock, and

Pilots had to exercise care when landing on floating ice because the weight of the helicopter could cause the ice to roll over without warning—or, on larger areas of decaying ice, the helicopter could break through the jagged ice, slashing the floats. This Bell G2 had canvas covers to protect the floats.

CANADIAN COAST GUARD PHOTOS

Canadian Coast Guard Bell 47-G2s carried considerably more radio equipment than their commercial counterparts. Bob Jones is at the controls in this 1960s photo.

Fuel for generators and heating plants could be moved quickly and easily by helicopters. Pads were built at lighthouses in the 1960s.

Pad-equipped Canadian Coast Guard ice breakers have telescoping hangars to protect their helicopters. With the hangar folded, there is sufficient space on the pad for the helicopter to land. The hangar can then be extended aft over the helicopter to permit maintenance and protect it from the weather.   D. N. PARKER

This Bell 212, with its considerable lifting and passenger capacity, has been one of the most useful aircraft in the B.C. Coast Guard inventory. Pouring concrete using a 212 might seem to be overdoing things, but in remote locations, it is more efficient to do it this way.

CCG PHOTOS

The Aerospatiale Alouette III served the Canadian Coast Guard well from the late 1960s to the mid-1980s, when it was replaced by the MBB BO-105 CBS.

R. D. TURNER

This MBB BO-105 CBS is shown being pre-flighted.

D. N. PARKER PHOTOS

The Canadian Coast Guard S-61 was photographed at Victoria International Airport in the mid-1970s. This large machine, the replacement for the one lost at Triple Island, is based at Prince Rupert. In the late 1990s, it was re-painted in the red livery and equipped with a rescue hoist.

adversity is accepted as a normal part of life. An example of the latter occurred in 1972 when on patrol in the Rasmussen Basin. It was a bad ice year, the thaw late in coming, and the winter ice extended almost shore-to-shore. We had a message from the settlement of Gjoa Haven on King William Island asking us to look out for one of their boats that had not been heard from for some time. Eleven people were on board, including a woman, a child and some young boys.

I took off in the helicopter and started searching in the area southwest of Gjoa Haven. After some time, we spotted the boat in a vast expanse of ice, looking like a black speck on a white sheet. As we approached, there was no sign of life, and we could see that the boat was heeled over at a bad angle. The vessel had been crushed and lifted out on the ice. Indications were that the party had camped on the ice but there was no sign of anyone now, nor as to what direction they had taken. A search of the closest shoreline drew a blank, so we headed for Godd Island, which seemed to be the next logical point to head for. This time, we hit the jackpot, locating the Eskimos with another Eskimo family.

The men of the party were still out on the ice dragging a canoe loaded with rifles, nets, an outboard motor and other supplies. Locating them with the helicopter, I flew the supplies back to the island, leaving them only the canoe. When I asked one of them if they wanted transportation back to Gjoa Haven, he seemed surprised and said that they had left home to fish, and fish they intended to do. He pointed out that they had the canoe, outboard and nets. I asked if they needed any help, and he suggested that they could use a little food to last them until they caught their first fish, so the ship gladly supplied some basic goodies for them. As I flew away, these resourceful people waved and smiled, and it occurred to me that had these been "civilized" folk, what a story of heroism and survival would have blazed across the front pages of newspapers!

Des O'Halloran at the controls of a Canadian Coast Guard Bell 47-G2.

While landings on board ship were fairly simple up north because the water was almost invariably calm, down south on the British Columbia coast they could prove interesting. It was generally easier to land while the ship was underway because it was possible to predict its motion. If the ship were at anchor, particularly in shallow water, it could roll from side to side, making a landing more difficult. Ivor Roberts explains the difficulty: "We did land under quite difficult conditions that made the ship pitch; it also rolled a little bit. How much roll you could handle was limited by the amount of lateral control you could maintain with your cyclic column because you were trying to keep the aircraft level. You'd touch one float down and then bring the other one down."

After 1961, the Coast Guard constructed a large number of helipads to service navigational aids with greater efficiency and safety. While using a helicopter for construction work did save considerable time over more conventional methods, it could prove extremely tiring for the pilot. This was especially true when a helicopter with a small payload, such as the G2, was used. Ivor Roberts did a great deal of construction work:

We built a helipad on Solander Island, on a little knoll about 300 feet [90 m] high with very limited space on which to land. Weather conditions were not good at times and it was difficult keeping the ship level. One day, though, when we did have reasonably good conditions, I can remember being up and down all day. I made non-stop trips up and down, so many men, so much material, water, food, and buckets of gravel and cement. The helicopter would act as a flying crane, placing materials exactly where needed.

When it was introduced into Canadian Coast Guard service in 1966, the Alouette III was a great improvement over the G2. It had more than twice the power, 800 shp derated to 550 shp, as opposed to the 200 hp of the G2's Lycoming. Apart from the improvement in performance, the Alouette had a greater passenger capacity, sometimes carrying up to six people.

While maintenance on Coast Guard helicopters is first class, things can occasionally go wrong. As with any complex machine, it can be difficult to diagnose the problems. Ian Duncan and pilot Doug Callen were returning home on one occasion, flying south from Cape Scott down the east coast of Vancouver Island. The Alouette experienced engine trouble and they put down in Port Hardy, near the northern tip of the island. Changing some parts, they continued south until the helicopter once again began having problems, this time near Campbell River. Ian changed one or two more components. With the problem apparently solved, they once again headed south. A few miles past Nanaimo, near Ladysmith, Ian heard the engine change its tone. He asked Doug if he'd heard the change, and got an affirmative answer, so they agreed that it would be a good idea to land–quickly. "He went down on the collective; the rpm didn't change, and then it started to get erratic and he couldn't control it. So he sort of half-power on, half-power off–he more or less autorotated–and landed on this point of land. Doug's face was white, and I guess mine was too; but we got it down right side up and changed some parts."

The next day Duncan and Ivor Roberts flew back to Victoria in another Alouette which had taken the spare parts up to Ladysmith. Bob Jones and the chief engineer, Sam Sirna, came back in the repaired machine. "So we took off together and we just followed behind them, and Jonesy came on the air. I remember he said, 'Well, we're okay now fellows; you go on in and land, if you want; we'll be right behind you.' So we went on and landed and saw this old girl come over the fence and it was just going to land when the engine failed again–just quit dead. He [Bob Jones] was about five feet off the ground and he just autorotated down and landed safely."

The defect was to remain a mystery, at least to the people concerned. The engine was returned to the manufacturer and no word was ever received, or at least passed on, as to what the problem was.

In January 1972, Coast Guard Sikorsky S-61N, CF-CGF, which had replaced the S-62 with the Prince Rupert agency in the late 1960s, experienced mechanical problems on a flight north from the lower mainland with 10 people on board. Ice had been ingested by the engines due to the absence of a shield. The pilot was able to make an emergency landing on Triple Island in Hecate Strait. The people were rescued and plans were made to recover the large aircraft. It was situated too far from the shore to be retrieved by means of a barge and crane, so a decision was made to bring it out by air.

A Canadian Forces Labrador from 442 Squadron at Comox, the only machine available with the necessary capacity, was pressed into service. With everything possible removed from the Sikorsky to reduce weight—engines, rotor, instrumentation and radios—the recovery operation went ahead. The wind increased in velocity and the stripped helicopter fuselage suspended below the Labrador began to "fly" on its own. The Labrador pilot had no alternative but to punch it off. The S-61 was written off and replaced in 1973. The replacement, also an S-61, was equipped for instrument flying (IFR) capability.

As had happened earlier, rumours abounded, and were denied, that the Coast Guard Air Service would be undertaking some responsibility for rescue. While Coast Guard hovercraft and cutters do have a vital role to play, the Air Service does not include search and rescue among its responsibilities, although the Rescue Coordination Centre has on occasion requested the assistance of its machines. The air service is almost exclusively concerned with the maintenance of aids to navigation. Nevertheless, the locations of Coast Guard helicopters are known at all times should an emergency occur in their vicinity; and, by the late 1990s, the Prince Rupert S-61 was equipped with a rescue hoist and the engineer trained to operate it just in case. Despite all, because its name is similar to that of the rescue-oriented United States Coast Guard, the Canadian Coast Guard has, in the public's mind, also been linked with search and rescue.

In addition to its tasks on coastal waters, the Coast Guard services navigation aids, all of which are unmanned automatic facilities, on northern inland waters using Victoria-based aircraft and aircrew. The entire Mackenzie River, from its source to its mouth, is marked. The Bell 212, a twin-engined development of the 205 produced for the Canadian Armed Forces, and designated by them as the CUH-1N, carries out the medium-lift assignments, usually working the Mackenzie River and Great Bear and Great Slave lakes during the early part of the season. Well liked by its crews, the Bell 212 has more power and capacity than the Alouette, as well as a much greater range. In Coast Guard configuration, it can carry nine passengers: five forward and four facing each other. The normal commercial configuration can generally carry four more passengers in space taken by extra auxiliary tanks on the Coast Guard machine. With

The new icebreaker
Sir Wilfrid Laurier is shown
in the background, along with
the Canadian Coast Guard base
in Victoria. The Helijet pad
at Camel Point is in the
foreground.

the Coast Guard 212, it is possible to carry three or four technicians, with their tools, equipment and supplies, to service three or four lights on one trip.

New ice breakers, including the *Sir Wilfred Laurier*, entered into service with the Canadian Coast Guard by the late 1980s. To complete the modernization, at least from the perspective of transportation, a new helicopter was chosen: the MBB Helicopter Canada BO 105 CBS, 16 examples of which were purchased for the Coast Guard, and were all delivered by early May 1988. The MBB plant in Fort Erie, Ontario, had only opened in mid-1986. The 105, which is powered by two Allison C28C turboshaft engines, has a range of 320 miles (515 km). Three of these new machines were assigned to Victoria and a fourth to Prince Rupert. One of the Victoria-based machines accompanies the icebreaker on its supply trip north.

In the late 1990s, Fisheries and Oceans Canada–the Coast Guard was no longer part of Transport Canada–decided to do away with manned aids to navigation. Conventional lighthouses are being progressively replaced with automated devices. However, air services have not been affected because the remaining manned lighthouses have to be serviced, as do the automated ones, and they have been able to continue with their very necessary work as before.

IN RETROSPECT

Immediately after the Second World War, when helicopters began to appear in public, the media, egged on by the manufacturers, extolled them as the ultimate vehicle. They could rise vertically (everyone assumed with a full load), hover motionless, move sideways or even backwards–there was nothing a helicopter couldn't do and confident predictions were made that within a few years there would be a helicopter in every carport. Yet in 1947, when the helicopter was first introduced into British Columbia, the technology was in its infancy as were the techniques for flying the new aircraft. It lacked the performance to achieve what the dreamers expected of it and, given both its virtues and its shortcomings, operators lacked the experience to market it effectively. Consequently helicopter operators had to develop techniques to overcome the myth of a helicopter's potential, and replace the myth with realistic expectations.

A Sikorsky S-76A of Okanagan Helicopters (now Canadian Helicopters) in the early 1980s.

OKANAGAN HELICOPTERS

Experimentation was the answer. Companies like Okanagan and individuals like Carl Agar, who risked his life to develop mountain flying techniques, made British Columbia one of the most significant regions for helicopter use in the world. Potentially useful roles for the helicopter that didn't work out–crop dusting was found to be infeasible at least in the Okanagan–were quickly discarded; while others, such as search and rescue, forest fire fighting and power-line construction, were further developed.

As helicopter operations expanded, new equipment, much of it developed in British Columbia, was introduced: Monzoon buckets for forest fire suppression, drip torches for slash burning and camera booms for forest inventory and evaluation. Helicopters were, by the mid-1970s, pulling old growth logs off otherwise inaccessible sidehills; transporting foresters, geologists, surveyors and biologists to worksites; maintaining aids to coastal navigation; carrying out search and rescue and medical evacuation missions; and acting as flying cranes in construction and industry.

The future may well see the start of offshore drill rig resupply operations like those on the east and Arctic coasts, an increase in the amount and scope of military flying and probably greater use of helicopters by corporations and the media. A scheduled intercity helicopter shuttle service seems likely to remain economically impractical for some time; and the other dreams of the forties—a helicopter in every garage, for example—never will materialize because of the complexity and cost of the technology (can you imagine the accident rate in crowded city skies if the average driver could move not only forward and backward but also up, down and sideways?).

Helicopters have by now assumed an important role worldwide. In British Columbia particularly, with its rugged terrain and vast distances, their contributions and those of the people who have operated them have been particularly outstanding. But perhaps the most persuasive evidence that helicopters have arrived was provided recently when a charter launch sank in Hecate Strait, just south of the Queen Charlotte Islands. Twenty people abandoned the launch and took to two rubber dinghies. Four hours later, bobbing around in 20-foot (6-m) waves, they were winched up into Canadian and US Coast Guard helicopters. The media, on this occasion, made very little comment about the helicopters; they had come to be accepted as run-of-the-mill rescue vehicles. The magic may have faded from the public consciousness but the value, in a case like this, is practically beyond measure.

Those were our predictions at the end of the first edition. Some have been realized; others we failed to foresee; and in one case we were wrong, i.e., in our pessimism about the future of a scheduled passenger service.

In the 1960s, the City of Victoria was bullish about a helicopter service between Victoria and Vancouver. It provided $35,000 for construction of a heli-pad a mile or so west of downtown, the land for which had been set aside in 1955. While used occasionally, there was no regular service until, in the late 1970s, Okanagan Helicopters made what appeared to be a token gesture: a Sikorsky S-61 made a single flight to the helipad with a load of politicians aboard, but this led nowhere and Okanagan announced in 1979 that it was no longer considering this service. Two years later, Southcoast Airways Ltd. of Vancouver made an attempt to start a service, but it, too abandoned the initiative.

The main problem was that any helicopter service would have to compete with the established scheduled fixed-wing carriers, notably Air West, which was then providing a floatplane service harbour to harbour. Fixed-wing operating expenses were considerably lower than an equivalent helicopter service. However, an important consideration in this equation was weather: frequent fog, high winds and often heavy rain handicapped float-planes because they had to land on the harbours without electronic

This Okanagan S-61 made a trial flight to the Songhees helipad in Victoria in the late 1970s in order to "test" the feasibility of intercity helicopter service. The photographer was "flattened" by the downwash.

D. N. PARKER

approach and landing aids. Fully instrumented, all-weather helicopters, on the other hand, could use lighted pads on land or, in Vancouver, on a barge anchored to the shore–both equipped with approach and landing aids.

Danny Sitnam and his two partners, of WM Aviation, came to this conclusion and, at the same time, realized the possibilities of a viable passenger density because the seat of government is in Victoria while the much larger industrial and commercial resources are in Vancouver. Consequently, there should be a viable market for both government officials and business people wishing to meet, using a reliable, virtually all-weather service from downtown to downtown.

WM Aviation tested the idea in June 1984 with this Dauphin. Their efforts resulted in success within two years.

D. N. PARKER

Sitnam and his partners announced in late July 1986 that a six-month trial for the intercity service, to be called Helijet, would commence in October. The service started with 14-passenger Bell 412s. Bases were established in both cities, the Victoria pad adjacent to the James Bay Anglers' boat ramp at Camel Point, and the Vancouver one on a barge anchored on Coal Harbour, just east of the foot of Burrard Street–so this was very much a downtown to downtown service. While there have been no problems at the Vancouver end, the Victoria base is close to residential buildings–mainly condominiums–and noise has been a contentious issue ever since. The replacement of the Bell 412s with quieter Sikorsky S-76s and a different approach pattern helped. In 1992, however, Helijet was still attempting to reduce the volume by building an earthen "berm."

By August 1987, three of the 13-passenger S-76s were operating. Flights were increased from 8 to 12 a day at that time, starting at 7:00 a.m. with the last flight at 7:30 p.m. In addition, a 7-times-a-day round-trip connection to Vancouver International Airport commenced. An attempt to expand the service into Whistler, the ski resort 70 miles (110 km) north of Vancouver, proved unsuccessful, perhaps because Whistler offers no LORAN blind-approach system to permit all-weather operations.

Helijet expanded its activities by purchasing Vancouver Helicopters, a company that had steady contract work for its fleet of six aircraft when it was taken over: traffic reports for local radio, pipeline patrols and an exclusive service to Grouse Mountain, a ski slope on Vancouver's north shore, among others. Finally, a service to Seattle, with one of the S-76s painted in a livery to honour the Mariners, is a feature of Helijet's highly successful operation. Those cynical about the company's prospects in 1986, and we were among them, were wrong.

Another development that was in its infancy when we last wrote was a helicopter ambulance service. Medical evacuation has, from their earliest use, been a role assigned

The Royal Canadian Mounted Police acquired their first helicopter on the west coast, a Bell 206 Jet Ranger, in September 1973. Tom Vickers is shown at the controls over Victoria.

JIM RYAN PHOTO, BCARS

Since 1994, the B.C. Ambulance Service has been using the Bell 222-UT, owned and operated by Vancouver Island Helicopters. Air ambulances operate in conjunction with standard road ambulances. This 222 is shown at Shaunessy Hospital loading an incubator.

D. N. PARKER

to helicopters; and, with the development of emergency pre-hospital care, their use has expanded beyond *ad hoc* transportation of victims. The British Columbia Ambulance Service was created in 1974 to provide the same level of emergency pre-hospital care to all citizens of the province regardless of where they lived. This included regions where roads were inadequate or even non-existent, thus making both surface and often fixed-wing air transportation difficult. While helicopters could be and were chartered to transport patients, often they were not well suited for this purpose. Paramedics were under severe space constraints with equipment to monitor the patients; bulky oxygen tanks in particular took up considerable room in the small cabins. If something went wrong during a flight, it was difficult to provide necessary care. Changes were needed.

Bell 222U
MODEL
ROTORCRAFT
FLIGHT MANUAL

In November 1988, Vancouver Island Helicopters was contracted to provide helicopter ambulance service to the Queen Charlotte Islands and into north and central B.C. from Prince Rupert. The first aircraft employed was a Bell 212, which conformed to the 2-2-2 formula demanded by the BCAS: two engines-two patients-two paramedics. The 212 began service on New Years Day, 1989, and proved successful enough even though VIH was not happy with it. It was noisy—a problem when a hospital was near the centre of a community; it was also comparatively slow and its capacity to carry medical equipment such as an installed oxygen system was compromised by the necessity for an auxiliary fuel tank in the cabin to increase range. The search for a replacement turned up a Bell 222A, which was soon in service. It performed well, but VIH felt that the more powerful 222-UT, with lighter skid gear, as opposed to the A's heavy retractable gear, would be a significant advantage. With some effort, affordable 222-UTs were acquired and, after considerable study with input from air paramedics, a conversion was developed that turned the standard 222-UT into a true advance life support, airborne ambulance. Refinements, such as the design of an "Easy-loader" device intended to prevent back injuries to the medevacs, have also been successful and both that and the overall ambulance conversion have resulted in sales for VIH.

By 1994, the British Columbia Ambulance Service, with four 222-UTs under contract, could provide 24-hour advanced life support medical service to citizens regardless of their location.

The Canadian Navy's use of helicopters was mentioned briefly in our previous effort: VU-33 Squadron operated three HUP helicopters on the west coast, but did not deploy any of them to its ships. In fact, the earliest operational use of helicopters was a long way from B.C., on board German navy ships during the Second World War. The Kolibri,

"Hummingbird" proved highly successful in an observation role when it was pressed into service. For the Germans, it was too little too late, but it did demonstrate just how much the effectiveness of surface units could be enhanced by the use of shipborne helicopters.

Serious consideration was not given to operating shipboard helicopters on the Pacific Coast until the mid-1980s, when the increasing importance of the Pacific Rim led to an upgrading of naval forces on the west coast. Then, more modern and more capable ships were transferred to Maritime Command Pacific: vessels capable of operating helicopters. Developed versions of the 1950s 205 class destroyer escorts, such as the *Annapolis* and the *Nipigon*, and the newer, larger 280 or "Tribal" class ships, soon appeared on the west coast; the former class could host a single helicopter, and the latter two.

In July 1989, 443 Squadron moved to the west coast and now makes its home at Victoria International Airport near facilities once used by VU-33 and VC-922 squadrons. Now, 443 Squadron can provide Maritime Command Pacific with three

A 443 (MH) Squadron CH-124A Sea King photographed in August 1998 at Victoria.

D. N. PARKER

detachments of aircrew and five aircraft when needed. The Sikorsky Sea Kings, which have been in service with the Canadian Navy since the early 1960s, are all-weather and night capable and can be safely winched down on board ship using the Canadian-developed Bear Trap. Crew for the Sea King consists of a pilot, co-pilot, navigator (tactical coordinator) and an airborne electronic sensor operator. The latter two crew-persons are trained in the use of the Breeze hoist, horse collar and Billy Pugh rescue net for search and rescue. The primary role of the squadron, redesignated 443 (Maritime Helicopter) in 1995, remains anti-submarine but with changes in the political and social climate at home, 443 has become more involved in sovereignty surveillance, fisheries, occasional search and rescue, and to support the "civil power"–the RCMP.

The Royal Canadian Mounted Police have, since before the Second World War, operated their own aircraft, such as the de Havilland Dragon Rapide, the amphibious Grumman Goose and various floatplanes, to get around British Columbia. This was especially the case in circumstances where speed was important, such as transporting forensic personnel or evidence for laboratory analysis, or taking part in searches. Helicopters joined the fleet in the 1970s, gradually replacing fixed-wing aircraft, and the number of helicopters in service has increased to nine in Canada. RCMP Bell 206s have been based at Victoria, Comox and Kelowna. In 1998, according to helicopter publications, serious consideration is being given to replacing the 206s with the new Bell 427 or Eurocopter Twin Stars, or other possible contenders.

Finally, one aspect we didn't consider previously was the use of helicopters for recreational purposes: heli-skiing and heli-hiking. In 1985, heli-skiing, which meant lifting skiers up into usually remote mountain areas, was regarded merely as a way to provide some work for otherwise idle helicopters in the slow winter months. Since then, it has blossomed into a significant and prosperous business. Large, luxurious lodges have sprung up all over the province and skiers from all over the world come to enjoy the uniqueness of gliding down very long slopes on genuinely virgin powder snow. While heli-hiking has not expanded to the same extent, the ability to be set down well back in the mountains to hike the ridges and alpine meadows before being picked up at the end of the day, is growing in popularity.

No doubt other uses have been and will be found. Meanwhile, the helicopter has long passed the magic toy stage; its versatility is still being exploited.

Triangulation often meant a brutal hike up a mountain, but the view was a definite bonus when you reached the top–if you weren't too tired to appreciate it. Helicopters revolutionized surveying, decreasing time and definitely fatigue. Often a pilot would help out, in part to pass the time.

A Bell 47-J2, in the Okanagan colours of the late 1950s. This model was originally designed as an executive transport version of the standard 47-G2 and did not work out well in the bush.

An Okanagan Bell 47-G2 transporting materials for the construction of a forest fire lookout tower on Mount Artaban, May 1959.

In the early 1960s, Sikorsky was promoting their new S-62, the commercial version of the US Coast Guard HH-52A. Alf and Lynn Stringer are in the foreground.

ALF STRINGER

There was an attempt in the 1950s to introduce the British Bristol Sycamore in Canada. Okanagan evaluated it but did not place an order. The faired-in fuselage and long, drooping main-rotor blades did not seem practical in the bush.

ALF STRINGER

A Bell 47-G3B-1 shown in 1974 hoisting high-value cedar blocks, later to be split into roofing shakes.

The late 1950s was a very busy period for Okanagan. These Bell 47s and the S-55s in the background–in RCAF red, white and blue–would soon be out earning money.

A Sikorsky S-64 high above Khutzeymateen Inlet. The base for this "show" is the barge, centre right.

BC MINISTRY OF FORESTS

Okanagan's first S-55 coming in for a landing. Okanagan was very fortunate in being able to acquire these large machines for the Kemano project. During the Korea conflict, priority was given to military rather than commercial orders.

ALF STRINGER

This Boise-Cascade-owned Sikorsky SH-3 was leased by Okanagan for heli-logging trials in the 1970s. It has been de-navalized for use in logging. A "land" undercarriage has replaced the naval floats to reduce weight.

BC MINISTRY OF FORESTS

An Okanagan Bell 206 Jet Ranger at work with a drip-torch in the Nelson district, 1976.

This immaculate Eurocopter Astar is shown on a typical job, transporting fuel drums. Helicopters of European origin have become increasingly numerous in North America.

It is every bit as close as it looks. Cone collecting for silvaculture.

BC MINISTRY OF FORESTS

The Bell 206 Jet Ranger series of helicopters are the workhorses of the industry. They are in use with commercial operators of all sizes, the military and even the police. As with earlier machines, the 206 is equipped with skids rather than wheels, making it possible to land on uneven ground.

G. CORLEY-SMITH

Equipped with a belly tank, this Frontier Bell 205 is approaching McNaughton Lake to refill its tank in August 1981. This operation is accomplished from the hover: water is pumped through the pipe to the tank. The tank has bomb-bay doors and the amount of water dropped can be regulated.

R. J. CHALLENGER,
BC MINISTRY OF FORESTS

A portable lake. This Frontier company Bell 205 is filling its Monzoon bucket from a "dam." Unlike a lake, the dam is portable.

D. WOODALE PHOTO, BC MINISTRY OF FORESTS

On July 27, 1992, a major brush fire broke out on Victoria's Mount Douglas. Aerial attack using both fixed-wing tankers and helicopters with Monzoon buckets proved necessary.

JOHN McKAY PHOTO, TIMES-COLONIST

Two liveries: the Alouette in the foreground displays the 1960s Canadian Coast Guard colours; the Bell 212 in the background is in the 1980s colours and has a decided SAR look to it.

A Helijet Airways Sikorsky S-76A lands at Victoria's Camel Point heliport.

British Columbia had its first dedicated helicopter ambulance in January 1989. Vancouver Island Helicopters put this Bell 212 – a twin-engine development of the 205 – into service in Prince Rupert to provide air evacuation service for the northern part of the province and the Queen Charlotte Islands. Before long it was replaced by a Bell 222A, and then a 222-UT. The 212 proved too slow, too noisy and too short-ranged.

BRIAN MYCROFT

This photo shows the enlarged fuel tanks to advantage. "Night Sun" is installed, but 113301 still lacks weather radar.

The Sikorsky CH-124A Sea King has been the standard Canadian shipboard helicopter since the early 1960s, and is due for replacement. In this 1980s vintage photo the Sea King has deployed its "dipping" variable-depth sonar. The livery of this aircraft as depicted is quite different from its late 1990s appearance, which is much darker with low visibility markings.

The United States Coast Guard replaced its ageing HH-52As
with the French-designed Dauphin, renaming it the Dolphin.

USCG

The Kamov KA-32's coaxial rotors swing impressive vapour trails in their wake. Both the Kamov and the Kaman have no tail rotor and so all the power available is provided to the main rotors and manoeuvrability is improved at the same time.

VANCOUVER ISLAND HELICOPTERS

The Kaman K-Max, with that manufacturer's characteristic intermeshing rotor system, is the latest helicopter introduced into B.C. heli-logging. Unusually, for a logging helicopter, it has only one pilot.

KAMAN

An advertising photographer's dream? The Bell 412 at the end of the rainbow. An Alpine Helicopters Bell 412, the penultimate stage in the development of the 204 – twin turbines and a four-bladed main rotor.

Eco-tourism in the 1990s, an important part of business for the helicopter industry: hiking in summer and heli-skiing in winter.

The federal government announced in January 1998 that EH Industries had won the contract for the new
Canadian Armed Forces Search and Rescue helicopter: the "Cormorant." This artist's impression of the large,
3-engined helicopter shows how it will look in Canadian Forces Search and Rescue colours.

AUGUSTA-WESTLAND

In the first edition of this book, we left the impression that Carl Agar was the one and only pioneer of helicopter mountain flying. However, additional research has revealed that four other pilots besides Carl Agar had begun to tackle the mountains at the same time as he did.

The first venture, early in August 1947, was by Carl Brady and Vern Montgomery, two pilots with Central Airways. Brady was Agar's instructor in Yakima, WA, and this attempted rescue took place just as Agar and Alf Stringer were returning from Yakima to Penticton with their first helicopter, a Bell 47B-3, CF-FZX.

George Williamson, who participated in a Luscombe (a 65-hp floatplane), describes what happened in a March/April 1998 article in *West Coast Aviator*. A group of climbers had fallen on Mount Waddington, the highest peak in B.C. One climber had been killed and another injured and, because of the area's remoteness, a helicopter seemed the answer to rescue the injured climber.

As it turned out, Brady and Montgomery could contribute little to the actual rescue, but they did land at the 4,000-foot (1 200-m) level of the Tiedemann Glacier–considered the uppermost limit for safety at the time. They flew two very experienced mountaineers, Neil Carter and Don Munday; the former was president of the Alpine Club of Canada, and the latter, with his wife, Phyllis, had pioneered routes to Mount Waddington since the 1920s.

Brady flew Don Munday up the glacier first, landing while he could still hover in ground effect. Dropping him at the 4,000-foot (1 200-m) level, he took Munday's pack another mile up the glacier. Montgomery then did the same with Neil Carter.

These certainly seem to qualify as the first mountain landings, and the Bell 47-B, NC 11H, as the first commercial helicopter to operate in British Columbia. In an interview, George Williamson reveals another first. He had cut out a landing pad for the helicopter at the head of Bute Inlet, by a slough just south of the mouth of the Homathko River, and cleaned out an abandoned cabin for accommodation. The only thing lacking was water–the slough was more than brackish. Fortunately, there was a trapper in a cabin nearby who did have fresh stream water, and he came by with two buckets of water. The next day, he came without the water and obviously in considerable distress. While putting a new cedar-shake roof on his cabin, he had slipped, put his hand down to save himself, and driven a large splinter, as thick as the lead of a pencil, right through the pad of his index finger. The pilots decided to operate. They gave the trapper half a tumbler of whisky, dipped his finger in a cup of the same beverage and pulled the splinter out with needle-nose pliers.

As George commented, "There was blood all over the place and we decided to get him to a logging camp across the inlet where they had a first-aid attendant. Brady flew him across and I guess this qualified as the first helicopter mercy flight in B.C. as well."

Another American pilot followed this with a much more impressive performance. In March 1948, he began to fly the first "experimental contract with the [U.S.] Department of the Interior [to] establish the feasibility of utilizing helicopters to transport personnel in geological survey work." The operation lasted from March 9 to March 15, and the results seem to have been remarkably successful. The venue was the Colorado mountains. The contract was with the Fabick Aircraft Company, St. Louis, Missouri; the helicopter was a Bell 47-B, and the pilot was Robert Angstadt.

Based at the Royal Gorge Airport, seven miles (11 km) northwest of Canon City, Colorado, elevation 6,320 feet (1 930 m), the helicopter carried one passenger and equipment with a total weight of 185-225 pounds (84-102 kg). Fuel was kept to the minimum and, while the first landings and take-offs were made at what are described as the lower altitudes of 7,000 to 8,000 feet (2 150-2 440 m), one landing was made at a density altitude of 11,000 feet, or 10,200 feet above sea level (3 350-3 110 m), but this time without a passenger. The optimum wind speed for these landings and take-offs was between 10 and 20 mph (16-32 km/h). Less than 10 meant insufficient lift; more than 20 introduced unacceptable turbulence (leaving a very narrow operating window for a longer project). The report, which is undated, was written by J. S. Dunne of the Bell Aircraft Corporation and, presumably, put things in the best possible light.

Finally, a Canadian pilot, Al Soutar, flying for Photographic Surveys Limited, part of the Kenting organization, was pushing into the mountains in July 1948. He was on a contract with the Dominion Geodetic Survey along the Alaska Highway in the Watson Lake-Teslin area of the Yukon. This was a well-financed operation: the helicopter was loaded into "a truck-hangar" and moved by rail to Dawson Creek before taking to the road. The truck-hangar housed, besides the helicopter, "a full machine shop."

While Soutar reported a successful operation of 210 flying

Carl Brady and Don Munday on Tiedemann Glacier, Mount Waddington, August 1947.

Carl Brady, Neil Carter and Vern Montgomery at the head of Bute Inlet, August 1947.

hours, hampered by bad weather, F. B. Steers, of the Geodetic Survey, was rather less than enthusiastic: he concluded that the operation was not a success, "due to extremely unfavourable weather and the very limited payload of the helicopter above 4,000 feet [1 200 m]." He ended by commenting that, "It was found last summer that a mobile maintenance unit mounted on a truck was practically indispensable. This presented no problem along the Alaska Highway, but would prove to be an almost insurmountable obstacle in areas where roads were non-existent." Soon, however, helicopter operators proved that this was an easily surmountable obstacle.

Al Soutar was the first Canadian helicopter pilot to fly commercially in Canada, operating a Bell 47-B3 for the Kenting organization in southern Ontario in March 1947. He went on to a long and successful career in the industry.

A little reminiscent of a flying bedstead, FZX drops down for a landing.

VERNON MUSEUM AND ARCHIVES

History of Helicopter Development

With the first successful flights of their "Flyer" in December 1903, the Wright brothers at last proved that powered, heavier-than-air flight was possible, and potentially at least, practical. But their solution to the problem of flight–the airplane–still did not entirely fulfill the dreams of visionaries and experimenters of preceding centuries. The hope, and indeed the expectation, of these early aviation enthusiasts had been that man would someday be able to control his movements in the air just as he could on land or at sea. The conventional airplane–one that needs forward momentum to fly–can neither take off nor descend vertically, nor can it hover. However, the elements of a machine that can–the helicopter–have existed for centuries.

Evidence exists from as early as the fourth century BC of a helicopter-like toy in use in China. It was a simple device. A short rod or stick was surmounted by a cork into which four feathers were inserted, each placed at right angles to its neighbour and "canted" or raised along one edge. When the shaft was twirled, the toy would rise high into the air. As further proof of their antiquity, similar toys have appeared with children in paintings dating from the fifteenth century, and similar types are in use today. As has been true throughout history, one idea or invention led to another.

Archimedes, the Greek mathematician, physicist and theorist of the second century BC, developed a machine which inspired the fifteenth-century artist and engineer Leonardo da Vinci to design a helicopter. Archimedes produced a type of screw which, enclosed in a tube and turned with sufficient speed, would raise water, a duty it has performed to the present day. These devices irrigate agricultural land in the Middle East. Da Vinci correctly deduced that air reacted like water, and the screw device developed by Archimedes would therefore logically be able to make its way through air as well. Necessary conditions were that the tube enclosing the screw was removed and the speed of rotation increased to compensate for the lesser density of air. Da Vinci's design for a helicopter or "helix," as it has been called by others, appeared in a 1505 manuscript. He wrote that

[i]f the instrument made with a screw be well made–that is to say of linen of which the pores are stopped up with starch–the said screw will make its spiral in the air and it will rise high. [He went on to explain that] when force generates swifter movement than the surrounding air, the air becomes compressed after the manner of feathers by a sleeper. And the thing which drove the air, finding resistance in it rebounds after the manner of a bell struck.[1]

No indication is given as to a power source. Probably da Vinci was simply testing the theory of a screw operating in air. It is uncertain whether or not he actually flew a model. Power was to remain a problem in flying until an engine was designed that was both light and powerful. However, the famous scientist did not view this as a problem. In the case of at least the majority of his flying machines, he believed that man, with his great strength compared to that of birds, would be able to fly with ease if only he were provided with a suitable machine; but he had misunderstood the manner and means by which birds fly. These principles were not understood until, in 1670, Giovanni Alfonso Borelli produced a book entitled De Moto Animalum, in which he proved that man's power-to-weight ratio was insufficient for flight. In short, he demonstrated that man was both too weak and too heavy, and lacked the appropriate muscles to enable him to fly. Inevitably, this realization limited experimentation.

The only successful investigation undertaken with helicopters until the 20th century was carried out with models. They could be powered easily in reduced scale, but the springs or bow strings used hardly would have been practical for full-sized machines.

Nevertheless, experimenters persisted. In 1754, Mikhail Lomonosov, known today within the Soviet Union as the "Father of Russian Science," demonstrated a helicopter device in model form that he had designed and built, before the Russian Academy of Sciences, the most prestigious body of its kind in 18th-century Russia. Called an "Aerodynamic" by Lomonosov, it was "to be used for the purpose of depressing the air by means of wings rotated horizontally in the opposite directions by the agency of a spring of the type used in clocks in order to lift the machine into the upper layers of the air."[2] The model was intended primarily to carry test materials aloft in the course of other experiments. Scientists, however, who had become interested in the helicopter as such, foresaw a different application.

In 1768, a Frenchman, J. P. Paucton, in his *Theorie de la Vis D'Archimedes*, described a machine capable of vertical flight – a "Pterophere." It was impractical, but Paucton is remembered as the first to suggest that a helicopter could carry a person. The English, not to be outdone by the Europeans, also began investigations into the problems of vertical flight. In 1796, 30 years after Paucton's experiments, Sir George Cayley, who was later to become known in Britain as the "Father of Aerial Navigation," turned his attention to a model that had been produced in France. Launoy and Bienvenue, respectively a naturalist and mechanic, had built and flown a device similar to Cayley's before the French Academy of Sciences in 1784. After some study, Cayley was able to improve the aerodynamic qualities of its airscrew, making it more efficient. This exercise marked the beginning of his investigations into the performance of airfoils – wings.

In 1799, Cayley developed the theory of the separation of lift and thrust – two of the forces working on an air foil – and within a decade, by means of a whirling-arm test device, the theories of streamlining, and of the changes in the centre of pressure of an airfoil. John Smeaton, the famous civil engineer, had inspired this investigation with his work on the effects of wind speeds and pressures on windmill vanes. Cayley, unlike da Vinci, had the advantage of being familiar with Borelli's work; he understood how birds fly. He appreciated the fact that feathers at the tips of the wings rotated as they beat the air.

The pace of technological progress and experimentation accelerated in the 19th century, making possible the refinements which would ultimately lead to powered flight. Robert Taylor, an Englishman living in the United States, and correspondent of Cayley's, had become intrigued with a marine propeller invented in the 1830s by John Ericsson, the Swedish-American naval engineer. Taylor felt that the marine propeller could be adapted to flight and that construction of a vertical lift machine was feasible. He wrote to Cayley in 1842 that the machine he proposed would

resemble an immense flat umbrella—the power and weight situated at the handle—the stem being hollow or double shaft revolving contrariweis [*sic*] when the vanes, of which the top is composed, are inclined, in ascension. The propeller or "compeller" is situated a little below the centre of gravity. . . .

The lateral movement of a large plane surface edgewise to attain and retain altitude is, I conceive, your original invention or idea. I divide the plane which is circular into fourteen vanes: eight susceptible of inclination in one direction, and six (the lower or inner series) in the other direction.

The rotary or ascensive action could be dispensed with if sufficient speed were attained by the rotary propulsive action with a general angle of the whole machine; but to start from the ground requires a perpendicular ascent, at first, and I consequently screw the plane up.[3]

There is a distinct similarity between Taylor's proposal and an 1843 design published by Cayley in *Mechanic's Magazine*. Both would seem to favour rotary wings – rotors – to raise their machine vertically into the air. In Cayley's aircraft, these flying surfaces would then have the blade pitch reduced so as to function as wings in forward flight. The design reflected the English inventor's earlier research and experimentation in that the rotor's blades were slightly cambered and given an angle of attack. Rotors on each side of the aircraft would turn counter to those on the opposite side. This design countered torque–the force which would otherwise turn the body of the aircraft in the same direction as the rotor–and the gyroscopic action which would invariably roll the machine over to one side. The design prepared by Cayley was at the concept stage–had he tried to build a full-sized working aircraft, problems quickly would have become apparent.

Cayley and Taylor would have experienced difficulty in designing the mechanism to drive their creations. A steam engine, the best power source that contemporary technology could provide, would have been both too large and too heavy with its boiler, firebox, fuel and water, to be practical. Cayley knew this and suggested that an internal combustion engine might be the answer:

It may seem superfluous to inquire relative to a first mover for aerial navigation, but lightness is of so much value in this instance that it is proper to notice the probability that exists of using the expansion of air, by the sudden combustion of inflammable powders or fluids with great advantage.[4]

At the time, a practical engine of that kind did not exist and attempts by other aircraft designers made use of existing types of power plants.

Models employing tiny steam engines were flown in 1863 by the Viscomte Gustave de Ponton D'Amecourt of France, and in 1878 by an Italian, Enrico Folanini. The Frenchman is often cited as being the first to use the term "Helicopter," doing so in a patent of 1861. His model featured two coaxial contra-rotating rotors–turning in opposite directions on the same shaft–and a small steam engine. Unfortunately, it didn't work. The patent that D'Amecourt was granted in Britain reads, in part, "The required ascensional motion is given to my aerostatical apparatus (which I intend denominating aeronef or helicoptere), by means of two or more superimposed horizontal hellixes combined together."[5]

During the 19th century, the United States provided an ideal environment for the inventor and so, inevitably, several individuals turned their efforts to developing vertical-lift aircraft. Their attempts were characterized by the optimism so prevalent in the Victorian age. One American proposal would have avoided the necessity of having to carry a steam-generating plant aloft. In 1849, J. Henry Smith envisaged a machine that he felt would be ideal for military purposes. Steam was to have been supplied via a long hose connecting a portable boiler on the ground and an engine situated directly below a rotor. An umbrella-like parachute was mounted above the rotor for safety in the event of an engine failure. The machine would, however, have been uncontrollable in any but the vertical mode, and so would have provided little or no advantage over balloons.

A New Yorker, W. J. Lewis, built and allegedly flew a model helicopter in 1876. It used two rotors, which looked much like horizontally-mounted sails, to raise it into the air, and others, vertically-mounted, to propel it forward. Wings attached to the roof of the passenger cabin were intended to provide lift in level flight. While a small clockwork motor proved to be sufficient to power the model, the inventor intended the full-sized version to be powered by foot pedals. Other inventors had similar proposals for propulsion.

The May 9, 1885, issue of *Scientific American* contained an illustrated article describing an aerial machine designed by Dr. W. O. Ayers of New Haven, Connecticut. Though the main driving force was to be compressed air under 3000 pounds (20 685 kPa) pressure, foot pedals were to assist in raising the machine via two horizontal "fans." The propellers were quite small but could be enlarged. It was necessary to experiment, in the inventor's opinion, to determine how large they would have to be and the speed with which they would have to be turned. Controlling the aircraft, which had its tubular steel frame filled with air for lightness, was fairly straightforward: "Thus far we have only two motions, vertical and horizontally direct: but our apparatus must be steered

An artist's concept of Professor Ayres' machine.

A Pitcairn autogiro in B.C. in 1931.

An attempt to design and build a helicopter in B.C. during the 1930s and 1940s. One of these was the Dubin Helicopter. Featuring a coaxial, contra-rotating rotor system that very effectively dealt with the problem of torque, the Dubin machine was, unfortunately, not successful.

Spaniard de la Cierva made major contributions with the drag and flapping hinges.

Henri and Emile Berliner, working in the United States, produced this vertical-lift aircraft in 1922 after more than 20 years of experimentation. The contra-rotating blades on the outriggers were powered by a single engine. Another horizontally mounted propeller situated behind the pilot above the fuselage decking controlled the attitude of the aircraft. SCIENTIFIC AMERICAN

Bell's Model 30, predecessor to the Bell 47 series.

BELL TEXTRON

Igor Sikorsky (*right*) built this crude-looking but effective vibration test stand in 1939.

UNITED TECHNOLOGIES/SIKORSKY AIRCRAFT

precisely like a boat, and it must ascend and descend obliquely."[6] In this imaginative design, elevators and rudders were basically flat plates intended to operate in much the same manner as the control surfaces of an airplane. It would apparently take off nearly vertically without "ground roll."

Clearly, there was no shortage of would-be helicopter inventors during this period, but the problems of power and control made all of their dreams an impossibility. There were many potential applications for a small, lightweight engine, however, and with all the experimentation going on in the 19th century, it was inevitable that someone would eventually succeed.

As mentioned earlier, Sir George Cayley had suggested that some form of internal combustion engine might be the answer. Some means by which a piston could be forced to move within a cylinder other than by steam pressure had to be developed. Gunpowder had been tried as early as 1680 by Christian Huygens, the Dutch physicist and astronomer, and Cayley himself had tried it in 1807. The explosive, however, had an obvious and unfortunate characteristic that led to a search for another solution. During the first half of the 19th century, experiments were undertaken with hot-air engines, it being reasoned that air, after all, was available everywhere and it was safe. Unfortunately, it was proven that an air engine, while it could be made to work, would have to be at least as large as a steam engine, thereby cancelling virtually all advantages it may have had.

A more positive step was taken in 1860 when Etienne Lenoire, working in France, produced the first somewhat practical internal combustion engine. It was practical in the sense that it could be made to operate, but not in two other important respects: it was far too large, and it consumed enormous quantities of illuminating gas as fuel. Though in-efficient, it was nevertheless a beginning and development continued. Ironically, the answer came from inventors who had no desire to become airborne.

"Horseless carriage" inventors shared some of the problems of the aviation enthusiasts: they needed an engine that was compact, self-contained, light, and that could produce enough power to move their vehicles. By the 1880s, success was at hand. Gottlieb Daimler and Carl Benz in Germany, working separately, each produced a successful automobile engine. By the end of the century, many gasoline engines were being produced and inevitably there were many innovations and improvements. It wasn't long before the automobile engine took to the air.

When Orville and Wilbur Wright and others reached that point in their flying experiments at which they could seriously consider powered flight, they naturally looked to existing engines as a basis for aero engines. By modifying a Pope-Toledo automobile engine, the Wrights solved the problem of powering an aircraft. Though far from efficient, or even from being as powerful as they could have made it, the engine was a starting point from which further experimentation could continue. Though the Wrights had proved an aircraft could be powered, a significant problem remained.

Means had to be developed by which the power produced by an engine could be translated into thrust–motion. Though da Vinci and others had proved that a screw propeller was the answer, surprisingly little scientific research had been undertaken into the operation of propellers even by the first decade of the 20th century. Improvements in marine propellers, the area where these screws were most commonly used, occurred more as a result of trial and error than scientific investigation. Virtually nothing was known about a propeller's operation, theoretically or otherwise, in the less dense medium. Orville Wright, in relating the problems involved in designing an airscrew, wrote that:

It is hard to find a point from which to make a start . . . for nothing about a propeller, or the medium in which it acts, stands still for a moment. The thrust depends upon the speed and the angle at which the blade strikes the air; the angle at which the air strikes depends upon the speed which the propeller is turning, the speed the machine is travelling forward, and the speed at which the air is travelling backward; the slip of the air backward depends upon the thrust exerted by the propeller and the amount of air acted upon. When any of these changes, it changes all the rest, so they are all interdependent upon one another. But these are only a few of the factors that must be considered.[7]

Once airborne, a whole new set of factors relating to control within a changing and changeable environment had to be considered. The Wrights were able to devise a system of control that countered the undesirable forces acting upon the aircraft, giving them the stability and the safety that they sought. Success was theirs because they had correctly combined the several necessary yet independent elements.

The success of the Wrights and others with powered, fixed-wing aircraft, prompted a number of helicopter enthusiasts to intensify their efforts, each wanting to be the first in his field. Surely, they thought, they must be at the threshold of success. But they were not as close as they had hoped.

On August 24, 1907, M. Volumard became the first man to be carried aloft in a helicopter. Designed and built by Louis and Charles Breguet and Professor Richet at Roubaix, France, the machine resembled a St. Andrews (diagonal) cross in plan form. The V-8 engine which could develop a maximum of 45 hp was situated at the mid-point of the framework–above the "aeronaut's" seat and below the fuel tank. It drove four, four-bladed biplane rotors, one situated at the extremity of each leg. A contemporary account of the flight stated that: "In the trials of the lifting power it was found that at the above speed of the planes (rotors, 48 rpm) the apparatus could rise in the air and keep itself off the ground at a height of a few feet."[8]

It was, however, apparently intended from the start that the machine would only test its lifting capacity because it could not be "steered." Once it had succeeded in lifting and holding 1169 pounds (530 kg) in the air for one minute, the machine was deemed to have accomplished all it had been intended to achieve. It had flown–but just barely, since it had been held down. Louis Breguet then built another helicopter and flew it to a height of 15 feet (4.6 m) on July 22, 1908, but it was wrecked. While he had been busy with his experiments, another Frenchman had also achieved a degree of success.

Paul Cornu designed and built a twin-tandem rotor helicopter in that same year. Powered by a 24 hp Antoinette engine, a common aero engine of the period, the Cornu helicopter was neither restrained nor uncontrolled. A moveable airfoil was situated at each end of the machine to permit it to climb or descend. Its only flight, on November 13, 1908, lasted a mere 20 seconds, but Cornu's helicopter was the first to fly without any attachment to the ground.

Experimentation with rotary-winged aircraft was not restricted to the West. In Russia, only two years after the first faltering flights of Breguet and Cornu, the son of a doctor began helicopter experiments. Igor Sikorsky, then a student, succeeded (if just barely) in getting an unmanned helicopter off the ground. Describing the helicopter years later, Sikorsky wrote that it

had a wooden frame similar to a large rectangular box, with a 25 horse-power Anzani engine on one side and the proposed seat or platform for the operator on the other. In the centre of the frame was the transmission box. A large wooden pulley was connected by a four-inch-wide [10-cm] belt to a smaller pulley on the motor. Two concentric tubular shafts were connected with the transmission box and were guided by an upper bearing at the top of the frame. On each of the shafts there were mounted two three-bladed lifting propellers, the upper one having a diameter of about fifteen feet [4.6 m], and the lower one sixteen and a half feet [5 m].[9]

The rotors turned in opposite directions, thus countering torque and dissymetry of lift. The machine was not powerful enough to lift both itself and a pilot, and it vibrated fiercely. Despite the problems with this machine and a second one built a year later, which was also unsuccessful, Sikorsky was grateful for the information acquired since he now realized, at least in theory, what he was doing wrong. Though he did not lose interest in vertical-lift flight, Sikorsky came to the conclusion that it was wiser to concentrate on fixed-wing aircraft, at least for the time being, since aviation technology was too primitive to solve the problems inherent in designing a helicopter.

While World War I brought with it tremendous advances in fixed-wing aircraft–including improved performance, increased size and better safety and reliability–no such claims could be made in the rotary-wing field. Not unreasonably, efforts and resources during wartime had to be expended on machines that had achieved a reasonable degree of refinement and for which a clear military value could be demonstrated. The helicopter, at this stage, was simply not worthy of intense development. Some experimentation did, however, continue.

A Danish pioneer, Jens Ellehammer, managed to get a twin coaxial-rotor helicopter of his design off the ground briefly in 1914. Like other helicopters of the period, it did not manage to get out of ground effect. One helicopter that did climb clear of the ground cushion was produced for the Austrian Army in 1915. Lieutenant Stephan Petrozy designed and built a machine that he intended would be used for observation, but it was incapable of leaving the ground until redesigned by Professor von Karman. Though it could rise vertically to a height of 150 feet (46 m) it was unable to move in any direction but down, from the hover. The only control feature was the ability to apply collective pitch, an equal angle of attack on all the rotor blades, to lift it into the air. In essence, nothing new had been developed in the difficult area of a control system.

Following the war, there was a renewed interest in helicopters. The April 1923 issue of *Scientific American* included an account of flights made by a United States Army-funded helicopter. In 1921, Georges de Bothezat, an ex-patriate Russian aeronautical engineer, managed to convince the United States Government that he could produce a practical helicopter for military use. It took him two years to design and build a machine basically like the Breguet-Richet helicopter of 1907 in configuration. Powered by a 170 hp LeRhone rotary engine—a type used extensively in WWI fixed-wing aircraft—the cruciform helicopter managed to lift 3600 pounds (1360 kg), including the weight of the pilot, fuel and aircraft.

It was claimed in the article that "the flight was steady and gave every assurance that the machine would perform at greater heights and would maintain remarkable stability in regular flight."[10] Directional control was achieved by means of small propellers—one for each manoeuvre. What would happen, the Army wondered, if one or more of the four main rotors quit? The resulting dissymmetry of lift would inevitably create serious problems for the pilot, rolling the cumbersome machine to the side where lift was lost. This potential difficulty and the complexity of the machine resulted in the cancellation of the project. De Bothezat, however, was undeterred and made a number of attempts to produce a workable helicopter over the next 20 years, being granted a number of U.S. patents for his ideas. Meanwhile, other experimenters were working without government assistance.

It seems characteristic of helicopter pioneers that they were highly determined. As with de Bothezat, the efforts of a father-and-son team of inventors, Emile and Henry Berliner, working in the United States, stretched over a period of two decades. Beginning in 1905, Berliner had built a machine which by 1909 had carried a man aloft a number of times. This was a significant achievement.

By September 1922, Henry had built and flown an aircraft based on his father's ideas. A contemporary account optimistically claimed that Berliner had "perfected the first successful helicopter which will rise perpendicularly from the ground, and when it has reached the desired elevation will fly ahead at whatever speed the operator desires."[11] It would fly ahead but still lacked the capability to manoeuvre in any other direction from the hover.

The fuselage resembled that of a contemporary fixed-wing aircraft—but there the resemblance ended. Vertical ascent was achieved by means of two bilateral, fixed-pitch rotors—one on each side of the fuselage at the end of the outriggers. Had a very tall pilot been employed, he may well have found himself abbreviated by the two-bladed rotors which turned uncomfortably close to his head. Forward motion was achieved by tilting the whole aircraft in the direction desired. A horizontally mounted propeller situated on the aft fuselage decking accomplished the evolution required. Lateral stability was assured by adjustable vanes situated below the rotors. Although the aircraft flew, it was a clumsy solution to the problem and difficulties remained. The builder admitted that a descent from high altitude could be unsafe, and while it might be accomplished with skilful use of the throttle, another solution was needed.

The solution came as a result of the stall and crash of an

airplane in Spain. Juan de la Cierva, a Spanish aeronautical engineer who had lost a friend in that crash, was determined to design an aircraft that was as near to being stall-proof as possible. If a fixed-wing stalled, lift would be lost and a crash was likely. The answer, it seemed to Cierva, would be to provide a number of wings rotating about a central axis. Using models with a two-bladed rotor, he began a series of experiments to test his theory. Each time, the model rolled to one side—the direction in which the rotor turned. Gyroscopic action and dissymetry of lift made this inevitable.

Then came a breakthrough. Cierva made some fundamental changes in the rotor, so that his models, and ultimately his full-sized aircraft, flew without the lateral rolling motion. Later, long after the major problems had been worked out, he wrote a book, *Wings of Tomorrow: The Story of the Autogiro*, in which he explained the reason for his success:

... the essential secret of the Autogiro's successful flight is the characteristic flexibility as applied to its wings ... if the blades were free to move, the current of air induced by forward motion would adjust them automatically into the correct position for flight.[12]

The rotor of an Autogiro was fully articulated; two hinges, one horizontal, the other vertical, attached the blades to the hub, allowing them full freedom of movement. They could rise on the side of the disc advancing into the airflow, providing lift, and fall on the opposite side where they were retreating and therefore losing lift. The vertically mounted hinges compensated for drag.

Few people at the time could understand how such a flexible and frail rotor could support a heavy aircraft. Cierva explained that ". . . the explanation lies in a very familiar fact—the fact of centrifugal force. The disc created by the revolving rotor is actually a very strong and stable flying surface."[13] Each rotor blade flew into the air exactly in the same manner as a conventional airplane's wing—both require forward motion to fly. Forward motion was, as in an airplane, provided by a vertically mounted radial engine and propeller mounted in the nose. The rotor which was always unpowered in flight was in "autorotation"; that is to say, its

blades had only a very slight positive angle of attack collectively and were turned by the flow of air coming from below while the aircraft moved forward. The means by which safe descents could be made had been discovered!

One problem with an Autogiro, or to be more accurate, gyroplane, was that it could not become airborne until its rotor was turning at least 180 revolutions per minute. To accomplish this, several methods were employed: the first involved a rather lengthy take-off run which decreased the aircraft's short take-off capability to almost that of a conventional airplane; the second, which reduced the length of run, employed a pull cord to get the rotor turning—this was clearly inadequate. A third used the deflected prop wash—the air thrown back by the propeller—to turn the rotor; and in the fourth and most effective method, the rotor was connected to the engine by means of a shaft and clutch. The engine drive had to be declutched before flight was possible.

Another development that was later used in helicopters was the "swash plate." This device made possible the tilting of the rotor to achieve directional control on all four axes.

Throughout the 1920s and the 1930s the gyroplane underwent a number of improvements. Raoul Hafner, an Austrian working in Britain, designed a type with workable collective and cyclic controls, both of which were used in helicopters by the mid-1930s. These machines could take off at a very steep angle—but not vertically. The Autogiro and its equivalents could accomplish all that Cierva had hoped and more. The Autogiro did not, however, even at its most sophisticated stage of development, have all the capabilities and features of a helicopter, but it was never intended that it should. In spite of this, its success was a major advance towards a true helicopter. Interest in developing a true helicopter persisted, and large corporations became involved in the late 1920s.

In 1927, Maitland B. Bleeker, an engineer with the Curtiss Aeroplane and Motor Corporation in the United States, undertook helicopter research with the full backing of his employer. Three years later the result, a rather strange-looking machine, was proclaimed in *Scientific American* as having some promise of vertical flight. Power was provided by a Pratt and Whitney Wasp radial engine, which was allowed to rotate, along with its oil and fuel tanks, above the fuselage on the mast. The rotor itself was turned by four small propellers, each mounted on the leading edge of a blade and driven by a complex system of shafts and gearing from the engine. This arrangement was intended to counter torque. Pitch control was accomplished by means of "Stabovators"–vanes situated at and below the trailing edge of each rotor blade. This helicopter did fly after a fashion under strictly controlled circumstances but proved so unstable and complex that further development was suspended.

In the early 1930s, a Dutch scientist, Dr. A. G. von Baumhauer, produced a helicopter similar in configuration to a type produced by a Boris Yuriev in Russia in 1912–a single main rotor for lift and control, and a single anti-torque tail rotor. A small radial engine, in the nose in the case of Baumhauer's machine, powered the main rotor via a long shaft, and a smaller engine in the tail drove an anti-torque rotor. This machine flew but later crashed, possibly as a result of control problems. It was, however, another step towards the comparatively simple yet most effective configuration which would soon prove so successful.

In 1935 and 1936, Louis Breguet briefly re-established France's leadership in helicopter development with his third rotary-wing design. Along with his co-designer, René Dorand, he produced a twin coaxial-rotor helicopter which was able to set several international records: height 518 feet (158 m), speed 27.32 mph (43.97 km/h), endurance 1 hr. 2 min. 50 sec.[14]

In 1935, Brough, England was the site for experiments by Dr. Oskar Asboth, which produced positive results. The Blackburn Company, a major fixed-wing manufacturer well known for its naval aircraft, claimed that the Asboth machine could climb 1500 feet/minute (450 m/min) and attain a forward speed of 100 mph (161 km/h). It, like the Breguet machine, was a coaxial type with the two rotors situated immediately behind the 2-seat cabin and adjacent to the machine's centre of gravity. Asboth had earlier built helicopters that attained heights of at least 50 feet (15 m) on a hundred occasions. Lauren D. Lyman of the *New York Times*, who submitted the report, suggested that helicopters could be used for forest protection patrols and topographic survey.[15]

The claims of some helicopter inventors were something less than modest. In Finland that same year, V. Louhia claimed he had invented a helicopter capable of 250 mph (400 km/h)–an enviable if not visionary achievement. He claimed that it ran noiselessly without a propeller or wings and that it was able to carry great loads. If tests in England were to prove satisfactory, the inventor declared, it would soon be put into production. Outlandish claims notwithstanding, progress was being made.

The German air force, the Luftwaffe, was rearming at this time in an environment that encouraged innovation. Professor E. H. Henrick Focke, who was at the time in disfavour with the Nazi regime, left the Focke-Wulf company and soon began work independently on a helicopter design. Focke, like a number of others, had gained experience with rotary-wing designs by building Autogiros under licence. The result of his own research, the Fa 61 of 1936, with its twin side-by-side rotors, proved to be a great advance over earlier types. In 1937, the 160 hp Brandenburg engine carried the small aircraft to new records at Hoyken Kamp near Bremen: endurance 1 hr. 20 min. 49 sec., speed 77.6 mph (125 km/h), distance 50 miles (80 km).[16] The German machine aroused considerable interest, and in 1938 a paper prepared by Focke, together with films of the Fa 61, were a feature of a meeting of mechanical engineers in New York. The 1939 World's Fair in that city was to be the starting point for a transcontinental flight to San Francisco by a new 5-passenger model helicopter by Focke-Achelis. It never took place.

The years just before and during the Second World War were critical to the development of the helicopter. Igor Sikorsky, who had cherished the idea of a direct lift aircraft since his first experiments in 1909, and had applied for a United States patent in 1931, was at last able to pursue

French aircraft builder Louis Breguet and his co-designer, René Durand, took the lead in helicopter development in 1935-6 with this machine. It was a twin-coaxial helicopter that captured several international records: height 518 feet (158 m), speed 27.32 mph (43.97 km/h), endurance 1 hr. 2 min. 50 sec.

The left and right side rotors of Focke-Achelis built helicopters were driven by a single engine.

serious studies with a view to actually producing a practical helicopter.

In the spring of 1939, Sikorsky was authorized to proceed with drawings for a helicopter.[17] United Aircraft Corporation, the parent company of Sikorsky Aircraft, was sufficiently impressed with the practicality of the project and, needless to say, with the engineering ability of Sikorsky, to commit company resources to the development of a helicopter. In view of the failure rate of others working towards the same end, it took courage to make this sort of commitment.

Having confidence in his own ideas, Sikorsky was undaunted by the high failure rate of others and went ahead with the design and construction of what came to be called the VS-300 (Vought-Sikorsky 300). By September 14, 1939, Sikorsky had completed the first version and was able to carry out a number of very brief hops; a remarkable achievement for less than six months' work. The term "hop" accurately describes the series of experiments since they were of too-brief duration to be called flights.

The machine was purposely kept extremely simple so that problems could be more easily isolated and corrected. The pilot sat right out in the open without protection of any kind. Development of the helicopter once again proved to be a process of constant revision. Severe vibration encountered in the first hops led to the rotational speed of the main rotor being reduced until the problem was corrected. By November 1939, hops of one or two minutes' duration were possible. But the control problems that had plagued other experimenters still had to be ironed out. Various tail-rotor configurations were tried and new flying techniques were developed. The latter were carried out using the helicopter, without its rotors installed, on a variable attitude test stand–a primitive simulator. It soon became obvious that in inexperienced hands the helicopter would easily roll to one side, so techniques were developed to counter this. Safety standards were soon improved to the point where restraints were no longer necessary. By mid-summer 1940, both the machine and techniques had developed to the point where

Sikorsky was flying the helicopter for periods of 15 minutes under reasonably good control. Considering the difficulties, this was a significant milestone in the development of the helicopter. On May 6, 1941, the VS-300 established a world helicopter endurance record of just over 90 minutes.[18]

While Sikorsky was experimenting with the VS-300, others were hard at work attempting to turn their ideas into practical aircraft. Configurations other than the single tail rotor and single main rotor were tried with limited success. The first helicopter purchased for the U.S. Army since that of de Bothezat in the 1920s closely resembled the German Fa 61 in form, with two contra-rotating rotors mounted on pylons extending at right angles to the fuselage, one from each side of the machine. The rotors were powered by an engine buried in the fuselage and driven by long shafts carried out through the pylons. The designer, W. Laurence LePage, had had access to data gathered by the Germans with the Fa 61. In 1938, he and Havilland H. Platt, a mechanical engineer with similar ideas regarding helicopter development, formed a partnership to produce a rotary-winged craft. Congress, under the Dorsey Bill, provided ample incentive for ventures of this kind by voting $300,000 for the development of rotary-winged machines other than Autogiros,[19] indicating that the United States government thought a breakthrough in helicopters was imminent. Convinced that they had the answer, the Platt-LePage company had begun construction of a machine at their own expense before a contract had been awarded by the army. Their helicopter, which the army had designated XR-1, flew by the summer of 1941, but control and performance problems were such that further development seemed unwarranted. The effect of Sikorsky's success by this time cannot be discounted.

Cut off from developments in the United States by WWII, the Germans continued helicopter research independently. Flettner succeeded in designing and manufacturing one of only two helicopter types to see operational service during the second World War. The Fl282 Kolibri (Hummingbird) had two rotors situated side-by-side above the fuselage which, when they rotated, were synchronized each to pass between the blades of the other. Torque was countered by making the rotors contra-rotating; a tail rotor was rendered unnecessary as a consequence. This configuration worked well except on those rare occasions when there were synchronization problems. Then, rotor blades could shear off right down to the hub and the helicopter would crash. The idea of synchronized rotors was taken up after the war by the Kaman company in the United States.

Meanwhile, another helicopter was under development. The prototype, which ultimately proved as successful as Sikorsky's VS-300, took to the air in Gardenville, New York, in the summer of 1943. An engineer, Arthur Young, had developed his ideas for a two- rather than three-blade rotor. The Bell Model 30, an aircraft which was every bit as rudimentary as the VS-300, like the Sikorsky aircraft initially showed an eagerness to roll over in inexperienced hands. Four large outriggers therefore were attached which imparted a greater degree of safety until tests solved control problems. The Model 30 was the progenitor of the extremely successful Model 47 series, the first commercial model of which came onto the market in 1946. This machine was available in two configurations: the open cockpit 47-B3 for agricultural use, and the fully enclosed 47-B, for other operators. The former type was purchased by Okanagan Air Services Limited in 1947 for use in British Columbia. Over the succeeding years, Bell took the intelligent course of progressively developing the basic Model 47. Meanwhile other manufacturers whose machines would be used in British Columbia were also hard at work giving substance to their ideas.

While these first successful machines were still somewhat primitive, the major problems had been solved. A "watershed" in the technology had been reached and improvements to existing helicopters and new designs came quickly. Stanley Hiller, who would go on to produce the versatile and successful Hiller 12E light helicopter, had begun experiments with rotary-wing craft at the age of 19 in 1944. He designed and built two coaxial-rotor machines—one of which crashed—before settling on the single main and tail-rotor configuration. The Hiller 360, similar to the 12E, was awarded its certificate of airworthiness on October 14, 1948.

There had always been helicopter designers interested in the twin-rotor configuration—coaxial, intermeshing, and side-by-side—but few tandem twin-rotor types had received attention. Undoubtedly the problems in developing a suitable power train had contributed to this. Frank N. Piasecki perfected this latter type and went on to produce designs such as the Vertol H-21A, in which tandem rotors were driven by a single engine. These helicopters came to be widely used in search and rescue, medium-lift transport and airline service. The Piasecki company was taken over by Vertol and eventually became Boeing-Vertol.

While the basic problems had been solved by the early 1950s, most helicopters were still limited in payload and performance. Manufacturers, naturally enough, took steps to improve their product. With the Korean War underway, there was considerable incentive. An automatic pilot was developed using a Sikorsky S-51 (H-5), and a self-contained navigational system was produced for the S-58. Though neither of these features would have much impact in British Columbia, where short-distance flights were the rule, other developments, such as the pitch, yaw and roll control system used in the Sikorsky S-55, would prove useful. Helicopters were becoming more sophisticated.

The introduction of turbines to helicopters in the mid-1950s greatly enhanced their versatility and capacity once some of the inevitable "teething" troubles had been worked out. Another advantage of turbines was that they were smaller and could free more space in the aircraft for passengers or internally stowed cargo. Other innovations such as skids to replace castoring landing gears, Monzoon buckets, bear paws and better cargo hooks and slings, when combined with innovative flying techniques, have made helicopters the most versatile aircraft in use today and a worthy fulfilment of the dreams of the ancients.

[1] Ivor B. Hart. *The World of Leonardo da Vinci: Man of Science, Engineer and Dreamer of Flight*. London, MacDonald, 1961, p. 328.

[2] Charles Gablehouse. *Helicopters and Autogiros: A History of Rotary Wing and V/STOIL Aviation*. Philadelphia, J. B. Lippincott, 1969, p. 3.

[3] J. Lawrence Pritchard. *Sir George Cayley: The Inventor of the Airplane*. London, Max Parrish, 1961, p. 197.

[4] *Ibid.*, p. 227.

[5] Svante Stubelius. *Balloon, Flying Machine, Helicopter: Further Studies in the History of Terms for Aircraft in English*. Göteborg, Göteborg Universitets, Arss Krift, vol. LXVI, 1960, p. 256.

[6] "A New Aerial Machine." *Scientific American*, vol. LII, no. 19, May 9, 1885, p. 291.

[7] John Evangelist Walsh. *One Day at Kittyhawk: The Untold Story of the Wright Brothers and the Airplane*. New York, Thomas A. Crowell, 1975, p. 114.

[8] "The Breguet Gyroplane," *Scientific American*, vol. 92, no. 20, November 16, 1907, p. 354.

[9] Igor Sikorsky. *The Story of the Winged "S": An Autobiography*. New York, Dodd, Mead & Co., 1967, p. 25.

[10] "Our Army's Helicopter," *Scientific American*, vol. 128, no. 4, April 4, 1923, p. 243.

[11] "A Helicopter that Flies: The Berliner Machine," *Scientific American*, vol. 127, no. 3, September 22, 1922, p. 160.

[12] Juan de la Cierva and Don Rose, ed. *Wings of Tomorrow: The Story of the Autogiro*. New York, Warren and Putnam, 1931, p. 91.

[13] *Ibid.*, p. 115.

[14] "Along the Far Flung Airways: New Helicopter Establishes World Records in Germany." *New York Times*, August 1, 1937, X1, p. 6.

[15] Lauren D. Lyman. "Helicopter Again Tried: British Are Building One Expected to Have a Range of Two Hours." *New York Times*, March 24, 1935, VIII, 17-1.

[16] "Professor H. Focke Claims World's Altitude Record, Distance and Speed Records: Bremen Germany." *New York Times*, July 4, 1937, 3: 3.

[17] In British Columbia there were attempts to develop a helicopter. John Hess and sons were hard at work. After 15 years of exhaustive tests and expenditure of $30,000 they felt that they were near success. They had, by July 1936, taken out patents for a four-rotor craft in 42 countries. Plans were a closely guarded secret. It was not successful. "New Westminster Man Perfects Helicopter." *Vancouver Sun*, July 15, 1936, p. 3.

[18] Sikorsky, *op. cit.*, p. 217.

[19] H. Franklin Gregory. *The Helicopter*. Cranbury, New Jersey, A. S. Barnes, 1976, p. 64.

Igor Sikorsky's successful VS-300 was, in its initial stages, quite rudimentary. One advantage was that new ideas could be tried and adopted or discarded readily. Parts such as tail rotors could be tried in various positions to determine which worked best. At one point, the VS-300 had three tail rotors— two were eventually removed.

UNITED TECHNOLOGIES/SIKORSKY AIRCRAFT

Books

Berget, Alphonse. *The Conquest of the Air*. London, William Heineman, 1911.

Cierva, Juan de la and Don Rose, ed. *Wings of Tomorrow: The Story of the Autogiro*. New York, Brewer, Warren and Putnam, 1931.

Fay, John. *The Helicopter: History, Piloting and How it Flies*. Newton Abbot, David and Charles, 1978.

Gablehouse, Charles. *Helicopters and Autogiros: A History of Rotating Wing and V/STOL Aviation*. Philadelphia, J. B. Lippincott, 1969.

Green, William and Pollinger, Gerald. *The Aircraft of the World*. London, Macdonald, 1965.

Gregory, H. Franklin. *The Helicopter: A Pictorial History*. Cranbury, New Jersey, A. S. Barnes, 1976.

Hart, Ivor B. *The World of Leonardo da Vinci: Man of Science, Engineer and Dreamer of Flight*. London, Macdonald, 1961.

Hubler, Richard G. *Straight Up: The Story of Vertical Flight*. New York, Duell, Sloan and Pierce, 1961.

Kaplan, H. R. and Hunt, James F. *This is the Coast Guard*. Cambridge, Maryland, Cornell Maritime Press, 1972.

Milberry, Larry. *Aviation in Canada*. Toronto, McGraw-Hill Ryerson, 1979.

Moolman, Valerie. *The Road to Kittyhawk*. Alexandria, Time-Life, 1980.

Pritchard, J. Laurence. *Sir George Cayley: The Inventor of the Airplane*. London, Max Parrish, 1961.

Sikorsky, Igor I. *The Story of the Winged "S": An Autobiography*. New York, Dodd, Mead & Co., 1967.

Stubelius, Svante. *Balloon, Flying Machine, Helicopter: Further Studies in the History of Terms for Aircraft in English*. Göteborg, Göteborg Universitets, Arss Krift vol. LXVI, 1960.

Taylor, Michael J. F., comp. and John W. R. Taylor, ed. *Jane's Pocket Book of Helicopters*. New York, Collier, 1981.

Turner, Charles C. *Aerial Navigation of Today: A Popular Account of the Evolution of Aeronautics*. Philadelphia, J. B. Lippincott, 1910.

Walsh, John Evangelist. *One Day at Kittyhawk: The Untold Story of the Wright Brothers and the Airplane*. New York, Thomas Y. Crowell, 1975.

Young, Arthur M. *The Bell Notes: A Journey from Physics to Metaphysics*. New York, Delacourt Press, 1979.

Canada's Navy. Calgary, Corvus, various years.

Canada's Air Force. Calgary, Corvus, various years.

Booklet

Dietrich Collins Equipment. *The ALCAN Story*. Vancouver, F. W. Lees, n.d.

Reference sources

"The Bell 212 Twin: It Makes Every Plane in Your Fleet More Effective." Fort Worth, Bell Helicopter, 1975, 18 pp.

"Construction By Air." Stratford, Connecticut, Sikorsky Division of United Aircraft, June 1958, 18 pp.

"S-62: First Turbine Powered Helicopter with Built-in Amphibious Capabilities." Stratford, Sikorsky Division of United Aircraft, n.d., 24 pp.

"The S-76." Stratford, Sikorsky Aircraft: United Technologies, September 1981, 32 pp.

"Air Search and Rescue: 63 Years of Aerial Lifesaving: A Pictorial History 1915-1978." Alexandria, VA, Department of Transportation, Coast Guard, 1978.

Articles-Signed

Diamond, Gordon, Miff Fletcher, and Hal Morrison, "S.O.S. *Prinsendam!* Rescue on the High Seas." *Sentinel*, vol. 16, no. 5, 1980, pp. 16-17.

Edwards, Les. "Okanagan Helicopters." *Air World*, March/April 1967, pp. 128-30.

Emerson, G. C. "Topographical Mapping by Helicopter." *Canadian Surveyor*, vol. X, no. 11, January 1952, pp. 3-11.

Graf, Cherry. "Heavy Lift Division Logs." *Rotortales*, vol. Z, no. 4, August 1981, pp. 1-3.

Foly, Dennis C. "Ode to the R4." *CAHS Journal*, vol. 18, no. 4, Winter 1980, pp. 112-15, 124.

Hanson, Phil. "West Coast Helilogging: Reaping the Harvest with Rotary Wings." *Canadian Aviation*, vol. 52, no. 8, August 1979, pp. 21-24.

Keith, Ronald A. "Okanagan Helicopters: World Wide Operations with 161 Whirly-birds." *Exxon Air World*, vol. 32, no. 2, 1980, pp. 26-29.

———. "The Versatility of Conair." *Canadian Aviation*, vol. 54, no. 3, March 1981, pp. 22-25.

Klemin, Alexander. "Sikorsky's Helicopter." *Scientific American*, vol. 163, no. 1, October 1940, p. 189.

Love, Myron. "Aerial Truck: K-Max Meets Midwest's Expectations." *Helicopters*, Issue 3, 1995, p. 24.

Meadows, Jack. "West Coast Heli-Commuters." *Helicopters*, Issue 4, 1996, pp. 26-28.

Morgan, David G. "B.C.'s Rapattack." *Canadian Aviation*, vol. 54, no. 7, July 1981, p. 39.

Pole, Ken. "EH101 Back in the Race. Now It's the Cormorant." *Helicopters*, October 1996, pp. 39-43.

———. "Cormorant Politics: Auditor General Gets Crack at Helicopter Contract." *Helicopters*, Issue 1, 1998, pp. 16-17.

———. "Eyes in the Sky: Helicopter Law Enforcement Roles are Varied." *Helicopters*, Issue 1, 1996, p. 29.

———. "MHP Delay: Recent Budget Forces 12 Month Wait." *Helicopters*, Issue 1, 1996, p. 29.

———. "On Guard Aloft: Bell Helicopters in Police Use." *Helicopters*, January 1997, pp. 47-49.

———. "The Front Runners. The Field Narrows in Race to MHP." *Helicopters*, Issue 1, 1996, pp. 31-32.

———. "Top Manufacturers Vie for Contract." *Helicopters*, Issue 4, 1996, pp. 30-36.

Randell, Keith. "Banner Year in '79 Prompts High Hopes for '80's." *Canadian Aviation*, vol. 53, no. 1, January 1980, pp. 20-24.

Reyno, Mike. "Heli-logging in Canada: It's Changed the Way Forest Operations Are Conducted." *Helicopters*, Issue 3, 1996, pp. 21-29.

———. "Shortsky: A New Lease on Life for S-61." *Helicopters*, Issue 3, 1996, pp. 30-34.

———. "Flight of the Dragon Fly." *Helicopters*, Issue 3, 1996, pp. 34-36.

———. "Transport Canada Gives Green Light to Russian Helicopter." *Helicopters*, Issue 4, 1996.

———. "Sea King Problems and Upgrades." *Helicopters*, Issue 4, 1996, p. 25.

Sims, Donald. "Out of a Lifeboat into the Air." *Air International*, vol. 13, no. 4, October 1977, pp. 190-96.

Tomey, Ralph. "Logging by Helicopter in B.C.: An Overview." *Canadian Forest Industries*, vol. 120, no. 3, March 1980, pp. 14-16.

Tower, Courtney. "Too Busy to Fly." *Canadian Aviation*, vol. 30, no. 1, January 1957, p. 56.

Wall, Rick. "Between a Rock and a Cold Place." *Approach*, vol. 27, no. 8, February 1982, pp. 2-6.

Watson, Gary. "Helicopters in the Movies: Versatility Enhanced for Aerial Shots." *Helicopters*, Issue 3, 1996, pp. 16-18.

Wenzel, Jan Udo. "Skyhook." *Western Wings*, vol. 4, June 1959, pp. 5-6.

Wilkie, M. "Bus: The 407 Works Well for Fletcher Challenge." *Helicopters*, January 1997, p. 54.

———. "Vancouver's ERT." *Helicopters*, Issue 2, 1996, p. 26.

———. "VIH Signs 3 Year Medevac Contract." *Helicopters*, Issue 2, 1996, p. 31.

Woodcock, Don. "The *Prinsendam* Rescue: An Account of the Greatest Marine Rescue of Modern Times." *Westworld*, vol. 7, no. 7, November 1981, pp. 21-23.

Articles-Unsigned

"Cormorant to be Canada's New SAR Helicopter." *Janes Defence Weekly*, January 14, 1998, p. 4.

"The Breguet Gyroplane." *Scientific American*, vol. 92, no. 20, November 16, 1907, p. 354.

"Driptorch: A New Technique Helps Slash Burning Problem." *Timberline*, vol. 4, no. 7, October 1976, pp. 4-5.

"A Helicopter That Flies–The Berliner Machine." *Scientific American*, vol. 127, no. 3, September 1922, p. 160.

"The Helicopter Triumphant." *Scientific American*, vol. 161, no. 1, January 1939, p. 30.

"A New Aerial Machine." *Scientific American*, vol. LII, no. 19, May 9, 1885, p. 291.

"Presentation of Awards." *Newsletter: Canadian Coast Guard*, Victoria, vol. 2, no. 17, May 1976, pp. 2-4.

"Rotary Wings Among the Mountains: The Story of Okanagan Helicopters Ltd." *Esso Air World*, November/December 1952, 4 pp.

"Trees from the Sky." *Harmac News*, December 1951, pp. 12-13.

Interviews

Art Johnson, January 15, 1981.

Ernie McMinn, February 5, 1981.

Bruce Payne, February 25, 1981.

Alf Stringer, April 1, 1981.

Eric Cowden, May 15, 1981.

Ian Duncan, May 29, 1981.

Bob Jones, June 9, 1981.

Lynn Stringer, June 26, 1981.

Bill McLeod, June 29, 1981.

Ivor Roberts, July 28, 1981.

Barney Bent, August 10, 1981.

Joan McLeod, September 8, 1981.

Ken Blackwood and Don MacKenzie, October 15, 1981.

Will Tompson, October 30, 1981.

Jock Graham, December 3, 1981.

Bob Taylor, March 14, 1982.

Mrs. Anne Agar and Mrs. Ada Carlson, March 16, 1982.

Lt.-Col. C.G. Diamond, CD, CAF, April 27, 1982.

Walter Palubiski, May 1982.

Hugh Lyons, June 3, 1982.

Commander Paul Milligan, USCG, Lt. Commander Dennis Maclean, USCG, and Ensign Jeff Vail, USCG, June 16, 1982 and July 1998.

Frank Norie, frequent: 1991-1998.

Ken Norie, frequent: 1991-1998.

George Williamson, July 1998.

Henry Stevenson, August 1997.

Sgt. Don Mackie, 443 (MH) Squadron, July 1998.

Lt. L. Brown, 443 (MH) Squadron, July 1998.

INDEX